The Mandate of Heaven

The Mandate of Heaven

Hidden History in
the *I Ching*

天命
一易
經祕
史

S J Marshall

Columbia University Press

Columbia University Press
Publishers Since 1893
New York
© 2001 S. J. Marshall

First published in the United Kingdom 2001 by Curzon Press

Library of Congress Cataloging-in-Publication Data

Marshall S. J.
  The mandate of heaven : hidden history in the I Ching / S. J. Marshall
  p. cm.
  ISBN 0–231–12297–7 (alk. paper)
  1. I ching. I. Title.

PL2464.Z7 M37 2000
299'.51282—dc21

                                                                00–059646

∞

Casebound editions of Columbia University Press books are printed on
permanent and durable acid-free paper.

Printed in Great Britain

c 10 9 8 7 6 5 4 3 2 1

Dedicated
to
Richard Wilhelm
(1873–1930)

Contents

Section III: Appendices

Preface

The Master said:
'At 15 I turned my mind to learning.
At 30 I had a firm foundation.
At 40 I was free of doubts.
At 50, I knew the Mandate of Heaven ...'
(*Analects* of Confucius 2/4)

King Wen is traditionally believed to have authored the judgments of the ancient Chinese oracle known as the *Yijing*, or *Book of Changes*. It is also said that he 'probably' combined the eight trigrams to form the 64 hexagrams during his imprisonment by the tyrant Zhou Xin, the 'bad last king' of the Shang dynasty. Some time after his release, King Wen received the Mandate of Heaven, *tianming*, to found a new dynasty, the Zhou dynasty; but he died before he could complete his plan to conquer the Shang, and his son King Wu took over the task.

This is the story frequently repeated by those with an interest in the *Book of Changes*. Rarely are any other details mentioned, yet there is a wealth of information scattered in ancient Chinese sources. Surprisingly, these fragments have never been properly pieced together into an unfolding narrative. In this book I examine the whole story, particularly with respect to allusions in the earliest layer of the *Yijing*.

When my work was almost completed, I came across a 'grand old man' speech given by the great sinologist Herrlee Creel when he was 81, in which he said there was one thing that the young scholar must *on no account* ignore: 'Be lucky!' This struck a chord with me, as luck has actually played a large part in the formation of this book. (There is a wonderful Chinese idiom to describe making a lucky find: 'A blind cat dragging a dead rat.')

The seed of this book germinated when I began to think about a small point that had emerged in a brief discussion at the inaugural meeting of the 'I Ching Society', held in the summer of 1995 in Bloomsbury, London. I was introduced to Steve Moore, author of *The Trigrams of Han*; we had both published reviews of a translation of the *Changes* by Rudolf Ritsema and Stephen Karcher and we compared our impressions of the work. He pointed out to me their odd translation of the second and fourth lines of hexagram 55. Instead of 'at noon seeing the Big Dipper' they had 'visualizing a bin' at midday, completely missing the reference to the constellation *Ursa Major*. Until he mentioned it, I hadn't noticed that a *specific* group of stars was referred to in that hexagram; I was too familiar with the more general rendering in the Wilhelm-Baynes translation, 'the polestars can be seen at noon'. As it was, even this reference had largely washed over me. I was too bound up in the orthodox Song dynasty commentaries to ask myself what it had originally meant; its literal value had been buried beneath the great weight of subsequent symbolic interpretation that had amassed over three millennia.

Intrigued how Ritsema and Karcher had arrived at their translation, I began thumbing through dictionaries and scribbling notes, planning to pen a footnote to an article I had just written, 'A Critical Survey of I Ching Books'. But the footnote expanded, and expanded, eventually leading to the discovery and dating of an overlooked total solar eclipse record from the eleventh century BC. This becomes the earliest datable record of a total solar eclipse from anywhere in the world. The eclipse is a significant factor in the story of the Conquest of the Shang that has otherwise dropped out of history. As a result of deciphering the true meaning of hexagram 55 a reliable date for the Conquest can now be established as 1070BC, the same year as the eclipse. A detailed analysis of hexagram 55 revealed that King Wu launched the invasion shortly after the eclipse, responding to it as an auspicious omen, a sign that he had the Mandate of Heaven. It became clear that the *Book of Changes* has an underlying narrative integrity that has thus far remained hidden and unappreciated.

According to contemporary modernist scholars, who have sceptically re-evaluated early Chinese history, the traditional association of King Wen with the *Book of Changes* is simply a myth, with no basis in historical fact. The modernist interpretation of the *Yi* began to gain strength in China in the 1930s with the *Gushibian* school of context criticism, and spread to the west in the 1980s via the PhD dissertations of Edward Shaughnessy and Richard Kunst. (*Gushibian*, 'Debates over Ancient History', is the title of the journal in which many modernist studies were published.) Though there are still a great many traditional scholars of the *Yijing* in China, they do not appear to have felt any necessity to defend their beliefs against the modern research that has undermined the tradition. Consequently, in the academic world the modernist view of the *Yi* is now pre-eminent. Tradition has effectively become moribund and a new consensus has taken hold. The interpretation developed in this study will, I hope, go some way to redress the balance. It is important to stress, however, that I do not believe that this debate is ultimately about the polarisation of modernist and traditionalist views, but rather about finding common ground and moving towards a fusion of ideas. In *The Mandate of Heaven* I turn modernist thinking and techniques to the task of sympathetically examining traditional beliefs about King Wen and the origin of the *Book of Changes*. This constitutes a fresh approach in contemporary sinology, in that the modern sceptical approach to ancient Chinese history has resulted in a reluctance to examine tradition seriously.

S J Marshall, London

A brief note on ancient sources

The Chinese text of the *Yijing* I have used is the Harvard-Yenching edition, found in *A Concordance to Yi Ching* (Harvard-Yenching Institute Sinological Index Series, Supplement No. 10, October 1935. Peiping, China). This is effectively what I refer to as 'the received text' or 'the transmitted text'.

I have quoted a number of ancient Chinese works of literature, the most used of which I will briefly describe here for the benefit of those to whom they may be unfamiliar. Two works with a time-span of composition approximately the same as the earliest layer of the *Book of Changes* (the earliest layer will be delineated in Chapter I) are the *Shujing* and the *Shijing*, the *Book of Documents* and the *Book of Odes*, respectively. These have been by far my most valuable sources. The *Documents* mainly takes the form of speeches and harangues of the early Zhou dynasty kings, the dynasty founded by Kings Wen and Wu, though the book also contains chapters purported to originate from mythological times. There is a problem with the *Shu*, it became the prime target during the Book Burning in 213BC, and clever forgeries of 'lost chapters' were later incorporated into it that were accepted as genuine for over a millennium. I have used predominantly the material that has been shown to originate from the Western Zhou dynasty. The *Odes* is a collection of 305 early Zhou dynasty folk-songs and poems, mostly reflecting the lives of ordinary people, some with overtones of political protest, which were supposedly chosen from a much greater number by Confucius. The *Odes* survived the Book Burning much better than the *Documents*. (The *Changes* was one of the few books exempt from being burnt.) Where I have made my own translations I have relied on the Chinese provided by Bernhard Karlgren for the *Odes*, and that provided by James Legge for the *Documents*, using Karlgren's extensive glosses for both.

There are a number of works of the 3rd and 4th centuries BC by various 'masters', or *zi*. The ones I have quoted most are the *Mozi* and the *Han Feizi*. Mozi, or Modi, believed in universal love and preached against war (unless it was sanctioned by Heaven). Mozi once walked for ten days and ten nights to persuade a ruler to call off an attack on another state. Han Feizi, on the other hand, was a Legalist who sought to advise rulers how to secure their states by fair means or foul, often with great wit. Han Feizi has been likened to Machiavelli, but he has far greater charm and his book is a joy to read. Han Feizi committed suicide in prison with poison supplied by his former student Li Si, who, as minister to the Qin Emperor, had recommended his imprisonment, either out of jealousy or because he was following Han Fei's own philosophy of protecting the state from a potential threat. This is extremely ironic, in that the *Han Feizi* is full of cautionary tales of treachery and double-cross. Li Si, a fellow Legalist, was the minister who masterminded the Book Burning. Both Legalism and Mohism died out, Confucianism and Daoism gaining supremacy.

The author of the *Xunzi* was a Confucian, and at one time the teacher of Han Feizi. Xunzi believed human nature was inherently evil and so stressed that man must become habituated to morality in order to offset this deficiency. The *Mengzi* is more commonly known by its Latinized title *Mencius*; it contains the wise and humanitarian counsel of Master Meng, or Mencius, widely recognised as second only to Confucius (Kongzi). *Mencius* has been an important source, particularly in that he quotes a number of genuine fragments from otherwise lost and subsequently fabricated chapters of the *Shujing*. The *Lunyu*, better known as the *Analects* of Confucius, consists of the sayings of the sage and his discussions with his disciples, which were gathered together as recollections after his death. Strangely, Confucius appears not to have directly written anything, though a number of texts have been attributed to him. I also refer to the well-known Daoist works *Zhuangzi* and *Daodejing* (sometimes called the *Laozi*), as well as the fourth century AD 'Yang Zhu' chapter of the *Liezi*, which is humorously hedonistic in outlook. The *Huainanzi* is an eclectic work compiled by a team of scholars that was completed in 139BC, containing folkloric and Daoist knowledge in the main.

There are several ancient works of history that have proved useful. The *Shi Ji*, or *Historical Records*, was compiled by Sima Qian, Grand Historian at the Imperial court, who suffered the indignity of being castrated after offending the Emperor. Because he was very poor he could not afford to pay to have the sentence commuted, and none of his friends would help, which greatly distressed him. As a consolation, he wrote one of the most valuable histories of ancient China. The initial research was begun by his father Sima Tan. Sima Qian promised him on his deathbed that he would complete the project, though he did not consider himself especially suited for the task. This massive text of 130 chapters, which has still not been fully translated into Western languages, is a history of everything that was known about the past up until the time it was finished, circa 99BC. The *Chunqiu*, or *Spring and Autumn Annals*, is a sparse record of events in the period 722–481BC from the state of Lu, birthplace of Confucius. The *Zuozhuan*, the *Chronicles of Zuo*, named after its compiler, deals more vividly with the despicable feudal behaviour of the period 722–468BC; the text itself dates from the third century BC and is probably semi-fictional in parts. Though originally a separate work, the *Zuo* was broken up and arranged to fit the entries of the *Spring and Autumn Annals*. The *Zuo* is of special interest because it contains a number of early records of divinations made by consulting the *Changes*, the quoted text of which is sometimes at odds with the received text.

A curious fourth century BC work known as the *Tian Wen*, which I believe should be translated as *Ask Heaven* though

Heavenly Questions is most often seen, forms part of the *Chu Ci*, an early poetry anthology from the southern state of Chu. The *Tian Wen* is a mysterious book of conundrums that is the *locus classicus* for some early Chinese myths and historical fragments.

The inscribed oracle-bones of the Shang were discovered at the turn of the twentieth century, after being buried for over 3,000 years. The form of divination practised by the Shang kings was to make cracks in tortoise/turtle shells and ox scapulae by the application of a glowing firebrand to carved notches in the shell or bone. The resultant cracks were then 'read'. These shells and bones were afterwards inscribed with the original enquiry and the king's prognostication on the cracks. I have also used inscriptions from early Zhou dynasty bronze vessels excavated since the 1960s.

Other works drawn on just once or twice I describe briefly on those occasions. For an introduction to ancient Chinese books, *Early Chinese Literature* by Burton Watson is recommended. For a more academic survey, see Michael Loewe, ed, *Early Chinese Texts: A Bibliographic Guide*.

Conventions employed

In order to refer to, say, the third line of hexagram 10, I will often write hexagram 10/3. A reference such as *Mencius* 2A/4 means Book 2, Part A, Verse 4. As the numbering of the verses of the *Analects* of Confucius differs slightly between various translations, my references are consistent with the translation of D C Lau. Chinese characters have been transliterated in *pinyin*; the actual characters are shown in a glossary at the back of the book, excluding the titles of texts and characters of no importance to the discussion. Where book titles and names of Chinese authors appear in the bibliography according to older romanisation systems, such as Wade-Giles, I have retained these forms in the text. In quotations where non-*pinyin* transliterations were originally used I have substituted *pinyin*; these alterations of the quoted text are indicated by square brackets.

Acknowledgements

I am particularly grateful to Steve Moore, who loaned me many rare works and hard-to-obtain sinological journals from his library. He read the manuscript as each chapter was written and offered numerous useful suggestions. He also typeset the glossary of Chinese characters.

Patrick Poitevin provided invaluable astronomical help in calculating the date of the total solar eclipse recorded in the *Yi*.

I also wish to thank Eric Smith, Rikki Joannides, Sean Hogan, Emily Rigge, Cliff Ashcroft, Sandra Mudge, William de Fancourt, Dr Edward Hacker, Prof Anne Birrell, Dr E C Krupp, and Richard Rutt, for their contributions at various stages of this work. Matthew William Jacobs and Seán Matthews helped me with the figures and maps. I am indebted to George T Keene for allowing me to use his photograph of a total solar eclipse on the cover, and to Wei Bing for her calligraphy. I am grateful for access to the collections of the British Library and the Warburg Institute. The bibliographic section of Waltham Forest Central Library assisted my research by procuring many books via inter-library loan.

Illustrations

Figures

Maps

Section I

The Mandate
of Heaven

Chapter I

The framework of the argument

'Announce the Mandate in your own city.'[1]

Defining terms

The subject of this study is the earliest layer of the *Yijing*. This is an independent work known as the *Zhouyi*, written roughly 3,000 years ago. The *Zhouyi* is the actual oracle. In 136BC, about 1,000 years after the oracle was created, the *Zhouyi* was embedded in a collection of seven appendices known since the Later Han as the Ten Wings, three of them being in two parts, and the resultant text was canonised as a *jing* or 'classic'. Thus the *Zhouyi*, or *Changes of the Zhou Dynasty*, together with the Ten Wings, make up what we today call the *Yijing*. The Ten Wings date back to approximately the third century BC, and do not represent well the original meaning of the *Zhouyi*.

In the Wilhelm-Baynes translation, the *Zhouyi* consists solely of those brief phrases printed in slightly larger type and indented under each line (the *yaoci*, also called the *xiaoci*, said to have been written by the Duke of Zhou), and the indented larger text that Richard Wilhelm labelled 'The Judgment' (the *guaci*, attributed to King Wen). Among the lines, for example, phrases such as 'There is no skin on his thighs, and walking comes hard' (hexagrams 43/4 and 44/3), and 'Flying dragon in the heavens' (1/5), are from the original 3,000-year-old text. These and all such sections date back to about the eleventh century BC.[2] The text in indented larger type referred to in Wilhelm-Baynes as 'The Image' has been stripped out of the Third and Fourth Wings, written seven or eight centuries later, and will not form a part of this essay.[3] Note that the unindented explanations found under each line and the judgment, in slightly smaller type, originate from Song dynasty commentaries collated by Wilhelm. In particular, these explanations are slanted towards ideas found in the works of the Neo-Confucianist philosophers Zhu Xi (AD1130–1200) and Cheng Yi (AD1033–1107).[4] Wilhelm also mixes in his own comments here, together with ideas derived from discussions with his honoured master Lao Naixuan (1843–1921) and other friends, according to his own understanding of the *Book of Changes*.[5]

When the *Zhouyi* was set down the *yin-yang* theory, together with the 'five elements', had not been conceptualised. These are Warring States (480–222BC) developments, a period when the feudal states were constantly at war with each other and the 'Hundred Schools' competed for philosophical supremacy. It was at this time that the philosophical notion of the *Dao* arose. Though the character *dao* appears four times in the *Zhouyi*, in the eleventh century BC it had the literal meaning of a path or way, not 'The Way'. Consequently, these later ideas will not form a part of the argument.[6]

The issues involved

In the time since Richard Wilhelm (1873–1930) made his German translation of the *Book of Changes*, published in 1924, and Cary F Baynes translated it into the influential English version published in 1950, a transformation of our understanding of the earliest layer of the book, the *Zhouyi*, has been taking place. I remember my own reaction over a decade ago when new translations started to appear in which hexagram 33, 'Retreat', was suddenly about a piglet, and hexagram 36, 'Darkening of the Light', was about a crowing or bright pheasant.[7] Being at that time unfamiliar with the scholarly debate I tried to ignore these aberrations, not realising that I had unwittingly become a 'traditionalist'. I later became aware that a new breed of *Yijing* scholar had emerged in China, the 'modernist', who no longer believed that King Wen 'doubled the trigrams' when he was imprisoned at Youli by the Shang tyrant Zhou Xin, or wrote the judgments of the hexagrams. The Duke of Zhou was no longer regarded as having appended the statements to the lines. Fuxi, the legendary creator of the trigrams, never existed. And Confucius most certainly never authored the Ten Wings, or, indeed, had any interest in the *Changes* at all.

The Modern School, an iconoclastic twentieth century reassessment movement, has a number of new beliefs. One of these is that the *Yi* is the work of anonymous court diviners who collated their collective knowledge of omens. An omen, for example, is the folk wisdom or superstition that says it is unlucky if a black cat crosses your path; or that a red sky at night is a shepherd's delight (a fine day tomorrow), but a red sky in the morning is a shepherd's warning (it will rain). When I first read Arthur Waley's 1933 essay 'The Book of Changes', which re-interprets the oracle in this vein, I was tremendously excited, and yet, not a little sad to be relinquishing my old views. It seemed the *Book of Changes* had changed beyond recognition; it was almost as if the *Yijing* had shed a skin, and no-one had quite witnessed how it had happened.

On reflection, however, I could not help feeling that the modernist characterisation of the *Zhouyi* as a simple omen-text was essentially a classificatory insight into aspects of the work that had been pressed into service as an explanation of the whole. The understated implication of modern thought appeared to be that there was no deeper significance to the text: it was just an anthology of naturalistic omens and prognostications upon them (such as 'auspicious' and 'disastrous'). It meant that the generations of traditional Chinese scholars who had sought to articulate the principles that govern the meaningfulness of the work in sublime and philosophical terms had effectively created the book anew. Given such a perspective, I could understand why the modernists might regard the legend of King Wen's authorship as a product of this endeavour, and feel fully justified in writing it off as pseudepigraphy. Numerous works of unknown authorship, for instance, were attributed to the Duke of Zhou in the Han dynasty that he could not possibly have written.[8]

When Waley wrote his essay, the *Zhouyi* was thought to date back to anywhere in the period 1000BC to 600BC. Eventually modernist scholars honed this estimate to 800BC. Though it was little more than a convenient average, a few modernists found reasons to assert it as an exactitude. This meant King Wen couldn't have had anything to do with the *Zhouyi*; even some traditionalist scholars began to move away from their former views. In Chapter IV, however, I show how the dating procedures that 'disproved' King Wen's association with the *Changes* are faulty.

As I grew more familiar with the modernist (post-*Gushibian*) view of the *Zhouyi* I began to see that it was all still an *interpretation*. It is necessary to emphasise this because issues that are still in great flux have taken on an appearance of being settled beyond question. Edward Shaughnessy, in his 1983 PhD dissertation, writing about two seminal modernist studies published in China in the 1930s, expressed his opinion in such a way as to reveal the new attitude, and bias, in a single sentence: 'Perhaps the most important contribution of both these works is that they served to thoroughly discredit the myth of the *Zhouyi*'s sagely authorship.'[9]

The modernists have taken full advantage of such research materials as the oracle-bone inscriptions of the Shang, discovered at the turn of the twentieth century, as well as the inscribed bronze vessels of the early Zhou dynasty that have come to light in the past few decades. These studies ought to have made it clear that there is nothing inherently naïve in the idea that King Wen created the *Zhouyi*. The Shang oracle-bone inscriptions, after all, exclusively record the concerns of the Shang kings put to the 'tortoise oracle'.[10] The language of the Shang oracle-bone inscriptions bears a close resemblance to the language of the *Zhouyi*. The Shang records have helped in deciphering obscure passages of the *Yi*, particularly by the recovery of the original etymologies of divinatory and sacrificial terminology. It is not unreasonable to suppose that the *Zhouyi*, the yarrow-stalk oracle, may possibly contain a transfer of knowledge from the tortoise divinations of the early Zhou kings, including King Wen. Yet because the initial thrust towards modernism began with an almost complete disavowal of tradition there has been a great reluctance to apply fresh thought in this area and turn back to tradition from a modern perspective. Instead, there has been a polarisation.

Direction of the argument

I propose that the *Zhouyi* does indeed preserve intact tortoise divinations of the early Zhou kings. The apparent absence of dates, names, and places—present in Shang inscriptions— suggests that specific details that originally appeared in the source materials from which the *Zhouyi* was constructed were at a later time removed by an editor, in order to generalise the text in the form we know it today. Traces remain, however, of these original oracles; dating clues, hidden names, and ancient places are still in the book, some having eluded discovery for the past 3,000 years.

Very few people are named in the *Zhouyi*, and some names have for a long time remained hidden because the characters forming them have been read according to their dictionary definitions without it being realised that a name was intended. The classic example of a name being missed is Kanghou, the Marquis of Kang, who does not appear in the Wilhelm-Baynes translation. In ancient Chinese literature Kanghou is referred to as Kangshu, *shu* meaning 'younger of brothers' (he was the ninth son of King Wen). He was enfeoffed as the Marquis of Wei, but it hadn't been appreciated he was enfeoffed twice and had previously been the Marquis of Kang, a fact now made clear by bronze inscriptions.

It was only when bronze vessels carrying the title Kanghou began to be excavated in the early decades of the twentieth century, such as the vessel known as the Kanghou *gui*,[11] that it was realised he is named in the *Zhouyi*. The character *kang* of his name means 'vigorous', hence in the judgment of hexagram 35 Wilhelm-Baynes translates *kanghou* as 'the powerful prince' instead of 'the Marquis of Kang'. The elusiveness of proper names in the *Yi* is a theme that will be returned to throughout the ensuing investigation.

I have sometimes wondered what would account for the rarity of names in the *Zhouyi*, and why those that are there have been overlooked for so long. It can, of course, be argued that when the book was written names such as Kanghou would have been instantly recognisable. But still, the nagging thought keeps arising: why are names in the *Book of Odes* and the *Book of Documents* so obvious, yet in the *Changes* those few that can be found appear to be virtually enciphered? If I were to speculate, it is almost as if they escaped the attention of the early redactors when other proper names were removed. Because Kangshu became the Marquis of Wei soon after the Conquest, for instance, his former title of Kanghou would have quickly become obsolete. If the *Zhouyi* was subjected to editing to remove proper names a century or two after his death it is quite conceivable that his early title would no longer have been recognised.[12] (This in turn forms a part of the evidence suggesting the *Zhouyi* was originally written at the time of the Conquest.)[13]

Several factors have contributed to our loss of understanding of the *Zhouyi* over time. The gradual evolution of the meanings of Chinese characters from their original concrete and substantive meanings to a great profusion of conceptual and abstract meanings has introduced numerous ambiguities, leading to the text being read in different ways at different times. By its very nature ambiguity requires insight in order to be resolved, hence those who have supposed they had it have created strikingly divergent interpretations of the same sentence. To an extent, ambiguity is a great aid to an oracle, enabling a multiplicity of possible readings. In a private consultation over a personal concern any interpretation that lifts doubts and aids decision is of value. When it comes to understanding the original meaning of the book, however, uninformed conjecture and inappropriate interpretation, not conforming to the conditions of philological accuracy, merely dulls the significance of the text. Down the centuries the *Yi* has been overlaid with explanations derived from the philosophical fashions of the day, some of which hardened into orthodoxy, particularly in the Song dynasty. Thus it became progressively harder to read the *Zhouyi* as a text of its own time. The modernist challenge to this 'hermeneutic sedimentation', as Richard Kunst called it, served to free the oracle from these anachronisms. But now modernism has itself become a new orthodoxy, and the right questions are no longer being asked.

Early sources linking King Wen with the *Changes*

In popular culture, the act of consulting the *Book of Changes* by tossing three coins six times has for centuries been idiomatically referred to as 'to enquire of Wen Wang'.

The text of the *Zhouyi* itself does not mention King Wen by name, nor does the character *wen* appear, which in its own right means 'writing, literature, culture, elegance, civil' as well as other meanings. Nor does his personal name appear, Chang, 'light of the sun'.

As King Wen is not named in the *Zhouyi*, we must search elsewhere for the origin of the tradition associating him with the book.[14] Eight centuries after the Conquest, in the third century BC, we find the first hard evidence that a belief has grown up that the *Yi* is actually about something that is not immediately obvious from the text itself. In the *Dazhuan*, the *Great Treatise*, it is all explained, almost in passing:

> The time at which the *Changes* came to the fore was that in which the house of Yin came to an end and the way of the house of [Zhou] was rising, that is, the time when King Wen and the tyrant [Zhou Xin] were pitted against each other. This is why the judgments of the book so frequently warn against danger.[15]

The tradition that has survived to the present day, namely that King Wen wrote the judgment texts and that the line texts were written by his son Dan,[16] the Duke of Zhou, is first found in the works of Ma Rong (AD79–166), an eccentric scholar of the classics.[17] Before that, however, the grand historian of China, Sima Qian (145–86BC), had recorded in 'The Biographies of the

Diviners of Lucky Days', Chapter 127 of his *Shi Ji*, the *Historical Records*, that 'ever since [Fuxi] devised the eight trigrams and King Wen of the [Zhou] expanded them with the 384 explanations of the lines, the world has been well ordered'.[18] He attributes this remark to the Former Han diviner Sima Jizhu. While in Chapter 4, his 'Basic Annals of the Zhou', Sima Qian sets down the most famous clue of all to the early existence of a tradition:

> The Earl of the West[19] probably held the throne for 50 years. It was when he was imprisoned at Youli that he probably combined the eight trigrams of the *Yijing* to form the 64 hexagrams.[20]

Richard Wilhelm noted that King Wen 'is said to have composed the judgments on the different hexagrams during his captivity'.[21] James Legge went further:

> I like to think of the lord of [Zhou], when incarcerated in [Youli], with the 64 figures arranged before him. Each hexagram assumed a mystic meaning, and glowed with a deep significance. He made it tell him of the qualities of various objects of nature, or of the principles of human society, or of the condition, actual and possible, of the kingdom. He named the figures, each by a term descriptive of the idea with which he had connected it in his mind, and then he proceeded to set that idea forth, now with a note of exhortation, now with a note of warning. It was an attempt to restrict the follies of divination within the bounds of reason.[22]

Such ideas persist, and are often repeated as fact.[23] The *Historical Records*, however, makes it clear that the idea King Wen wrote the explanations during his captivity at Youli is an unwarranted leap, conflating Chapters 4 and 127 to become a 'Chinese whispers' version of the tradition. Sima Qian actually says that King Wen probably combined the trigrams into hexagrams during his imprisonment, *i.e.* the 64 lineal figures, but it is not specifically stated when he is supposed to have set down the explanations in writing.

The *Great Treatise* may imply that King Wen wrote the judgments when he was imprisoned by reference to their frequent warnings against danger; but danger was present both before and after King Wen was imprisoned. I shall, in any case, be arguing that it is highly unlikely that the judgments and the line statements were 'written' at all, in the sense, that is, of an author writing a book. It is more reasonable to suppose that the text originated from words *spoken* by one or more of the early Zhou kings as they interpreted cracks made in tortoise shells, and that the *Zhouyi* was constructed from a store of such divinatory materials, scribes having recorded both the king's enquiry and his comment after the divination had been performed. It is in this sense that the 'traditional authorship' may be shown to have a factual basis after all.

Chapter II

The title of the oracle

It is only with the discovery of the Shang oracle-bone divination record in the twentieth century that the original meaning of *Yi* is becoming clear. The etymology of *jing*, on the other hand, is straightforward. The character refers to the warp of a fabric. The word was applied to a selection of ancient texts besides the *Yi*, such as the *Shujing* and the *Shijing*, the *Book of Documents* and *Book of Odes*, respectively, in order to distinguish them from the rapidly accumulating apocrypha devoted to their explication. *Jing* is usually translated as 'book' or 'classic'. The apocrypha are referred to as the *wei* texts, which means the weft of a fabric, the threads woven into and crossing the warp. The canonical status of the *Yi* has ensured that the text has been faithfully transmitted from the Han dynasty onwards.

But what exactly does *Yi* mean? This is more problematic, the character has a far greater antiquity. What kind of change is implied? For much of this book I will dwell on the change of the Mandate of Heaven, the replacement of the Shang dynasty by the Zhou dynasty, but this is still an abstract idea, abstract concepts generally coming into a language as extended meanings of concrete images. It is an original concrete image we are in search of. There are a number of ideas as to what this might be. The modern form of *Yi* has remained the same for over 2,000 years:

One of the dictionary meanings of *Yi*, besides 'change', is 'easy'. Fung Yu-lan proposed that the name of the book was 'the Easy', because divination by the manipulation of yarrow stalks was much easier than divination by oracle-bone.[1] It required many man-hours to produce cracks in tortoise/turtle plastrons and carapaces, and ox scapulae.[2] First the bone or shell had to be scraped and pre-bored or chiselled on the back, producing a series of round or oval hollows for the tip of a brightly glowing bronze poker or hardwood firebrand to be applied. Carbon deposits found in the hollows suggest a hardwood brand was used, kept glowing by some kind of bellows or simply blowing.[3] The hollows on the back served to locate the sites where hairline cracks were desired on the polished front, the bone or shell being thinner at these places and so more amenable to cracking. Even so, present-day attempts to reproduce Shang techniques have shown how hard it is to crack a shell by this method.[4] On this basis, Fung Yu-lan's idea that the title of the yarrow oracle is 'the Easy' does appear to have much to commend it; it is, however, simply a guess, and is unsupported by any ancient textual source.

The earliest known etymological derivation of *Yi* appears in the *Shuowen*, a dictionary compiled by Xu Shen, completed in AD 100, which suggests that the primary form of the character is a pictograph of a lizard, probably a chameleon, which can change its skin coloration, and hence, by extension, 'to change'. This early character does indeed bear a resemblance to the modern character:[5]

A further notion is that *Yi* is a composite of the characters for sun, *ri*, and moon, *yue*, with the sun at the top and the moon at the bottom, appearing thus:

This idea suggests the natural cycle of change through the image of day and night, and is attributed to Yu Fan (AD164–233).[6] James Legge followed this line of thought, but without mentioning its source.[7] This derivation cannot hold, because it depends on a resemblance to the form of the character as it is known today. *Yi* was written differently at the end of the Shang and the start of the Zhou. The lizard derivation fails for the same reason.

Wilhelm-Baynes does not discuss the etymology of the character, but does give a broad hint that the answer is to be found in a study of the Shang oracle-bone inscriptions. On the Chinese title page of Wilhelm-Baynes, and on the cover of the UK edition, the following two characters appear, which read *Zhouyi* in oracle-bone script:

The original calligrapher was Dong Zuobin, who was the first archaeologist to survey, in 1928, the Shang remains at the Yinxu site near present-day Anyang, in Henan. K C Chang, in *Shang Civilization*, translates a marvellous account, in Dong Zuobin's own words, of how local dealers in ancient relics tried to fob him off as to the location where the inscribed oracle-bones in their shops had been found. Dong finally foiled the dealers by hiring a guide of unsullied innocence, a small child, to accompany him around the areas thought likely. The child pointed to a sand-dune where Dong found oracle-bones, on the strength of which he recommended that excavation of the area begin immediately.[8]

The oracle-bones had first come to light in 1899. They had been sold to apothecaries as 'dragon bones', a traditional Chinese medicine. In one sample prescribed for a Beijing scholar, Wang Yirong, who was sick with malaria, the bones had been insufficiently ground up, and his house-guest, Liu E, the famed author of the novel *Lao Can's Travels*, noticed they appeared to be inscribed with an unknown ancient script. The two scholars eventually managed to trace the supplier, which finally led to the discovery of the archaeological site near Anyang, where local farmers had been digging up the bones and selling them. This story itself has become something of a modern legend, existing in several versions. The above account comes from Dong Zuobin.

The uppermost of the two characters on the Chinese title page and cover of Wilhelm-Baynes is how the name of the Zhou state appears on both Shang oracle-bones and early Western Zhou bronzes. The lower is the original form of *Yi*.[9] In the Shang oracle-bone inscriptions this character refers to 'a *yi* sacrifice to the sun', the context suggesting a ritual intended to change overcast conditions and rainy weather, and bring the sun out again. In the inscriptions the character precedes *ri*, 'sun', literally meaning 'change to sun' or 'change to sunny weather'.[10] When I realised this, immediately I noticed that the original character appears to be a drawing of the sun just emerging on the right from cloud cover on the left, with three slanting rays of sunshine breaking through.[11] I found out later that the contemporary Chinese scholar Yang Shuda had already explained the character in this way.[12] Hence, this is the original concrete image of 'change'. When combined with the name of the dynasty in the original title of the *Book of Changes*, the *Zhouyi*, it is the 'change' of the Zhou dynasty, the change of the dynasty from Shang to Zhou reflected in the imagery of the brightness of the sun emerging from behind the dark clouds of an oppressive regime.[13]

The fourth century BC *Mozi* quotes the *Tai Shi*, 'The Great Harangue', a chapter of the *Book of Documents*, which says: 'King Wen was like the sun or moon, shedding his bright light in the four quarters and over the western land.'[14] Richard

Wilhelm makes a similar comparison: 'The more the tyrant [Zhou Xin] gave vent to his fury and perverse cruelty, the more did men turn to the guardian of the West, Wen, whose lustre was all the brighter for this dark setting.'[15] The personal name of King Wen, Chang, actually means 'the light of the sun'. This imagery of the emerging sun is appropriate, then, both to the actual meaning of the word *Yi*, and to the particular historical circumstances surrounding the book's composition.

Chapter III

Imprisoned for a sigh

My aim in this chapter is to reconstruct the events leading up to the Conquest of the Shang as they are *traditionally* understood, and to trace the sources of that tradition. It has to be borne in mind that these sources are of varying value as true historical record. Western Zhou texts such as the *Documents* and the *Odes*, and archaeologically excavated materials originating from the time of the Conquest, obviously have the greatest veracity.

According to the *Historical Records*, Zhou Xin, the last ruler of the Shang, was a tyrant possessed of extraordinary powers of discernment who used his quick wits to find sophisticated reasons with which to refute the advice of his counsellors. He had immense physical strength and liked to fight wild animals with his bare hands, being able to lay them out on the ground with a single blow from his fist. He used dissembling tactics to present his wrongdoings in a light few could find fault with. Those who knew him to be a hypocrite kept their feelings to themselves, knowing King Zhou would turn their outspokenness against them. Ambrose Bierce defined a hypocrite as: 'One who, professing virtues that he does not respect, secures the advantage of seeming to be what he despises.' But Zhou's aim was solely to keep official censure at bay, his hypocrisy was conscious and calculating. By boasting about his virtues to his courtiers he ensured that those who saw the truth remained afraid of openly opposing him.[1]

There is an old Chinese idiom, 'Calling a stag a horse', meaning to talk up black into white, to deliberately confound right and wrong. It comes from a story told by Sima Qian about the prime minister of the second Emperor of China, who wished to usurp the throne. Being uncertain whether other ministers would yield to him he tested them out by bringing a stag to court as a gift for the Emperor. Presenting it, he said it was a horse. The Emperor laughed and said: 'Why do you call it a horse? It's a stag.' He then turned to his ministers and asked them whether it was a stag or a horse, whereupon those fearful of the prime minister fawned and said it was a horse, while some remained silent. Those who called it a stag were later killed, one by one, by the prime minister. Such was also the atmosphere at the court of the Shang tyrant, except that it was the king himself who exacted this effect. In consequence, only slanderous reports reached his ears, and his honest advisers fell silent. Petty men drew close to him, kow-towing to serve their own ends. Honourable men eventually took their leave.

In the closed world of the Shang court, King Zhou drank heavily and organised lavish feasts, collected exotic objects to fill his palace rooms, and stocked his gardens with all manner of wild animals and colourful birds, with the result that his residence became known as the Deer Pavilion.[2] He raised taxes and called for larger and larger tributes from satellite states in order to fund his extravagance. Zhou is even said to have shown flagrant contempt for the ancestors by ignoring his duty to offer them sacrifices. This charge against King Zhou is frequently repeated in early Chinese literature as being a significant factor in the downfall of the dynasty. Its earliest extant formulation appears to be in the fourth century BC *Mozi*, quoting a lost section of the *Documents*:

> [Zhou] sits with his legs sprawled out and refuses to serve the Lord on High. He neglects the spirits of former kings and fails to sacrifice to them. And yet he insists, 'I have the Mandate of Heaven!' He gives himself up to tyranny, and Heaven therefore casts him away and will not protect him.[3]

It has often been remarked that it was Zhou's insatiable lust for his seductive concubine Da Ji that inspired him to the acts of depravity that moved Heaven to withdraw its Mandate.[4] Drinking wine with Da Ji late into the night, Zhou presided over orgies; he made a lake of wine and hung up joints of meat throughout the forest, forcing young boys and girls to cavort naked with each other amidst the meat-laden trees while his musicians played licentious music with pornographic lyrics.[5] According to the fourth century AD 'Yang Zhu' chapter of the *Liezi*, King Zhou once 'let loose his desires in a night four months long', referring to an orgiastic banquet that lasted 120 days without cease, known as the 'Drinking Bout of the Long Night'.[6]

Han Feizi told a story in the third century BC illustrating one such occasion, which also shows the wisdom of the Viscount of Ji, whose example of fortitude in adversity, when the tyrant later imprisoned him, is traditionally regarded as being the subject of the fifth line of hexagram 36. Zhou got so drunk he couldn't remember what day it was. He asked those ministers who were with him, but they didn't know what day it was either. So he sent an attendant to see the Viscount of Ji, as he would surely know. The Viscount of Ji thought to himself: 'If the Lord of All-under-Heaven doesn't know what day it is, and neither do his ministers, then the state is in danger. If I alone know what day it is, then I am in danger.' So he pretended to be drunk and said he had no idea what day it was.[7]

Gradually rumours reached Zhou's ears that his acts were resented by the people and that some among the nobility plotted sedition against him. So Zhou increased the severity of his punishments to silence open criticism of his ways. He devised a new punishment to amuse Da Ji. A greased bronze pole was laid over a pit of burning charcoal, those he wished to punish were forced to walk barefoot across it. Zhou became intoxicated by the obvious delight on Da Ji's face as those he judged to be miscreants fell to their death in the red-glowing embers.

The vices of King Zhou litter the pages of history. Wang Chong of the Han noted in his *Lunheng*, *Doctrines Evaluated*, that Zhou once offended the sensibilities of his adviser the Viscount of Ji, who burst into tears one day on seeing Zhou using ivory chop-sticks.[8] Wang Chong says they were used for eating dragon liver and leopard foetus. Han Feizi's earlier version of this story explains Jizi's reaction. Apparently when Jizi saw Zhou was having ivory chop-sticks made this was the moment he 'knew the seeds' and foresaw the end of the Shang dynasty. This was the reason he became frightened. By seeing the origin he knew the outcome; by seeing the obscure he knew the manifest. Jizi's train of thought on this occasion illuminates the concept of knowing the seeds:

> Ivory chop-sticks would not be used with earthen-wares but with cups made of jade or of rhinoceros horn. Further, ivory chop-sticks and jade cups would not go with the soup made of beans and coarse greens but with the meat of long-haired buffaloes and unborn leopards. Again, eaters of the meat of long-haired buffaloes and unborn leopards would not wear short hemp clothes and eat in a thatched house but would put on nine layers of embroidered dresses and move to live in magnificent mansions and on lofty terraces. Afraid of the ending, I cannot help trembling with fear at the beginning.[9]

The *Mozi* states that Zhou Xin 'cast aside the aged, murdered little children, roasted innocent men alive, and cut open pregnant women'.[10] As Arthur Waley pointed out, the legend of King Zhou's vices evolved over time. The charge made in the *Documents* and the *Odes* that Zhou drank excessively is amplified in later sources, where he makes a lake of wine; he does not merely disregard the advice of his officers of state, he has them pickled.[11] Challenges to this consensus are rare, but do exist, cautioning one against accepting fables as history, such as Zigong's comment: 'Zhou was not as wicked as all that. This is why the honourable man is loathe to live downstream, because all the sordid imaginings of the Empire wash up there.'[12]

Zhou installed three senior lords to rule in his name in outlying territories: the Marquis of E, the Marquis of Jiu, and Chang, the future King Wen, who became the Earl of the West, Xibo. The Marquis of Jiu had a pretty daughter who he presented to King Zhou, but not being a woman of dissolute tastes she refused his passionate advances. In a fit of anger Zhou killed her and ordered that the Marquis of Jiu be minced up and made into a meat stew. The Marquis of E, moved to indignation, remonstrated violently with the tyrant and for his pains was sliced up into strips and made into pemmican. The earliest reference to King Zhou's predilection for bringing his vassals to this grisly end is found in the fourth century BC poem, the *Li Sao*, 'On Encountering Sorrows', where the poet Qu Yuan says: 'Zhou cut up and salted the bodies of his ministers; and so the days were numbered of the House of Yin.'[13] King Zhou is said to have distributed among his feudatories, as a warning to others, pickled portions of those who had had the temerity to admonish him.

In Sima Qian's version of events, the Earl of the West, who had cultivated his virtue and was loved by his people, when told about these events could not contain a deep sigh, but made no open protestation. Nonetheless, Hu, the Marquis of Chong, who for years had harboured an acute jealousy of Chang, heard about this sigh and duly reported it to King Zhou, adding a slander of his own creation: 'The Earl of the West is secretly hatching a plot against you, he is accumulating good deeds; the feudal lords are all turning to him, this is not to your advantage.' Zhou had the Earl of the West imprisoned at Youli, where, according to the *Zuozhuan*, he remained for seven years.[14] It was during this time that Sima Qian says he 'probably' formed the hexagrams of the *Yi*.

In an alternative version, according to Qu Yuan in the *Tian Wen*, *Ask Heaven*, a minister named Mei Bo was 'sliced and salted' by King Zhou.[15] Sima Qian doesn't mention Mei Bo in the *Shi Ji*. Qu Yuan later notes: 'When Zhou bestowed that flesh on him, the Earl of the West declared it to Heaven.'[16] Presumably this was the flesh of Mei Bo. The Earl of the West offered the flesh as a sacrifice in the temple of the ancestors in order to declare King Zhou's wrongdoings to Heaven. One tradition has it that Zhou heard about King Wen's shudder of disgust on receiving this ghastly package, and that this was the reason he had him imprisoned.

The *Qin Cao*, or *Compositions for the Lute* compiled by Cai Yong (AD133–192), here expands on Sima Qian's bare outline of the events resulting in the release of the Earl of the West.[17] Fearing that Chang was about to be executed, King Wen's ministers went to visit him at Youli. King Wen, unable to speak freely, spoke in gestures. He winked and slid his right eye round, as one man might silently point out to another an attractive girl passing by, indicating King Zhou was a womaniser and doted on the ladies. He patted his stomach with his fine archery bow to hint that King Zhou had a great appetite for coveted possessions and exotic ornaments. He mimed the frail jittery steps of an old man, meaning that time was fast running out and his ministers should gather such items to offer as a ransom without delay. With no words spoken openly to this effect, King Wen's ministers correctly interpreted the message and scoured the land, going to every village, until they found two beautiful girls, a large water-cowrie, and a fine white horse with a red mane.[18] They hurried to the Deer Pavilion and displayed them in the central courtyard. When King Zhou set his eyes upon them a great excitement was aroused within him: 'How gorgeous they are! Who is their owner?' One of King Wen's ministers rushed into the courtyard and said: 'They are the prized possessions of the Earl of the West. We have brought them as a ransom because he has been condemned to death.' King Zhou said: 'How generous he is to me!' In the *Shi Ji* version a minister of King Wen makes use of the offices of Zhou's favoured counsellor, the sycophantic Fei Zhong, in order to present the ransom. King Zhou, on seeing the gifts, said: 'Just one of these would have been enough to secure the release of the Earl of the West, how much more is possible with this amount.'[19]

King Wen was immediately pardoned, released from Youli, and reinstated as Xibo.[20] King Zhou ceremonially bestowed upon him bows, arrows, hatchets, and battle-axes, and increased his powers by granting Xibo the authority to launch punitive military campaigns and expeditions under his own prerogative. Some commentators make the mistake of thinking that this investiture is what is meant by King Wen 'receiving the Mandate'. It is a rationalisation disingenuous to the vast body of early literature that makes it clear that the populations of both the Zhou and Shang nations implicitly believed that King Wen had received the Mandate from Heaven to form a new dynasty. The *Book of Documents* even says that 'Heaven grandly ordered King Wen to kill the great Yin and grandly receive its Mandate'.[21] The Mandate of Heaven, *tianming*, can only be bestowed by Heaven; the 'command' or 'charge', also *ming*, that was given to King Wen by the Shang ruler, was the granting of a fiefdom.

After King Wen's release, Sima Qian has King Zhou saying to him: 'The one who slandered you, Xibo, was Hu, the Marquis of Chong.' But in the *Qin Cao* King Zhou tells one of King Wen's ministers: 'The man who acted behind the back of the Lord of Qi[22] has a hook nose and a disfigured ear.' When King Wen heard this description of the traitor he knew it was the Marquis of Chong. The Earl of the West gave King Zhou a gift of land west of the Luo River,[23] and used his new-found influence to request that the 'roasting pillar' punishment be abolished, to which Zhou agreed.[24]

The Earl of the West returned to his own territory and discreetly continued his virtuous deeds, while at the Shang court King Zhou appointed the scheming Fei Zhong to administer the state, who used his position to amass personal wealth, helped by E Lai, who was skilled at defaming his rivals. Both of these ministers are named in the fourth century BC *Mozi*, which appears to be the earliest mention of them.[25] The third century BC *Han Feizi* makes the perverse claim that 'King Wen financed Fei [Zhong], made him stay around [Zhou], and told him to disturb his mind'.[26] Han Feizi also claims elsewhere in his essays that King Wen gave Fei Zhong a gift of carved jade plates because he loved his usefulness, which immediately calls to mind the Viscount of Ji's fears over the ivory chopsticks. King Wen had earlier refused to give the jade plates away when King Zhou had sent a worthy minister to get them, because King Wen disliked to see an honourable man advance his career under the tyrant.[27] How much of this account is reflective of Han Feizi's own Machiavellian political cunning, and how much is a genuine indication of King Wen's long-range strategy, will probably never be known. But Fei Zhong

was undoubtedly a slippery figure. There is a picturesque
Chinese idiom used of those who rise in life by means of other
people: 'The leech attaches itself to the legs of the egret.' Han
Feizi also says it was Fei Zhong who tried three times to
persuade King Zhou to censure King Wen, as he would be
trouble in the future, but Zhou would not listen, resulting in
the fall of the Yin.[28] This presumably refers to Fei Zhong
trying to dissuade the tyrant from releasing King Wen, before
he was bribed to change his stance.

The feudal lords grew more and more disaffected by the
corruption at the Shang court and began to turn away, looking
to the Earl of the West, whose reputation was rapidly spreading.
He was known as a good man who took care of the elderly and
respected the young, who was willing to humble himself before
those of wisdom and ability. In the *Wu Yi* chapter of the
Documents, 'Against Idleness', the Duke of Zhou says King Wen
dressed in coarse clothing and personally took to farming. He
was so dedicated to uniting and harmonising the people that
'from dawn to noon, and from noon until the last rays of the sun
were slanting in the west, he did not allow himself leisure to
eat'.[29] The *Shi Ji* says that at midday he would forego his meal
in order to make time to receive petitioners. Those with
disputes to settle turned to him as an arbiter who showed no
personal bias.

The Yu and Rui peoples had a legal case they were unable to
resolve so they made their way to the Zhou court. As they
crossed the boundary into the Zhou state they were immediately impressed by the way farmers were not protective of their
land, giving way to all who wished to cross their fields, and that
the custom of the people was to yield to their elders. Before the
Yu and Rui delegations had reached the Earl of the West they
grew ashamed of themselves, turning to each other they said:
'What we are struggling for between ourselves is what the Zhou
people consider dishonourable. Why then are we going to see
them? We will only bring ignominy upon ourselves if we
continue further.' Whereupon they settled their differences,
ceased to contest with one another, and returned to their own
lands. When the feudal lords heard about it they began to say

among themselves: 'Perhaps the Earl of the West has received the Mandate.' Mozi says:

> In former times King Wen was enfeoffed in [Zhou] at Mount [Qi]. Making allowances for the irregular boundary line, his domain measured only a hundred square *li*.[30] He worked with his people for universal love and mutual benefit, and shared with them what was in abundance. So those nearby found security in his government and those far away were won by his virtue. All those who heard of King Wen rose up and went to him, and the morally weak, the unworthy, and the crippled who could not rise stayed where they were and pleaded, saying, 'Couldn't the domain of King Wen be extended to our borders, so that we too could benefit? Why can't we too be like the people of King Wen?' Therefore Heaven and the spirits enriched him, the feudal lords became his allies, the people loved him, and worthy men came to serve him. Before he died he became ruler of the world and leader of the other lords.[31]

This was how King Zhou gradually lost his hold on power. Confucius praised the temperance of King Wen by saying that even when he had possession of two-thirds of the Empire he still continued to serve Yin as a vassal.[32] King Wen was a man of remarkable foresight and content to bide his time as a 'hidden dragon'. Mencius, who also says King Wen began his rise from a territory of just a hundred square *li*, and that this was why it was so difficult, remarks on his sense of timing by quoting a saying: 'You may be clever, but it is better to make use of circumstances; you may have a hoe, but it is better to wait for the right season.'[33] The year after the Yu and the Rui settled their dispute the Earl of the West chastised the Quan Rong, the barbarian tribe known as the 'Dog' Rong.[34] He followed this up by other military expeditions to secure a strategic foothold. Eventually he chastised the traitor Hu, the Marquis of Chong, and then the following year moved his capital from the foot of Mount Qi 70 miles south-east to Feng, an advance post for the Conquest of the Shang. A further 380 miles march away east-north-east lay Dayi Shang, 'Great City Shang'.[35]

In Feng King Wen built what Arthur Waley translated in ode 242 as a 'Magic Tower', and Bernhard Karlgren translated as a 'Divine Tower'. The actual expression used in the ode is *lingtai*. Soothill translates it as the 'Skyward Tower' in his book *The Hall of Light*. King Wen's *lingtai* contrasts with Zhou Xin's *lutai*, 'Stag Tower' or 'Deer Pavilion'. Chapter 12 of the second century BC *Huainanzi* suggests a reason why King Wen built his tower:

> On his return home (from imprisonment at [Youli]), Wen Wang simulated an infatuation for building doors inlaid with jade and lofty towers, played with girls and spent his time dilly-dallying with drums and music; but really he was waiting his chance to fall on [Zhou]. When [Zhou] heard of these infatuations, he said: '[Chang] has changed his ways and altered the course of his life. There will be no more disquiet for me.'[36]

King Wen's motive for building his tower was far more serious than to fool the tyrant into thinking he had embraced hedonism and was no longer a threat. King Wen, having been active all day long, at nightfall was apprehensive, watching the skies for heavenly movements from a ritual platform raised high above the ground. A *lingtai* is an astronomical observatory.

Observatories in ancient China kept diligent watch on the skies for portents, such as meteors, comets, and eclipses, all of which in increasing degrees can be omens of the fall of the ruling dynasty. Comets were referred to as 'brush stars', brushing away the old, whereas a meteor is referred to in the astronomical chapters of the *Jin Shu*, the *History of the Jin Dynasty*, as *mingxing*, a 'mandated star', which carried the command of Heaven for implementation below. If an unusually bright meteorite lands directly in the camp of an army it is likened to a heavenly missile, and, according to the *Tang Shu*, the *History of the Tang Dynasty*, it is an infallible sign that the army is doomed. From the *Shi Ji* we learn that an eclipse of the moon is an indication of moral deficiencies on the part of ministers; whereas an eclipse of the sun indicates a need for moral rectification by the ruler, a sign which, on occasion, was actually heeded.[37] At the beginning of the Tai He reign period

(AD 227–232), the court astronomer advised the Emperor of an impending eclipse of the sun, submitting a memorial to the throne to the effect that both he and the prime minister be granted leave to offer sacrifices at the *lingtai*. The Emperor replied:

> I have heard that when the Emperor is at fault the heavens are alarmed and manifest portents as warnings to him to amend his ways. When the sun or moon is veiled or totally eclipsed errors in his rule are implied. Since I came to the throne I have failed to exemplify the fine example set by my forebears as a guide for my subjects. I have offended the ancestors. When the heavens remind me of my shortcomings I must make recompense in response to their sign. The heavens are to man as father to son; I have never heard it said that a son, when admonished by his father, may appease him by offering him a banquet. Similarly, it would be ill-befitting to send my prime minister and court astronomer to offer sacrifices to avert the calamity. I hereby issue an edict that all officials, from senior minister to minister and grandee, should attend to their duties with extra diligence; I shall honour and promote all who can help compensate my neglect.[38]

Ancient Chinese history books could almost be reduced to a compendium of eclipse records and downfalls of dynasties, but so far as I know no-one has yet correlated the data to show the success rate of this method of foretelling the future. The oldest debate in the study of omens is whether celestial phenomena cause events or simply forewarn those sufficiently enlightened to understand them. The correlation of eclipses to worldly disasters certainly stands out in the study of military history, but whether the catastrophe is caused by the effect the event has on the participants, or is fated to happen, is a challenging question.[39]

The *Book of Documents* recounts, in the chapter entitled 'The Earl of the West Subdues Li', what appears to have been King Wen's last campaign against the Shang before he died, the final Conquest being completed by his son King Wu. In the wake of Xibo taking the Shang garrison at Li,[40] a Shang vassal warns the tyrant Zhou that 'Heaven has made an end to the Mandate of Yin'. Even the state oracle will not presume to foresee any luck for the Yin: 'The tortoise dares not oppose it.'[41] The vassal implores: 'It is not that our former kings do not come to the aid of us later men, but that the king is dissolute and tyrannical and hastens his own end. Therefore Heaven has cast us off.' The vassal tells Zhou that the commoners wish for the dynasty to fall into ruin, that they say among themselves: 'Why does Heaven not send down its terrors? Why does he who has the Great Mandate not make his appearance? What has the present king to do with us?' To which the Shang king replies: 'Oh, was my life not decreed in Heaven?' Exasperated by Zhou's defiance, the vassal returns to his own city, uttering as a soliloquy his response: 'Your crimes, which are many, are registered above, how can you make Heaven accountable for your life? When Yin perishes, if you carry on with your deeds, you cannot help but be killed in your own state.'

So steadfastly did King Zhou cling to the notion that everything he did was at the behest of Heaven once the Mandate had been given to his House, that he could not countenance its end. When the Shang were defeated and the Zhou dynasty was installed, the invaders were anxious to inculcate in the conquered people the belief that Heaven's Mandate was not forever, but depended upon the actions of the ruling House. Herrlee Creel put forward the view in *The Origins of Statecraft in China* that the very doctrine of *tianming* was an invention of the Zhou to justify their take-over, a propaganda ploy, and that it did not previously exist in the mind-set of the Shang. He hypothesises that the strange absence of any surviving genuinely Shang literature may indicate that the Zhou destroyed it to eradicate evidence that *tianming* was an alien concept.[42]

The Henan oracle-bone record, a textual source only becoming available to Chinese historians in the twentieth century, contains little to imply that *tianming* was known to the Shang. It may, however, be seen as a new name for an old idea. The meaning of *tianming* would not have been lost on the Shang. Their theology did include the concept that the ancestors could curse the living if they were dissatisfied with their behaviour,[43] such as laxity in providing them with sacrifices, a charge levelled at Zhou Xin. As to whether the Zhou destroyed Shang literature, William G Boltz has questioned the extent of literacy beyond, and even within, the Shang court. He points out that there is nothing in the archaeological evidence that requires us to assume the existence of a wide variety of now lost Shang written texts.[44] The extremely short inscriptions on excavated Shang bronzes, often no more than two or three characters, when contrasted with the lengthy and historically detailed inscriptions of the early Zhou that appear almost immediately after the Conquest, suggest that the Shang may have had no 'books' to destroy in the first place.

If Creel is right, however, that the Mandate of Heaven sprang into existence with the Zhou Conquest, and was not known to Tang the Completer who, according to the Zhou, received the Mandate to conquer the Xia and found the Shang, then the unquestioning acceptance of the concept for three thousand years of Chinese history must stand as the crowning achievement of King Wen, King Wu, and the Duke of Zhou. The idea of *tianming* set before the people and their rulers alike the principle that humanitarian standards of government succeed and corrupt government ultimately fails because Heaven wills it, with the bold implication that revolution against an hereditary Emperor can actually be sanctioned by Heaven. *Mencius* 1B/8 defends the idea of permissible regicide by likening it to punishing an outcast (in Japan, which knew no dynastic changes, this passage was deleted from texts of *Mencius* used in schools in the period of ultra-nationalism before and during the Second World War). The very term for 'revolution' in China is to this day *geming*, which literally means 'changing the Mandate' or 'transferring the Mandate'.[45] The same character, Ge, is the title of hexagram 49, translated in Wilhelm-Baynes as 'Revolution'. Originally *ge* referred to moulting or the hide of an animal, leading to its translation in modernist renderings of this hexagram as 'leather' or 'rawhide'. That 'Revolution' is the true reading of hexagram 49 is implied by the presence in the fourth line of the expression *gaiming*, which also means 'to change the Mandate', an action accorded the prognostication 'auspicious'.

In the Shang capital, shortly before the Conquest, King Zhou's indulgence in wicked deeds grew all the more wildly out of control. Zhou's elder step-brother Weizi, the Viscount of Wei, several times warned that the dynasty was on the brink of ruin, but King Zhou would not listen. After seeking the counsel of the Senior Master and the Junior Master, the Viscount of Ji and Bi Gan, respectively, Weizi went into voluntary exile. Sima Qian does not record their discussion, but it can be found in the chapter of the *Book of Documents* entitled 'Weizi':

The Viscount of Wei spoke thus:

Senior Master and Junior Master, the House of Yin can no longer sustain rule over the four quarters. What our founding ancestor[46] achieved was at the behest of Heaven, but we have undone his good work by stupefying ourselves with wine. The people of Yin, small and great alike, are thieves, villainous and treacherous. The nobility and office-holders compete to violate the laws; they are all guilty so how can anyone ever be brought to justice? Is it any surprise that commoners rise up in violence against each other? Yin is drowning, like one wading to cross the great water without having found a ford, who cannot now find a bank. Yin is at the point of perishing; the time has come.

Senior Master and Junior Master, the old men of our House have withdrawn to the wilderness,[47] and you do not indicate any course of action to me, but speak only of impending ruin. What is to be done?

The Senior Master spoke thus:

Son of our former king, Heaven is striking a massive blow to waste the state of Yin. The king does not fear that which should be feared, and he offends the elders, those who have long been in office.

The people of Yin now even steal the pure sacrificial animals, long promised to the spirits of Heaven and Earth, for their own cooking pots—all without fear of disaster.[48]

Yet when I survey the people of Yin I find them shouldering the burden of heavy taxes, which has led to hatred and resentment without cease. The crime is that of one person. Multitudes are starving with no-one to whom they can make their appeal.

Shang will now have its disaster; I will be a part of that. When Shang has lost its laws, I will not serve the new House. But I tell you, son of our former king, make your way away from here. What I said long ago will bring injury upon you.[49] If you, king's son, do not go away then our sacrifices will utterly perish. Let us each do our duty to the spirits of our former kings as is appropriate.[50] As for myself, I do not think of making my escape.[51]

Following this meeting, Weizi fled the capital. Bi Gan, the Junior Master, approached King Zhou at court and courageously expressed his concern about the way the state was degenerating: 'As an official I must register my disapproval, even at the risk of death.' King Zhou, knowing Bi Gan's reputation as a sage, said: 'I have heard that the hearts of sages have seven apertures, shall we see?' He had Bi Gan's chest cut open to examine his heart.[52] Han Feizi says that Bi Gan knew the course of events but not the mind of his master, whereas Zhou's more obsequious ministers did not know the course of events but certainly knew the mind of their master. Han Feizi adds that the honourable man who knows both will always be secure.[53] This description fits the Viscount of Ji, the Senior Master, who had foreseen it all. He grew afraid, and feigned madness, like Claudius at Rome. King Zhou had him imprisoned.[54] The example of Jizi, who, in Richard Wilhelm's words, 'did not allow external misery to deflect him from his convictions', is seen in hexagram 36/5 as providing 'a teaching for those who cannot leave their posts in times of darkness'.[55]

The earliest reference to Jizi feigning insanity appears to be in the fourth century BC *Ask Heaven*.[56] *Analects* 18/1 simply says Jizi was made a slave; the same section substantiates that Weizi left the capital and that Bi Gan lost his life for remonstrating with the tyrant, not mentioning, however, the manner of his death. The earliest reference I have found to Bi Gan having his heart cut out is in the third century BC *Xunzi*, which also says Jizi was imprisoned and mentions King Zhou's punishment of the roasting pillar.[57] The *Han Feizi* says that 'Zhou made request for Bi Gan's heart'.[58]

Mencius makes the point that it was only because King Zhou was assisted by fine men of the calibre of the Viscount of Wei, Bi Gan, and the Viscount of Ji, that it took such a long time for the dynasty to fall.[59] They are referred to as the 'three men of perfect virtue' (*sanren*). News of the death of Bi Gan and the imprisonment of Jizi reached the Zhou capital from musicians who fled the Shang court. In the next three chapters the focus will shift to King Wen's city of Feng in the west, the homeland of the Zhou. But before that, below is ode 255, which captures the spirit of the time like few other texts of the period:[60]

Vast is Shangdi,[61]
Ruler of the people below;
Terrible is Shangdi,
His Mandate has many rules.
Heaven gives birth to the multitudes of people,
But its Mandate is not to be relied on;[62]
To begin well is common,
But to end well is rare indeed.

King Wen said: 'Alas!
Alas, you Yin-Shang!
You are unruly,
You are oppressive,
You men of office,
You men of power.
Heaven makes you reckless,
To exalt it with violence.'

King Wen said: 'Alas!
Alas, you Yin-Shang!
You should hold to what is right and good,
Your violence is resented.
You uphold slanderers,

You give office to henchmen,
Who stand up and imprecate,
Without limit, without end.'

King Wen said: 'Alas!
Alas, you Yin-Shang!
You shout and bawl in the central kingdom,
You make a virtue out of heaping up hatred.
You do not make your virtue enlightened,
You do not distinguish the loyal and the perverse;
No, your virtue does not shine bright,
You do not distinguish your true ministers.'

King Wen said: 'Alas!
Alas, you Yin-Shang!
It is not Heaven that steeps you in wine,
It is you who are bent on impropriety and use it,
Most vulgar are your manners.
You make no distinction between light and darkness,
You shout and clamour,
You turn day into night.'

King Wen said: 'Alas!
Alas, you Yin-Shang!
You chirrup like cicadas, like grasshoppers,
You foam and froth like bubbling waters, boiling broth;
Small and great alike are on the brink of ruin,
But still you pursue your course.
When you are overbearing in the central kingdom,
It is felt as far away as Guifang.'[63]

King Wen said: 'Alas!
Alas, you Yin-Shang!
It is not that Shangdi bestows no blessings,
It is that Yin does not follow the old ways.
Though there are no longer any wise old men,
Still there are the statutes and laws.
You have not heeded them,
So the Great Mandate is tumbling down.'

King Wen said: 'Alas!
Alas, you Yin-Shang!
The people have a saying:
"When a tree crashes down and its roots are lifted,
The branches and leaves are as yet unharmed;
It is the root that is the first to be disposed of."[64]
The mirror for Yin is not far off,
It is in the age of the Xia king.'[65]

This vitriolic reproach to Shang rule was written, I suspect, after the Conquest, although it is made to sound as if it was said by King Wen in the run-up to the invasion. It is nonetheless a powerful indictment that reflects what was to come. And, of course, it is not beyond the bounds of possibility that the anonymous poet was quoting an oral tradition passed down about what 'King Wen said'.

Chapter IV

An overlooked solar eclipse record

It is my contention that a total eclipse of the sun occurred shortly before the fall of the Shang dynasty, which was perceived by King Wu as an auspicious omen signifying the transfer of the Mandate of Heaven to the Zhou. This is not a generally appreciated aspect of the Conquest story because, so far as I have been able to ascertain, the eclipse was recorded in only one place, hexagram 55 of the *Zhouyi*.[1] Though the eclipse is clearly referred to, those searching ancient Chinese annals for astronomical data have tended to ignore the *Yi* as an historical resource. Because the original literal meaning of the *Changes* was buried beneath layers of symbolic interpretation the sense of the eclipse as something that actually happened has been completely overlooked. For instance, Richard Wilhelm was one of the few who fully realised hexagram 55 was about a solar eclipse, but he treated it as if it was intended to be a metaphor, presumably because of the seeming absence of any detail to firmly establish it as an historical event; in general, though, he favoured a symbolic reading, not a literal one. The implications of the literal reading, however, are more far-reaching. We are able to reconstruct a lost pivotal moment in the great historical event from which tradition asserts the *Book of Changes* emerged, the Conquest of the Shang by the Zhou, and establish the year for the fall of the Shang dynasty simply and accurately as 1070BC, a date that supersedes all previous concocted chronologies. All this provided, that is, that the following literary analysis proves a persuasive argument.

In its broader ramifications, this elucidative study of a single hexagram and its solar eclipse episode serves to illustrate that the *Zhouyi* does indeed have a concealed narrative integrity underpinning many of its enigmatic statements. Once the story is supplemented by other sources much that initially appears obscure makes sense. Marcel Granet made use of this method when he brought out the courtship festivals that were hidden, yet obvious once realised, in the love songs of the *Shijing*: 'Studies such as these, being inductive, assume part of the hypothesis which it is desired to prove, but the conclusions which have been drawn may be verified by comparison.'[2]

The journey towards this fresh interpretation began in the smallest of ways. A bemusing translation was pointed out to me in the work of Rudolf Ritsema and Stephen Karcher.[3] In the second and fourth lines of hexagram 55 they have translated *jian dou* as 'visualizing a bin'. Wilhelm-Baynes gives this same expression as 'the polestars can be seen'. More correctly, this is a reference to seeing the Big Dipper, or the Plough as it is called in England, the seven-star asterism (a group of stars) that is part of the larger constellation of the Great Bear or *Ursa Major*. The Dipper is regarded by Daoists as synonymous with 'the polestars'; the Dipper is at the centre of their cult of polar star magic. Legge rendered *dou* as 'the constellation of the Bushel' in 1882, which he identified as corresponding to *Ursa Major*, or, in a footnote, 'perhaps part of Sagittarius'. The Big Dipper is also known to the Chinese as the Northern Ladle or *beidou*, which distinguishes it from *nandou*, the Southern Ladle, a six-star asterism in Sagittarius. The Southern Ladle, a grouping not noted by western astronomers, is not to be confused with *Ursa Minor*, a ladle with the north celestial pole at the end of its handle, which similarly went unobserved by the Chinese who saw two different constellations in this region of the sky.[4] Only de Harlez, in his 1889 translation of the *Yijing*, rendered *dou* as Sagittarius, thinking it *nandou*.

Clearly it is first of all important to be sure that it is *beidou*, the Big Dipper, that is referred to in hexagram 55. Fortunately, we can be. In the *Shijing* ode 203 establishes an early precedent for referring to the Dipper by the character *dou* alone. This ode is traditionally ascribed to the reign of King You (r.781–771BC), the 'bad last king' of the Western Zhou, as Arthur Wright dubbed the motif; though Arthur Waley argued the ode must date back to a time when the dynasty was still powerful if it is to make sense. The traditional chronology for the Western Zhou is from 1122BC to 771BC, when the capital was removed from Hao in the west, in modern Shaanxi, to Luoyang 200 miles to the east in Henan, marking the beginning of the Eastern Zhou. In the ode a man of the east complains bitterly that all the best jobs go to the sons of the men of the west, the hangers-on in the capital (the young noblemen 'foppishly mincing' in all their finery, in Waley's turn-of-phrase), while the sons of the men of the east do all of the hard work but get none of the pay. Though the Zhou aristocracy are descended from the noble Kings Wen and Wu they have left their virtues far behind and the dynasty has already fallen into decadence. The narrator of the ode accuses the Zhou court of nepotism in handing out high-sounding titles to the sons of petty henchmen, who are placed in lucrative offices where they are wholly incompetent, lazy, and useless. Employing what is possibly the earliest usage of the simile 'mere luminaries', he compares them to stars that are named after useful things but cannot perform the function their title implies. The 'Weaver Girl' (Vega) is idle at her loom and spins no material, the 'Draught Ox' (Altair) cannot be used to hitch a cart, while 'in the south is the Winnowing Basket, but it cannot sift, or raise the chaff; in the north there is the Ladle (*dou*), but it cannot scoop wine or conjee'.[5]

The 'Winnowing Basket', *ji*, is a four-star asterism in Sagittarius, the seventh and last mansion of the Azure Dragon.[6] It shares its name with Jizi, the Viscount of Ji, the minister who was imprisoned by Zhou Xin.[7] Pertinent at this point in the discussion, however, is the reference to the Ladle in the north, which establishes beyond doubt that *dou* is *beidou*, the Northern Ladle or Big Dipper. While *dou* can indeed be a 'bin', a receptacle for grain, ten *dou* being the typical capacity of a tub of rice, Ritsema and Karcher entirely omit to mention its stellar connotation. This double-meaning arose because *dou* is essentially a 'dry measure', often translated as a peck where this is a suitable rendering from the context; hence Legge named the Big Dipper the Bushel, which is four pecks in quantity. In Zhou times, however, the exact capacity of a *dou* was not yet standardised. It was used in a figurative sense to refer to any set measure; examples include the cup of an acorn, still used to this day by Chinese apothecaries for measuring out powdered drugs, and a ladle. Thus we arrive at the constellation of the Ladle, which its shape resembles. In France it is known, by the same principle, as *La Casserole* or the Saucepan.

The second and fourth lines of hexagram 55 refer to an 'obscuration', *bu*, that resulted in the Big Dipper being seen at noon.[8] Yet despite this clear description of an unusual astronomical observation, many translators besides Ritsema and Karcher, even those who correctly identify the Dipper, seem not to realise it is an actual record of a solar eclipse: something that really happened. The concise style here is reminiscent of the *Chunqiu* or *Spring and Autumn Annals,* the chronicle compiled for the period 722BC to 481BC. This brief text intersperses solar and lunar eclipse records between cursory mentions of political assassinations, raids, deaths, burials, murders, plagues of locusts, lightning strikes, sacrifices for rain, and curious omen-phenomena such as, for the year 644BC: 'There fell stones in [Song], five of them. In the same month, six fish-hawks flew backwards, past the capital of [Song].'[9] The former appears to be a fall of meteorites, while the *Zuozhuan* (the *Chronicle of Zuo,* covering roughly the same period) speculates that the latter was occasioned by a high wind so strong the hawks could not make headway against it and were carried back, struggling, against its current. Later the same year the youngest daughter of the duke died, as did two other notables, and in the winter the duke met with dignitaries of the feudal states. The details of when and who are not important here, it is the style of the work that commands attention. Just as in the *Chunqiu,* in hexagram 55 a web of sparsely-worded seemingly disconnected political events is woven around the omen of the Dipper being seen at noon. An unnamed king offers a sacrifice. Tortoise divinations are performed. There is a meeting with another lord, probably to form an alliance.

Someone's right arm gets broken. And, in the top line, there is a description of a person in a 'mourning hut', a record to which a 'disastrous' prognostication has been attached. This characterisation of the sixth line was first suggested by de Harlez and has been ignored ever since. Though he mistakenly identified the occupant as the Shang king Wu Ding, whose time in the mourning hut was auspicious and is mentioned in 'The Charge to Yue', a chapter of the *Book of Documents* the authenticity of which has been challenged, the basic insight is sound.[10]

In the Shang and Zhou dynasties a young king, mourning for his deceased father, was expected to undergo austerities for a nominal period of three years; in practice this was 25 months, *into* the third year. He exchanged the comforts of the palace for a rough hut erected in one of the courtyards, screened off from his family, seeing and speaking to no-one during the time of mourning, when the state was under the control of the prime minister. The *Mozi*, in a chapter entitled 'Moderation in Funerals', describes how the occupant of the mourning hut was expected to live:

> He must . . . sleep on a straw mat, and use a clod of earth for a pillow. In addition he is urged not to eat so as to appear starved, to wear thin clothes so as to appear cold, to acquire a lean and sickly look and a dark complexion. His ears and eyes are to appear dull, his hands and feet lacking in strength, as though he had lost the use of them. And in the case of higher officials we are told that during a period of mourning they should be unable to rise without support or to walk without a cane. And all this is to last for three years.[11]

Confucius appears to approve of such practices,[12] whereas Modi ridicules the custom in the *Mozi*. The phrase in hexagram 55/6 translated in Wilhelm-Baynes as 'for three years he sees nothing' is literally 'three years not admitting to audience'. The character *di* here means 'to see face to face; to be admitted to audience'. The only sensible way to understand this much-misunderstood sixth line is to see in it a depiction of a regal mourning hut.[13] For some strange reason this knowledge was lost very early on and never recovered. In the *Zuozhuan*, in a conversation referring to the *Yi* that purportedly took place in 603BC, one of the participants says: 'A worthless fellow who has high ambitions appears in the *Zhouyi* in the line of Feng (hexagram 55) that changes it to Li (hexagram 30).' This interpretation has been taken for granted since then. Wilhelm's comment is in the same vein and most people cannot see the line as meaning anything else, illustrating the degree to which the *Yijing* must be reinvigorated by fresh thought.

The major difference between the *Chunqiu* and the *Zhouyi* is that the *Chunqiu* identifies people by name, specifying places and dates, whereas events in the *Yi* seem to float in an indeterminate sea stripped of points of reference. As Kidder Smith put it, the *Yi* 'lacks narrative, narrator, and an implicit audience—anything that might identify a human voice or persona'.[14] Though this overstates the case, as sinological research can discover concealed people, place-names, and indications of time (which it is the object of this essay to decipher), nonetheless it is true that the Chinese do not regard the *Yi* as a history-book. Scholars who do not make it the sole focus of their attention seem to see only its obscurity.[15]

Herrlee Creel, who became an unrivalled authority on the Western Zhou dynasty, felt moved to write in 1936, in his youth, that the unusually cryptic 'cabalistic' language of the earliest layer of the *Book of Changes* 'makes one wonder if it was written at a time when the [Zhou]s had not yet learned to write very clear Chinese'.[16] Henri Maspero, in his time the foremost western scholar of ancient China, even went so far as to say in his 1927 book *La Chine Antique*: 'There are several translations of the [*Yijing*], all bad: by its very character, the work is almost untranslatable.'[17] Arthur Waley makes the point that in early China writing was essentially no more than an aid to memory, 'its purpose was to help people not to forget what they knew already; whereas in more advanced communities the chief use of writing is to tell people things that they have not heard before'.[18] In the early years of the first millennium BC it is highly unlikely a book of oracles created out of the act of divination would have changed hands without the accompaniment of an oral instruction in its meaning. This may explain the enigmatic style of the *Changes,* and why prolonged study and meditation upon its mysteries can give rise to an intuition into its meaning that restores to it what appears by its depth and consistency to be the original sense, while to others less enamoured of it it appears utterly opaque. Kidder Smith observes that 'the *Yi* may be judged the quintessential written text—pure residue, bereft of context, syntax, voice, and intentionality'.[19]

This difficulty is reflected in the fact that of western translators of the *Yijing* only Richard Wilhelm makes satisfactory mention of a solar eclipse in among the events of hexagram 55, though even he passes quickly over the literal image to draw out the symbolism of 'plots and party intrigues, which have the darkening effect of an eclipse of the sun'. In this he reflects the attitude of the Chinese literati since the time of Wang Bi (AD226–249). Just as the habits, habitat, and life-cycle of the dragon, crucial to understanding hexagram 1, were bred out of the *Yijing* and the Emperor substituted as the primary symbol instead, similarly the chronicle of a solar eclipse omen was taken as a metaphor, and the original sense, though perfectly preserved, was no longer seen.[20]

The eclipse as an actual event even eluded the Protestant missionary Alexander Wylie, whose list of 925 solar eclipses recorded in Chinese literature was published in 1897.[21] Ignoring for a moment his earliest eclipse, the list runs from 776BC up to AD1785. The 'ugly' solar eclipse of ode 193 in the *Shijing* was thought to be 776BC. This eclipse was taken by commentators to refer to a dire omen, in the middle of King You's ten-year reign, that portended the fall of the Western Zhou dynasty. But the date of the *Shijing* eclipse was later 'corrected' to 734BC, meaning that this interpretation of ode 193 no longer holds. This need not delay us here,[22] being subsidiary to the argument in hand, namely the proposal that a total eclipse of the sun occurred as an omen near the end of the Shang dynasty, and was incorporated into the *Yi.*

Alexander Wylie's academic credentials for compiling a list of eclipses were formidable. Wylie was the first to translate the differential and integral calculus into Chinese, and it was he who noticed that Horner's method for solving algebraic equations, submitted to the Royal Society in 1819, was known in China five centuries earlier. So for Wylie to miss from his list the solar eclipse in the *Book of Changes*, one of the five Confucian Classics of Antiquity, was a remarkable oversight, indicating that no Chinese scholars at the time were particularly aware of it despite several thousand years of scholarship devoted to the *Yi*. This is truly a strange state of affairs. The only eclipse listed by Wylie before 776BC, which he dates 2127BC, noting it is disputed, appears in 'The Punitive Expedition of Yin', a chapter of the *Shujing* or *Book of Documents*, where there is the phrase, in Legge's translation: 'On the first day of the month, in the last month of autumn, the sun and moon did not meet harmoniously in Fang.' Fang, meaning 'a chamber', consists of four stars in Scorpio close to the flaming red heart of the Azure Dragon, Antares, the Fire Star. (Antares, incidentally, is one of the few stars referred to in Shang oracle-bone inscriptions.)

For the sake of comparison it is worth briefly examining the supposed eclipse in the *Shujing*, given that numerous scholars have devoted so much time to it while paying no attention at all to the completely genuine eclipse in the *Yijing*. The document recounts the story of a punitive expedition led by the Marquis of Yin against Xi and He, ministers of the Board of Astronomy, who had neglected their duties by failing to observe a solar eclipse. According to Joseph Needham their failure, as magician-priests, was actually to prevent the eclipse. Others have suggested their failure was to calculate a correct calendar whereby it might have been anticipated, solar eclipses only being possible when there is a new moon. This is said to have taken place during the reign of Zhong Kang, 2159–2147BC, according to the traditional chronology, but the authenticity of this document was discounted by Bernhard Karlgren in 1950. The time of the eclipse was also recorded as an exact date by the third century BC *Bamboo Annals*, equivalent to October 28, 1948BC. John Knight Fotheringham noted in his 1921 Halley Lecture,[23] however, that there was no eclipse that day, nor even a new moon. The Tang dynasty astronomers calculated a date of 2155BC, which was widely accepted, until Largeteau in 1840 showed that the eclipse of that year was not visible in China. John Knight Fotheringham preserves a satirical epitaph inspired by this discovery (Wade-Giles romanisation retained):

Here lie the bones of Ho and Hsi
Whose fate though sad was risible,
Being hanged because they could not spy
The eclipse which was invisible.

Others have attempted to date the *Shujing* eclipse, but both Fotheringham, and Herbert Chatley in 1938, conclude that the evidence does not permit of a positive identification. Chatley adds that it 'may not even be an eclipse'.[24] I found this statement puzzling at first, until I checked the original Chinese myself and was surprised to find that the sun and moon are not even mentioned in the text at all, and that this was simply a classical interpretation of a difficult character (*chen*) of uncertain meaning in this context. Guy van Esbroeck translated the passage as follows, on the basis of a strained etymology, my italics highlighting his interpretation of *chen*: 'Then on third autumn month first day *observation* not harmonious as-far-as Chamber.'[25]

My own research has brought to light an additional factor to show that the 'sun and moon' rendering cannot hold. The knowledge that the moon had something to do with a solar eclipse was not set down before Shi Shen in the fourth century BC. The correct view in all particulars is not extant before Liu Xiang's *Wu Jing Tong Yi*, or *The Fundamental Ideas of the Five Classics*, circa 20BC, where it is stated: 'When the sun is eclipsed it is because the moon hides him on her way.' And though the correct theory that the lunar shadow is cast on the earth's surface was widely known in Wang Chong's time, circa AD80, he himself favoured the view, like Lucretius, that sun and moon have intrinsic rhythms of brightness of their own: 'If you say that eclipses of the sun are due to the moon consuming it, then what is it that consumes the moon in a lunar eclipse? Nothing, the moon fades of itself. Applying the same principle to the sun, the sun also fades of itself.'[26] Thus, to describe a solar eclipse by the phrase 'the sun and moon did not meet harmoniously' is anachronistic in a document that is supposed to be Western Zhou or earlier in origin, and so *chen* cannot sustain such a reading.[27]

This is all old hat now, sinologically speaking. Henri Maspero, followed by Joseph Needham in 1959, effectively closed the book on the matter by dismissing 'The Punitive Expedition of Yin' as a fourth century AD forgery. Though the eclipse was also mentioned in the *Bamboo Annals* in the third century BC, this record was buried underground for nearly 600 years before it was discovered by a grave robber in AD281, when it appears to have served as inspiration for a forger. And as Creel noted well about the *Bamboo Annals* itself: '... even if we did possess the text that was placed in the tomb at the end of the third century BC we would still not have a chronicle of unimpeachable veracity, as some have seemed to suppose.'[28] Forgeries of ancient literature came about because rewards were offered by the Imperial court in the Han and later for the recovery of textual fragments that had survived the Book Burning in the Qin dynasty (221–206BC); particularly for material from the *Shujing*, which for a short period completely disappeared from the world. Creel accepts only 12 writings from the 50 chapters of the *Book of Documents* found in Legge's translation as reliable source materials for the Western Zhou.

The solar eclipse in the *Yijing*, by contrast, is on safer ground. The *Yi* belonged to an exempted class of literature—books of 'medicine, divination, agriculture, and arboriculture'—that was spared the Qin conflagration, so it does not suffer from problems of authenticity in quite the same way as the *Shujing*. The line of transmission of the *Yi* down the centuries—at times by single pairs of hands—is beyond the scope of this essay, suffice it to say that Herrlee Creel provides a good summary of the evidence establishing the authenticity of the *Yi* and concludes: 'There appears to be a sound basis for the opinion that has been generally held, from antiquity to our own day, that the original text of the *Book of Changes* was produced during the Western Zhou.'[29] The few references to named people that have already been recognised, such as the Shang kings Wu Ding (hexagram 63/3) and Di Yi (11/5 and 54/5),[30] and the aforementioned Viscount of Ji and the Marquis of Kang, together with discernible allusions to events associated with the end of the Shang period, the Zhou Conquest, and the early years of the new dynasty, and nothing thereafter, suggests that the beginning of the Western Zhou is the most likely time of composition.

There is good reason to suppose that the judgments of the hexagrams, said to have been written by King Wen, rather than being conventionally authored may in a number of cases record words actually *spoken* by him over cracks in tortoise shells, which were preserved by a school of diviners. In the Western Zhou dynasty the tortoise oracle and the yarrow oracle were both consulted over the same enquiry, and the results compared. At first the tortoise oracle took precedence, but later it fell out of favour because of the hard work involved in preparing the shell and the *Zhouyi* was consulted on its own. It seems likely that a proportion of diviner's lore that was originally obtained from tortoise divinations found its way into the *Yi*. In the Shang dynasty the tortoise oracle was extemporised directly from the shape or angle of the crack in the shell when heat was applied, in essence no more than an elaboration on a yes-or-no answer, but later a tortoise manual appears to have been compiled that resembled the *Zhouyi*. In the past few decades there has been a consensus of opinion among scholars that the *Zhouyi* is solely the work of anonymous diviners, but it has been forgotten, or insufficiently emphasised, that the king alone was responsible for the prognostication in Shang and early Zhou tortoise divination, and that answers were sought about the king's concerns only. The standard introductory formula in Shang oracle-bone prognostications was: 'The king, reading the cracks, said: . . .'[31] The task of diviners at this time was solely to prepare and crack the shell; only later did diviners also prognosticate, when written manuals on both the tortoise oracle and the diagrams of the *Yi* had been compiled.[32]

I do not know of any early references to divination with yarrow stalks without the *Zhouyi* text. There is no evidence either that the 64 hexagram diagrams were ever used on their own for divination, without the text, nor is there a satisfactory explanation of their origin. It is not known whether they came into existence at the same time as the text, or whether they had an independent existence before the text was conceived. The idea that the hexagrams were formed by 'doubling the trigrams' appears to be an aetiological story; all the evidence suggests that the notion of trigrams came long after the hexagrams. One thing, however, does seem self-evident: it is reasonable to suppose that all 64 hexagram figures were invented simultaneously, and presumably, therefore, by a single human mind.

Various attempts have been made in recent years to date the text of the *Zhouyi*. Both Richard Kunst and Edward Shaughnessy in their PhD dissertations settled on circa 800BC. Kunst couched his statement cautiously in 1985, saying that the *Zhouyi* 'did not have a single identifiable author or even authors, but was the result of gradual accretion over centuries. The most that could be claimed is that a single editor, working in the waning years of the Western Zhou dynasty, that is, roughly 800BCE, wrote down the text and subjected it to extensive polishing'.[33] Shaughnessy, on the other hand, writing in 1983, believed the book was composed in its entirety in the early years of the reign of King Xuan (r.827–782BC), 'most probably the last two decades of the ninth century BC'.[34] So set on this idea does he appear to be, because he has a personal theory on the meaning of the text relating to King Xuan's reign, that he either overlooks the holes in his method or is careful not to discuss them. Relying entirely on dating a small sample of isolated two-character expressions, not once does he acknowledge that they could easily be interpolations: polishing by Kunst's postulated editor, for instance.

The existence of whole quotations from the *Zhouyi* in the *Zuozhuan* that differ from the respective sections in the received text shows either that emendations were made in places or that variant texts circulated that were subsequently lost.[35] Forced as we are to accept the possibility of textual emendation, this means that no cast-iron conclusion as to the date of the *Zhouyi* as a whole can ever be reached by dating selected minutiae.

So hedged about with special pleading is Shaughnessy's thesis that he feels able to say, for example, grounding his argument on what he claims is the first dateable appearance of the term *tianzi*, 'Son of Heaven', in bronze inscriptions, that its presence in the third line of hexagram 14 'is firm evidence that the composition of the *Zhouyi* must date no earlier than the reign of King Mu' (the fourth king after King Wu, 1001–947BC according to the traditional chronology).[36] This is a sweeping statement on the basis of two characters appearing together in a single line of a single hexagram.[37] Not only this, Shaughnessy's dating of the term *tianzi* is dubious in itself. Richard Kunst, citing Chen Mengjia, says that the presence of the term in hexagram 14/3 'argues for a Western Zhou date no earlier than the time of King Cheng'.[38] Herrlee Creel also pointed out in 1970 that the royal title 'Son of Heaven' was 'extremely common in the bronze inscriptions beginning as early as the reign of King [Cheng]'.[39] This takes us back to within living memory of the Conquest, King Cheng was King Wu's son.

It becomes necessary to subject these dating criteria to criticism because 800BC has gained wide acceptance as the date of the *Zhouyi*, purely on the say-so of scholars given to a magniloquent framing of their views, without the question ever being seriously addressed, or a vested interest in dating the text to a particular time being taken into account. Sarah Allan is quite damning of Shaughnessy's standards of scholarship in her review of his 1991 *Sources of Western Zhou History*. She accuses him of writing to a hidden agenda under the guise of objectivity, suspecting his interpretations of problematic bronze inscriptions are made solely to establish his own research into military history and chronology as authoritative.[40] In my reading of Shaughnessy's books and papers I too am inclined to think that he pushes his own pet theories against the grain of the evidence. The most that can be said for 800BC is that it is a reasonable estimate for a time by which the *Zhouyi* had attained a form more or less as we know it today, but this date has no bearing whatsoever on the age of the individual fragments comprising the work. This becomes an important consideration, of course, when attempting to date the eclipse in hexagram 55, which is why I have discussed this matter first of all.

The title of the hexagram, Feng, surprisingly enough, provides a solid dating clue. Though Feng is generally translated as 'Abundance' or 'Fullness',[41] more specifically in the context of hexagram 55 it is the name of the Zhou capital city that King Wen built and removed to from the former capital at the foot of Mount Qi.[42] Feng was a strategic advance post established just before the Conquest of the Shang; as soon as the victory was won it was vacated for King Wu's new capital of Hao, eight miles away on the east bank of the River Feng. The archaeologically excavated site of the city of Feng is on the west bank of the River Feng, approximately 15 miles southwest of the present-day city of Xi'an in Shaanxi Province, latitude 34°16′N, longitude 108°54′E.[43] In the first reports from the site in the 1930s, Feng was said to resemble a military marching camp more than a fully functioning city.[44] In the past few decades, the excavations have been cautiously described as being 'in the Feng area', in order to acknowledge the possibility that more startling finds directly pertaining to Kings Wen and Wu may lie nearby. K C Chang, in the 4th edition of *The Archaeology of Ancient China*, states that Feng was built 15 years before the Conquest, but does not identify his source. My reading of Sima Qian suggests it was built 12 years before, although his chronology of this early period does contain a number of contradictions and conflations. Such questions aside, it is clear that Feng was only inhabited as the Zhou seat of government for a very short period.

Now we may realise that what has been translated by Wilhelm-Baynes in the second and fourth places of hexagram 55 as 'The curtain is of such fullness that the polestars can be seen at noon', translating Feng here as 'fullness', is better rendered: 'The city of Feng was so obscured at noon the Big Dipper was observed.'[45] The sacrifice offered by the king in the judgment is also located in Feng, as is the mourning hut in the top line: 'His living quarters in Feng were screened off from his family. He peered through the door, on his own, without any others. Three years not admitting to audience. (Prognostication:) Disastrous.'

We are left with two major questions that need to be dealt with. Can the solar eclipse be reliably dated? Who was the unnamed king in mourning at the time? In the next chapter I will detail the procedure for dating the eclipse, and in the chapter after that I will continue the literary analysis of hexagram 55, showing my reasons for believing that this eclipse took place in the same year Wu Wang attacked the Shang.

Chapter V

Darkness at noon, June 20, 1070BC

The quest to find the year of the Conquest of the Shang has occupied the minds of scholars since the fourth century BC, with activity in this field at its most intense in the twentieth century. The last time I counted, no fewer than 22 candidate years had been proposed, ranging from 1127BC to 1018BC, all of them based on late deductive evidence. In the next chapter—'The army carries the corpse'—I aim to prove that the solar eclipse witnessed in King Wen's city of Feng immediately preceded the Conquest,[1] without a gap of years, meaning that dating the eclipse also dates the year of the Zhou invasion. In the present chapter I discuss the actual dating procedure, and address the belief held by some that there isn't an eclipse at all in hexagram 55. I shall also advance a number of possible interpretations of the perplexing third line to find its congruence with the eclipse.

Edward Shaughnessy, in 'The Absolute Chronology of the Western Zhou Dynasty',[2] provides a detailed critique of 15 different criteria that have been used in the past for establishing the year of the Conquest. He himself advocates 1045BC, which several authors have since followed. The previous favourites were 1122BC, the 'long chronology', simply because it was traditional, and the 'short chronology' of 1027BC, which, though it was accepted by Bernhard Karlgren, is now universally agreed to be too late.[3] The solution currently adopted by many scholars is to give the year for the Conquest

50

simply as 'circa 1050BC' and leave exactitude to the speculators. The trouble has been that up until now only relatively late and possibly corrupt texts of contestable authenticity, often requiring tortuous interpretations, have been used to arrive at a date. In particular, the *Bamboo Annals* has attracted a virtual gold-rush in recent years with its supposed reference to the five-planet conjunction of 1059BC. Those who follow this line of thought claim this phenomenon marks the bestowal of the Mandate of Heaven on King Wen.[4] With the overlooked solar eclipse in the *Zhouyi*, however, we have a secure text contemporaneous with the event it records, and a precise astronomical calculation.

My initial approach to the astronomical community was by e-mail to NASA, putting me in touch with Fred Espenak who recommended the 1986 book *Atlas of Historical Eclipse Maps: East Asia 1500BC–AD1900*, by F R Stephenson and M A Houlden. Stephenson's name was familiar to me because I had recently read in a clipping from *New Scientist*, Jan 15, 1987, that the so-called 'double dawn' eclipse mentioned in the *Bamboo Annals* had been dated to April 21, 899BC, using a computer program devised by him.[5] I also placed a notice on an astronomical bulletin board on the Internet: 'Author seeks help in precisely dating a total solar eclipse in ancient China circa 1100BC.' I received a response from Patrick Poitevin, chairman of the Eclipse Section of the Belgian Astronomical Association and a renowned eclipse-chaser, having witnessed over 20 around the world. He also holds sole licence on the eclipse-calculation programs of Jean Meeus, the famous theorist, who has variant ideas on the motion of the moon to those of F R Stephenson. As well as calculating the date of the eclipse, Patrick, by asking hard questions—'How do you *know* the eclipse was total? Is there a reference to the solar corona?'—acted as a devil's advocate continually pressurising me to look deeper, which has benefited this essay enormously.

Initially casting the net widely between 1150BC and 1010BC, we came up with the following list of total solar eclipses, partial and annular eclipses being excluded because of the reference to seeing the Big Dipper.[6] Because there is no year zero in the BC/AD system, the year after 1BC being AD1, astronomical convention is to present dates in this early period preceded by a minus sign, and so, for example, −1069 is 1070BC. The candidates coming within a broad sweep of the city of Feng, taking the specified 'noon' as between 11am and 2pm local time, were:

- −1116, June 28
- −1069, June 20
- −1062, July 31
- −1031, November 14

Maps of the path of totality across China for all these dates are shown in Stephenson's *Atlas*. It has to be borne in mind, however, that while the hour, day, month, and year for each eclipse can be established with certainty, and so of course these agree on the calculation-programs of both Stephenson and Meeus, the actual track across the earth can only be an approximation, albeit a good one, without a chronicle stating that an eclipse in this period was observed from a specific place. This is because the rate of rotation of the earth in antiquity is not known precisely. For instance, the total solar eclipse observed in Babylon in 136BC, April 15, would have been seen in Europe if the rate of the earth's rotation was the same as it is today. This is why ancient observations are so important, because they fix the track to a known location. The solar eclipse in the *Zhouyi*, because we know it was witnessed at Feng, serves to pin down the track of the eclipse with greater certainty, which in turn tells us a little more about the rotation of the earth three thousand years ago.[7]

There was actually a total solar eclipse I haven't listed above on September 21, 1122BC, the orthodox year for the Conquest, but this was filtered out early on as it took place in the late afternoon when the sun was at a low altitude. After consideration of the calculated paths of totality for the eclipses of 1117BC and 1032BC, they were filtered out on the basis that the lunar shadow would have been too distant from Feng. This left 1070BC and 1063BC as the prime contenders. And there the matter had to rest; there seemed to be no astronomical means of resolving the two target years any further.

At first, it also appeared unlikely that any textual evidence could be found to separate the two eclipses and tip the balance of probability towards one date over the other. Nonetheless, within a week I happened upon several academic papers detailing how, according to oracle-bone scholar Dong Zuobin, in the fourth century BC (circa 370BC) the *Yinli*, or Yin Calendrical School, had calculated 1070BC as the year of the Zhou Conquest. Apparently they used exactly the same textual criteria that Liu Xin (46BC–AD23) used to arrive at 1122BC, the year that became traditionally accepted.[8] The reason that identical data could give rise to two different years is because the exact definitions of the crucial 'lunar phase notations' used in the calculation were lost and became subject to re-interpretation by Liu Xin's time. A discussion of these notations is beyond the scope of this book, suffice it to say that, regardless of the method employed by the *Yinli* calendricists, their date for the Conquest, coinciding with one of the two candidate solar eclipse years, must be regarded as pre-eminent because it antedates Liu Xin's calculation by over three centuries, making it the earliest known. And, as David Pankenier has hinted (by openly wondering whether 1070BC was the starting point for the calculation or the result, after noticing oddities in the mathematics), there is always the possibility that the *Yinli* chronology may have been determined by means other than those available to Liu Xin or extant today.[9] All of which lends weight to 1070BC over 1063BC. When the evidence of the next chapter is assimilated into the argument, proving, I believe, that the eclipse occurred in the same year as the Zhou invasion, 1070BC will also become the most favourable possibility for the Conquest year when set against, for example, the excessively complex and far-fetched reconstruction of a five-planet conjunction supposedly referred to in the *Bamboo Annals*. Pankenier used this reconstruction to arrive at a Conquest year of 1046BC,[10] and Shaughnessy claims the conjunction 'guarantees that the Zhou conquest of the Shang necessarily post-dated 1059[BC]'.[11]

I had settled on 1070BC as the most probable of the two eclipse years, when Patrick Poitevin dropped a bombshell that

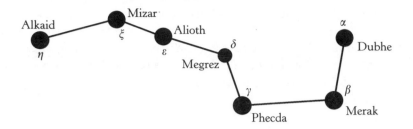

Figure 1: *The seven stars of the Big Dipper in* Ursa Major.

shattered my assumptions. He told me he was having grave doubts that the ancient Chinese would have been able to see the Big Dipper at all during a total solar eclipse. He had never seen it during his long experience travelling to solar eclipses all over the world, and was doubtful that any star less bright than second magnitude[12] could ever be seen by the naked eye during totality. This would mean that even supposing ideal 'long and deep' conditions only the stars Dubhe, Alioth, and Alkaid of the seven making up the Big Dipper, which are in a straight line, could possibly become visible, from which the rest of the constellation would not have been recognised (figure 1). Patrick had sounded out other expert opinion on my behalf, including Dr E C Krupp of the Griffith Observatory in Los Angeles:

> At the risk of repeating the obvious concerning the visibility of stars during a total eclipse, I'll add that it should be apparent that the best way to assess this possibility is through modern eyewitness accounts. The 11 July 1991 eclipse was very long and provided an opportunity to search for stars and planets. Those who observed from Baja California enjoyed very good atmospheric conditions, and some persons confirmed sightings of the brightest stars: Sirius (-1.46), Betelgeuse ($+0.5$), Rigel ($+0.12$), and Capella ($+0.08$). We also now have reports of Regulus ($+1.35$). To get to the three brightest Dipper stars we have to drop another half-magnitude or so. That was also about the brightness of Mars ($+1.8$), and Mars, recall, went unseen in 1991.

Tutored by the late George Abell, I have worn an eyepatch through the partial phases of total solar eclipses to increase the sensitivity of one eye. Although this technique has revealed remarkable details in the corona, it has not enabled me to pick out more than a star or two. I have deliberately looked for them. In 1991, I did spot Sirius. I believe Ron Smith, who also had previous eclipse experience, also wore an eyepatch, and he reported seeing the seven bright stars of Orion. This gets you down to Saiph at +2·06 and Mintaka at +2·19, but I would judge the 1991 eclipse shows us we are close to the limit. The other four stars of the Big Dipper are +2·27, +2·37, +2·44, and +3·31. It is possible that a darker sky might be observed if totality took place close to the horizon, but the Chinese eclipse in question was said to be at midday.

All this suggests that ideal conditions, including a long central eclipse at midday with transparent air, might allow you to see four stars of the Big Dipper. The next three get harder. An eclipse close to the horizon could help but maybe not enough.

There is little detailed commentary on the visibility of stars in the general eclipse literature. In *The Understanding of Eclipses* (1991), Guy Ottewell asserts: '. . . people who took the precaution of wearing sunglasses during partial eclipse have been able during totality to see stars as faint as fourth magnitude.' He provides no documentation, however, and I am dubious. Water vapor and atmospheric dust also modify the air's transparency and raise the threshold of visibility. The time in totality is short in the best of circumstances, and most observers do not retain the presence of mind to search for stars when the corona is so attractive. I don't blame them.

That famous bottom line: Maybe some of the Big Dipper stars were seen in that ancient eclipse in China (probably would also depend on the disposition of the Dipper), but it seems unlikely all seven would have been visible.[13]

This unexpected setback had me stumped, until, after a few nights pondering it, I realised that it simply didn't matter whether the Dipper was visible or not; so long as there was something to see in the darkened sky that the ancient Chinese *thought* was the Dipper then the observation still stood as a valid record. Patrick, as if waiting for me to fathom it out, told me he had already done the calculations, based on the book by Jean Meeus, *Astronomical Algorithms*. During the 1070BC eclipse the planet Mercury was positioned in a configuration with the bright stars Castor (+1·6) and Pollux (+1·1) in Gemini that matched the shape of the three-star 'bent handle' of the Dipper. The night before he told me this, walking home late, I had recognised the Dipper easily by its handle alone, the other four stars being covered by cloud (I checked by a planisphere to make absolutely sure). Jupiter, Mars, and Venus also formed a straight-line configuration at the time of the 1070BC eclipse, resembling the three stars of the Dipper brighter than second magnitude, Dubhe, Alioth, and Alkaid, which gave a further alternative for a mistaken identification. By contrast, the 1063BC eclipse showed no star-planet configurations of this nature whatsoever. So, ironically, what at first appeared to be an insurmountable obstacle casting all my research in doubt—the Dipper not being visible—turned out in the end to be a spur to find an astronomical means of resolving the two eclipses in favour of 1070BC, in addition to the sinological criterion of the *Yinli* chronology.

There may be another reason for the Zhou to have believed it was the Big Dipper they saw. Evidence exists in Han dynasty works that the constellation was perceived as a potent cosmic weapon. Chapter 3 of the *Huainanzi* states that 'what is attacked by the Northern Dipper cannot withstand it'. The *Han Shu* records that the Yin-Yang militarists 'follow the strike of the Dipper'.[14] Wang Mang, in the last desperate hours of his usurpation in AD23, attempted to make use of the apotropaeic powers of the Dipper to repel the Han troops.[15] While this is no proof that the Dipper was regarded as having such powers in the eleventh century BC, it nonetheless seems a reasonable conjecture, because it provides a plausible explanation why a configuration of stars or planets visible during the eclipse might naturally be identified as a military omen enhancing the meaning of the total solar eclipse, itself the classical omen for the fall of a dynasty.[16] To reiterate: it does not matter whether the Dipper can actually be seen during an eclipse, what matters is what the ancient Chinese thought they saw and what it meant to them.

We should not, in any case, be so stringent in judging the astronomical capabilities of our ancient colleagues. In an account of the solar eclipse of 1737 observed at Edinburgh, one of the first truly scientific reports of an eclipse, the astronomer Colin Mac Laurin writes in the *Philosophical Transactions* of the Royal Society: 'One gentleman is positive, that, being shaded from the Sun, he discerned some Stars Northwards, which he thinks by their Position were in *Ursa Major.*' If this was a reasonable assertion for a scientifically-trained mind in 1737, how much more so in the eleventh century BC.

Wu Jing-Nuan has argued in his translation of hexagram 55 that because the character meaning 'eclipse' is absent from the text that an eclipse is not meant.[17] He proposes that the Dipper may have been seen during the daylight hours from the bottom of a well, a phenomenon first noticed by Thales of Miletus.[18] This idea doesn't stand up. Though it is true that the early term for 'eclipse', *shi*, meaning 'to eat' as in 'eating the sun', does not appear in the *Zhouyi* as it does on the Shang oracle-bones,[19] nonetheless in the *Historical Records* of Sima Qian the solar eclipses of 442BC, 382BC, and 300BC, are also referred to without the use of any character meaning 'eclipse'. In each case it is stated: 'The daylight was so darkened that the stars could be seen.' In actual fact, the presence of the term 'eclipse' in ancient Chinese records more often than not confuses the issue, because it is not always apparent whether a real eclipse was witnessed or a prediction of one was made. Hexagram 55 clearly records an observation made during an eclipse; had the text contained just the term 'eclipse' on its own we could not be as certain that one had actually taken place.

Another important question is whether the eclipse was total, annular, or partial. Venus, the Morning and Evening Star, can be seen at dawn and dusk in relatively bright skies, and can also be seen in big partial and annular eclipses. So it used to be the case, in the early years of the twentieth century, that a mention of *some* stars in an historical report, *i.e.* stars in the plural, meaning one or more stars other than Venus, was taken to indicate totality when classifying solar eclipses in ancient literature. It was realised by John Knight Fotheringham in 1921, however, while he was investigating the eclipse of Thucydides in 431BC, which records 'some stars' being seen despite the fact that the eclipse only progressed to the crescent stage, that it was unnecessary to suppose that this claim was an exaggeration, as he had written earlier in the *Monthly Notices* of the Royal Astronomical Society. No sooner than his former opinion had appeared in print, he witnessed a very similar eclipse to that of Thucydides at Oxford and he noticed that both Vega and the planet Mercury were visible.[20] These days, Patrick Poitevin points out that only a description of the solar corona is an absolute guarantee that an eclipse was total, as a mere statement that the eclipse was total is a subjective opinion. Many observers of the 1927 total solar eclipse in the UK thought they saw totality when they were not at all in the path of totality. Thus a description of totality is beyond doubt only when there is an identifiable reference to the corona, though this is not a necessary condition for the eclipse to have been total. Many bona fide total solar eclipses in ancient records lack a description of the corona.[21] This creates an intriguing difficulty for the *Zhouyi* eclipse, as in the third line of hexagram 55 something further is reported seen at noon in addition to the Dipper in the second and fourth lines, but what it is is far from clear.

Let us first familiarise ourselves with the stages in the progression of a total solar eclipse (figure 2). 'First contact' designates the moment when the disk of the moon, invisible against the background of the bright sky, just touches the disk of the sun. The partial phase then begins, a small indentation in the western rim of the sun becomes noticeable, observed safely in ancient China through semi-transparent jade, smoky quartz, or by the reflection of the sun in water.[22] The dark disk of the moon gradually moves across the face of the sun. When the sun is reduced to a crescent the sunlight, shining through tiny gaps in foliage that act like pinhole cameras, forms little crescents of

Figure 2: *The phases of a total solar eclipse. The dark disk of the moon slowly moves across the disk of the sun from west (right) to east (left). (1) first contact; (2) partial phase; (3) second contact, onset of totality; (4) third contact, end of totality; (5) partial phase; (6) fourth contact.*

light on the ground, images of the source. The drawn-out darkening of the sky as the sun is progressively obscured stirs thoughts of evening, but at noon, when the eclipse in the *Zhouyi* occurred, the shadows would not have lengthened; they would have remained short, gradually blending eerily into a uniform greyness. Long before totality is reached, Venus usually appears. As totality approaches the direct light from the sun diminishes rapidly. The closer the onrushing lunar shadow gets, the darker the sky becomes, though along the horizon the earth's atmosphere still appears bright because the umbra of the moon's shadow, the corridor of totality, extends over only a narrow band of the earth's surface (figure 3). D Justin Schove put it well:

> Totality occurs where the dark cone of the Moon's shadow reaches the ground. As this cone is only just long enough, the

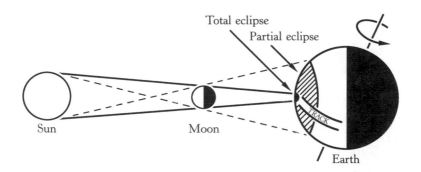

Figure 3: *The path of totality produced by the lunar shadow.*

diameter of the terrestrial region affected is never greater than
about 270km at any one moment. Moreover, the Earth rotates
from west to east and the shadow races eastwards, varying
slightly to north or south because of the moon's own movements;
at the equator the speed of this dark shadow is about 365 metres
per second. Among primitive peoples this is a path of panic.[23]

Birds and animals become disturbed; birds may go to roost as
they do at sunset, and dogs bark wildly.[24] As the tiny crescent of
the sun disappears, small bright specks remain where depres-
sions in the moon's edge, the limb, are last to obscure the sun.
These are known as Baily's beads, after the eighteenth century
English astronomer who first made an accurate study of them.
The beads vanish at the moment of 'second contact', when
totality sets in. The temperature drops by a few degrees, as a
result of which dew may form, wetting the ground. Some stars
and planets may be seen, but for most observers their attention
will be fixated on the solar corona, the appearance of the sun
described by Patrick Poitevin as 'a black eye of the gods'. The
white gossamer of the corona itself is one of the most beautiful
of natural phenomena: it 'shines like finely etched white frost
against the deep blue of the eclipse-darkened sky', in the words
of Jakob Houtgast.[25] At the moment of 'third contact' these
phenomena are repeated in reverse order: Baily's beads first
appear on the other side of the moon, the sun's crescent grows
again, the corona disappears, daylight begins to reappear and
stars fade from view. About an hour and a quarter later 'fourth
contact' comes when the moon's disk breaks away from the rim
of the sun. Totality itself rarely lasts more than five minutes,
though it can be as long as seven and a half minutes. During the
eclipse of 1070BC it lasted four minutes, which would have
seemed like hours to those who did not know what had
happened.[26] I shall in due course describe, as I perceive them,
the events on the ground in the Zhou capital of Feng that this
cosmic event interrupted. But before that, we must deal with
the enigmatic third line of hexagram 55.

Henry Wei translated the observation: 'At noonday, the Mo
star is visible.' Thomas McClatchie was the first to translate it

in this way, having 'the small *Mo* star', which he claimed was in *Ursa Major*. Yet it is by no means clear that *mo* is a star. The character actually means 'saliva, froth'. Wilhelm points out that *mo* means 'foam, drizzle', though he renders it as 'the small stars' (*die kleinen Sterne*), stating that this interpretation 'seems to suit the context better'. This it may do, but unfortunately we shall see that *mo* does not mean 'small stars'.

One interesting definition not in the dictionary I came across by chance in my reading. Mo was the name of the nearest Shang city to Muye, where the decisive battle of the Conquest was staged.[27] Conceivably the city of Mo could have come into view as King Wu marched on the Shang capital, but the reference to noon ties in with the Big Dipper being seen at noon in the second and fourth lines. Making a foray into a completely different interpretation opened up by the possibility that the events of hexagram 55 could be situated not in the city of Feng but on the outskirts of the city of Mo, I experimented with the idea that the reference to the Dipper might refer to a battle-flag with the constellation emblazoned on it. The third line contains the character *pei*, which has a number of meanings that various translators have struggled with. Some have played the substitution game and replaced the actual character with a homophone meaning 'a pennon'. Legge, Wei, and Whincup follow this reading. Though their translations of hexagram 55 are generally vague and confused, and they make no mention of Dipper flags, nonetheless this substitution did give me food for thought as it is known that in the late Zhou dynasty star-patterned royal battle-flags were indeed used to signalise the position of the Son of Heaven amidst the sea of banners carried by his army. The most famous of these was the 'Seven-Starred Banderole', to use Schafer's attractive translation.[28] This flag depicted the Big Dipper, which was hoisted aloft at the appropriate time as the 'Command of Heaven' for the awaiting army. The phrase 'to serve under a banner' derives from this practice as carried on by the Manchus. Dipper flags may still be seen to this day waving in the wind outside Daoist monasteries.

So, perhaps 'at noon the Dipper was seen' was not a reference to a solar eclipse at all, but simply the raising of the battle-flag.

But my foray into an alternative reality did not last long; not only did this interpretation make no sense when put together with other aspects of hexagram 55, there is absolutely no evidence that King Wu possessed a Dipper flag. In fact, according to the *Shi Ji* of Sima Qian, King Wu used a large plain white banner at the Battle of Mu. White being the colour of the Shang, it is said that by this tactical manoeuvre he intended to show the Shang nobles and ordinary troops of the enemy army that it was the tyrant Zhou Xin he marched against, not the common people. And in the *Mu Shi*, or 'The Harangue at Mu', a chapter of the *Documents*, King Wu waves a white ensign in his right hand while addressing his army on the eve of the Battle of Mu. These details effectively scupper what might otherwise be a challenge to the eclipse interpretation. Besides, the actual character *pei* that appears in the *Yi* does not mean 'pennon'. Wilhelm translated it as *das Gestrupp*, meaning 'undergrowth, brushwood', which Baynes combined into the familiar 'underbrush'. I can only think that 'The underbrush is of such abundance that the small stars can be seen at noon' refers to something like the effect of seeing small chinks of light through a dark dense canopy of leaves, which can resemble the night sky. I noticed this effect through the thick bush at my window as dawn came up one morning after pondering the supposed meaning of this very translation all night. Otherwise, the phrase is meaningless.

If we recall that Feng is not to be translated as 'abundance' but as the name of the Zhou capital city before the Conquest, where there is an 'obscuration' (*bu*) in the second and fourth lines, it all fits together when we turn to Karlgren's *Grammata Serica Recensa*, where the meaning of *pei* in the *Yi* is defined as 'darkened'.[29] Hence, one possible way the third line may be translated: 'The city of Feng was so darkened at noon *mo* was observed.' This rules out the Shang city of Mo as the intended meaning. It appears to be a further astronomical sighting, the parallel phrasing echoes lines 2 and 4, typical of the 'incremental repetition' found in other hexagrams and in the *Book of Odes*.[30] The question is whether *mo* is the solar corona. Patrick Poitevin has given his opinion that its meaning of 'foam,

'froth' could be a description of the corona. The Mawangdui
manuscript substitutes a homophone meaning 'white jasmine'.[31]
In Patrick's opinion this could also refer to the corona. But it is
hardly decisive, and there is always the possibility that this
character has become corrupt down the millennia and that we
shall never know what was originally intended. Yet the mystery
of *mo* does not end there.

To complicate matters further, Legge translated the character
as 'the *Mei* star', adding that it was a small star in or near the
Bushel. De Harlez also translated it as the *Mei* star, but placed
it in Sagittarius, following his mistaken identification of *dou* as
the Southern Ladle. *Mei*, a virtually identical character to *mo*, is
actually a town in the state of Wei and the name of a river. I can
find no authority by which it can be reliably confirmed as the
name of a star. Axel Schuessler, defining it as such in his 1987
Dictionary of Early Zhou Chinese, clearly takes Legge's
translation of the *Yijing* as his reference. Bernhard Karlgren
also offers 'name of a star' as one of the definitions of *mei* in his
Grammata Serica Recensa,[32] but he doesn't say which star and I
get the impression that here he departs from his usual
philological rigour and is merely following fashion.[33] Two
works available to Legge and Karlgren appear to have gone
unchecked. The *List of Chinese Stars* compiled by John Reeves
in 1819 mentions no *mei* or *mo* star among the 380 identified,
either in its published form in Morrison's Dictionary, which is
arranged according to occidental constellations, or in the
original hand-written notebook with the star characters brushed
one per page plus pencil annotations, which is kept in the
Oriental Room of the British Library.[34] And Gustave Schlegel,
in his monumental *Uranographie Chinoise* of 1875, which
records 759 stars and asterisms known to the Chinese, similarly
does not mention any such star. Nor does it appear in
Alexander Wylie's comprehensive list of 2,871 stars named by
the Chinese, which was published in his *Chinese Researches* of
1897. And none of the stars in the entirety of *Ursa Major*,
specified by Legge and McClatchie, are indicated by any
character remotely resembling the one in question. I have also
checked the *Jin Shu*, *Shi Ji*, *Huainanzi*, *Yue Ling*, and the

Xia Xiao Zheng, but none of these early works mention this star. The Purple Mountain Observatory in Nanjing to this day has no such star listed in its charts. Nor is it a planet. The character *xing*, 'star', often used in star names, does not appear in hexagram 55. In the oldest chapter of the *Shujing*, the 'Canon of Yao', contemporaneous with the *Zhouyi*, the names of the four stars that established the equinoxes and solstices are unambiguously labelled by *xing*. All this means that *mo* or *mei* is most definitely *not* a star, but rather appears to be a translational fudge.

How then is the character to be translated? I believe that Greg Whincup, among others, has the answer. In *Rediscovering the I Ching* Whincup asserts that *mei* in the received text means 'weak light', which is supported by Karlgren's 'a faint light' in addition to his definition of a star-name. Though Whincup repeats the familiar lore that most commentators associate this 'weak light' with 'the minor stars of the Dipper',[35] he himself favours, along with Richard Lynn and Richard Kunst, a slightly different character, also pronounced *mei* but meaning 'dark' or 'dim', which appears in several ancient versions of the text. In other words, there was 'darkness at noon'. Literally the third line would then read 'Feng so darkened, midday see dark/dim' but the sense of it could be tentatively translated: 'The city of Feng was so darkened at noon one could only see dimly.'[36]

Yet Whincup undermines the obvious narrative integrity revealed by this reasonable small emendation by proposing a wild substitution for *dou*, the Dipper. Following the Manchurian scholar Gao Heng, who has been sharply criticised for the profligacy of his textual substitutions, Whincup relies on one Han dynasty version of the text that has *zhu* instead of *dou*, which means 'lord'. It might be noted that the Mawangdui silk manuscript has the Dipper just as in the transmitted text. Gao places his interpretation on even shakier ground by reading *zhu* not as 'lord' but as 'candlewick', despite the fact that *zhu* already occurs in its own right as 'lord' twice in the received text of hexagram 55. Whincup further stretches 'candlewick' to 'lamp'. This reading involves great difficulties for the sense of the passage, because it is not clear why it is dark at noon, why

lamps have to be lit; Whincup, by substituting the reference to
the Dipper, takes away the solar eclipse. Whincup tries to get
round this by supposing that there are 'so many banners' flying
that the daylight is obscured. In the second and fourth lines he
appears to visualise a tented enclosure: 'So great a canopy that a
lamp can be seen at noon.' This means very little.[37] But
Whincup's translation at least attempts to make sense. Kerson
Huang, who also follows Gao Heng, tries to have it both ways,
with a candle seen at noon in the second line but the Dipper in
the fourth line, despite the fact that the two lines are identical in
the Chinese. In the third line, again following Gao Heng, he has
a ghost being seen at noon, the entire hexagram collapsing into
a ludicrous collage of modernist shots in the dark with no
binding meaning at all.

Richard Kunst's translation of the *Zhouyi* in his 1985
unpublished PhD thesis, on the other hand, must be seriously
examined. Kunst was the first western translator to seemingly
disavow the straightforward sense of the eclipse by interpreting
it instead as a calendrical observation: 'At the equinox we see
the Dipper.' Others have since followed this reading, without
crediting Kunst, necessitating a critical appraisal of the idea. It
is based on a usage of *rizhong* found in the *Yao Dian*, the
aforementioned 'Canon of Yao'; *ri* is 'sun' or 'day', *zhong* 'mid-
point', hence 'midday' when the sun reaches its zenith, or
'noon'. But in the context of the *Yao Dian* calendar it is used in
the sense of 'day of middle length', *i.e.* the equinox. But to
render it this way in the *Zhouyi* is specious, as shown by the
proverbial saying of great antiquity in China, attributed to the
pre-Han *Heguanzi*: 'When the handle of the Dipper points east
at nightfall it is spring throughout the land; when it points
south, it is summer; when west, it is autumn, and when north,
winter.' In ode 203 the handle of the Dipper is pointing west at
a time when hoarfrost lies on the ground, providing good
evidence for the knowing use of this constellation as a seasonal
indicator in the Western Zhou.[38] Kunst's translation, by
contrast, cannot specify the Dipper's disposition in the sky.
Unlike some stars such as Sirius, the heliacal rising[39] of which in
Egypt warns each year of the imminent flooding of the Nile, the

Dipper neither rises nor sets as viewed from China: being circumpolar it is always visible in the night sky. And, as Chalmers pointed out: 'It is well to keep in mind that the body of the Great Bear was in ancient times considerably nearer to the north pole than it is now, and the tail appeared to move around the pole somewhat like the hand of a clock or watch.'[40] So the mere sight of the Dipper, without reference to the position of its handle at nightfall, does not establish an equinox. Therefore Kunst's translation is a nullity because it has no calendrical value.[41]

At the end of this chapter, it should be obvious that the evidence supporting the eclipse interpretation of hexagram 55 is overwhelming, and that the equinox interpretation has not been thought through. As noon approached on the morning of June 20, 1070BC, the sky became progressively darker over the Zhou capital of Feng, and the inhabitants grew anxious. They wondered, what is the meaning of this dire omen ...? And then, an excited cry went up: *'Look! The Big Dipper!'*

Chapter VI

The army carries the corpse

Returning to the reconstruction of historical events in hexagram 55, I will discuss now the reasons I believe the solar eclipse directly preceded, without a gap of years, King Wu marching on the Shang. The judgment of this hexagram is much misunderstood, and mistranslated in Wilhelm-Baynes. The famous 'Be not sad, be like the sun at midday' means nothing of the sort in the original Chinese. Not only does this translation use the single character *ri* twice, both as 'sun' and as 'day' in 'midday', it imposes an incorrect interpretation on the hexagram. This error is very early: Part 2 of the 'Commentary on the Decision', the *Tuanzhuan* or second of the Ten Wings, which possibly dates to the third century BC, interprets this phrase as referring to the fact that when the sun is at its zenith at midday it can only turn towards its setting. Thus it is seen as a concrete image of cyclical change. Wilhelm naturally followed this interpretation and tailored his translation to fit, though it cannot be justified by the Chinese. Although the judgment is set at noon, the point has been missed that a solar eclipse is happening at this time, which we know by the evidence of the lines. So this is not the sun at midday on a normal day: this is the black sun, the direst omen of ancient peoples.

The Chinese simply reads: 'Not mourning. Noon appropriate.' Its terseness is typical of a tortoise divination about the significance of the omen. I thought at first that 'noon appropriate' meant that what happened at noon, the eclipse, was deemed an 'appropriate' (*yi*) sign for the downfall of the Shang, as opposed to a foreshadowing of disaster for the Zhou. Paul L-M Serruys draws attention to a Shang oracle-bone divination concerning a solar eclipse: 'Is it inauspicious (literally: is it not disaster?), or is all fine?'[1] An enquiry followed as to whether they ought to make a ritual announcement about the eclipse to the ancestor Father Ding, with a sacrifice of nine oxen. The more I pondered the meaning of the key character *yi* in the judgment, however, the more dissatisfied I became with this interpretation. *Yi* means 'appropriate, suitable, fitting, ordered rightly',[2] and while 'noon appropriate/ordered rightly' makes some sort of sense, in that we know a solar eclipse is occurring at this time and there would of course be a concern to determine if everything was all right, I couldn't help feeling it was a lame way to refer to a cosmic event of this magnitude. I began to wonder if the character had some other meaning in eleventh century BC China. Eventually I looked up *yi* in Bernhard Karlgren's *Grammata Serica Recensa* and was astounded to discover that in Zhou China it was the specific name of the 'sacrifice to the deity of the soil'.[3] The reason this had such an impact on me was because I instantly recalled a passage from Henri Maspero's *La Chine Ancienne*:

> If an eclipse of the sun occurred, it was necessary to go to the sun's assistance. The king went in haste to the mound of the God of the Soil and tied it with a red cord, which he wrapped three times around the tree of the god. Followed by his grand officers, he arranged them in battle formation, had the drum beaten, and himself loosed arrows with 'the bow which aids the sun'. At the same time a victim was sacrificed to the God of the Soil, in the same way as was done whenever arms were taken up near him.[4]

Maspero further points out that this sacrifice, *yi*, was made to the God of the Soil whenever armies set out to go to war. Drums were presented to the god as the troops lined up, and were smeared with blood. All military expeditions had to start out from near his altar.[5] So, it was not 'noon appropriate' at all; rather at noon the *yi* sacrifice was hastily performed by the king to allay the eclipse. The fragments of the story were beginning to fall into place to reveal a richness of meaning in the hexagram Feng hitherto unsuspected: 'Not mourning. *Yi* sacrifice at noon.' It sounded even more like a line from an oracle-bone inscription. But what did it refer to? Was it possible to find out? This is the subject of the rest of this chapter.

Compelling evidence that a tortoise shell was cracked in hexagram 55 comes from an expression used in the first line: 'In the (next) ten days there will be no calamity.' This is very similar to a formula commonly seen in Shang oracle-bone divinations. Shang kings sought to establish that there would be no calamity or disaster in the next ten days, the *xun* period or ancient ten-day week, on the last day, *gui*, of the *xun* preceding it. This is what the first line appears to refer to, using the character *xun* for 'ten days' just as in the Shang inscriptions. The only real difference, in fact, is that the Shang used the character *huo* for 'disaster/calamity' instead of *jiu*, which appears in hexagram 55/1 and means the same.[6]

The judgment 'not mourning' seems to be the response to a typical 'perhaps/perhaps not' testing out of alternatives seen so many times in oracle-bone inscriptions. One of the more frequent examples, for instance, poses on the right-hand half of the shell the positive charge 'it will perhaps rain', and on the left-hand half the negative charge 'it will not perhaps rain', with cracks being made routinely for each in turn to assess the situation.[7] The phrase 'not mourning', I suggest, is the recorded response to just such an enquiry over alternative courses of action, one half of the shell testing the proposition 'perhaps mourning' and the other 'not perhaps mourning'. I shall return to the loaded meaning of 'not mourning' in the further unfolding of the argument.

In the remaining text of the judgment 'the king approached it', *wang jia zhi*. What exactly he approached is left unsaid, though in the judgments of hexagrams 45 and 59 where the first two characters again appear together, 'the king approached his ancestral temple', *wang jia you miao*. In addition, in all three cases a sacrifice is offered, *heng*. Sacrifices usually followed oracle-bone divinations. One of the major findings of the

Modern School is the reading of *heng* as 'sacrifice' or 'sacrificial offering', instead of 'success' as in Wilhelm-Baynes.[8] In hexagram 55 the sacrificial offering takes place in Feng. The Lord of the Soil, Hou Tu, had his mound in the palace grounds facing the ancestral temple. In ancient times this was a flat, open-air, square mound of earth, with a tree or trees growing on it.[9] The identity of the king who performs the sacrifice is not specified as such, but of course the city of Feng immediately suggests King Wen.

Although orthodox Chinese history holds that King Wen was a title bestowed posthumously, and that he could not have called himself *wang*, 'king', while he was supposed to be acting the part of a loyal vassal of the Shang (there cannot be two kings under Heaven, as the ancient Chinese saying goes[10]), there is good evidence he was at least known as a king, if not Wen, in his lifetime. Though Sima Qian does indeed say that the Earl of the West, Xibo, was posthumously entitled 'King Wen', which is the origin of the orthodox view, the full quotation is: 'It was probably in the year he received the Mandate that he proclaimed himself king... Ten years later he passed away and was posthumously entitled King Wen.'[11] Sima Qian adds that Xibo probably held the throne for 50 years,[12] and that the year he received the Mandate was the same year the Yu and Rui delegations made their way to his court to have their dispute settled by him, described in Chapter III. This was when the feudal lords began to say among themselves: 'Perhaps the Earl of the West has received the Mandate.'

Both King Wen's father and grandfather ruled the Zhou under the title *wang*, King Ji and King Tai, respectively. Ode 300 says that it was in the reign of King Tai 'when the clipping of Shang began', and that in the process of time 'Wen and Wu continued the work of King Tai'. Tradition asserts that King Tai, the ruler who took the Zhou to live at the foot of Mount Qi,[13] recognised the outstanding abilities of his young grandson Chang, the future King Wen, and longed for him to rule, though he was not in the normal line of succession.[14] Knowing their father's wish, the two elder brothers of King Ji left the court to live among barbarians to ensure that King Ji gained the succession, not because he was better suited for the role but so that his son Chang would ultimately accede to the throne.[15] King Ji had a Shang wife, Tairen,[16] and fought on behalf of the Shang in Shanxi Province, being appointed 'Master of the Herds', lord over a cluster of minor states, only to be put to death by the Shang shortly afterwards.[17]

King Wen exhibited great restraint in making an outward show of loyalty to those who had murdered his father. Though King Wen is often praised as being more peace-loving than his son King Wu, because he refrained from attacking the Shang, this is not an entirely accurate portrayal. He died awaiting the decisive moment, but while alive he led several preparatory military campaigns to consolidate his power, chastising in full view of the Shang the traitor Hu, the Marquis of Chong. Hu's slander had brought about King Wen's imprisonment at Youli. Ode 241 records the Siege of Chong. The following extract is from Waley's translation:

> God said to King Wen,
> 'I am moved by your bright power.
> Your high renown has not made you put on proud airs,
> Your greatness has not made you change former ways,
> You do not try to be clever or knowing,
> But follow God's precepts.'
> God said to King Wen,
> 'Take counsel with your partner states,
> Unite with your brothers young and old,
> And with your scaling ladders and siege-platforms
> Attack the castles of [Chong].'
>
> The siege-platforms trembled,
> The walls of [Chong] towered high.
> The culprits were bound quietly,
> Ears were cut off peacefully.
> He made the sacrifice to Heaven
>   and the sacrifice of propitiation.
> He annexed the spirits of the land, he secured
>   continuance of the ancestral sacrifices,
> And none anywhere dared affront him.

The siege-platforms shook,
So high were the walls of [Chong].
He attacked, he harried,
He cut off, he destroyed.
None anywhere dared oppose him.[18]

'God' is Di, otherwise called Shangdi, the Lord on High, the principal deity of the Shang but also worshipped by the Zhou, whose 'deity' was known as Tian, simply 'Heaven', as in *tianming*, the Mandate of Heaven.[19] The *Zuozhuan* also records the Siege of Chong, saying the Zhou withdrew after 30 days before launching their final assault, when the city fell.[20] Sima Qian notes that Feng was built a year later.[21] Ode 244 describes the construction of Feng, which, we are told, was a walled city built at Heaven's bidding according to the ancient plan. This ode even provides the location of Feng by saying 'the River Feng flowed to the east'. Probably King Wen's last campaign against the Shang before he died was the taking of their garrison of Li, mentioned in the *Book of Documents*, which I referred to in Chapter III. I say 'probably' because Sima Qian appears confused on the issue of the timing of King Wen's death and conflates the details from this section of the *Documents* with an entirely different campaign.

The most indisputable evidence that Xibo was known as a king in his lifetime only came to light in July and August of 1977. Approximately 17,000 oracle-bone fragments were unearthed from a Zhou palace at Qi Shan, or Mount Qi in Shaanxi, King Wen's seat of government before he removed his capital to Feng. The bones that are inscribed are quite unlike those of the Shang; some of the characters are no bigger than a millet seed and require a magnifying glass to read. In the Zhou inscriptions the man known to the Shang as the Earl of the West is referred to simply as 'the king'. Clearly then, 'the king' of hexagram 55 could well be King Wen. Indeed, I worked on this assumption at first, until, quite suddenly, I saw that it was King Wu, full of sadness that his father had just died. The character *you* in the judgment, often translated as 'sad' and generally meaning 'grief, melancholy, mournful', has the more specific meaning of 'mourning for a parent'. This is relevant because King Wu is infamous for his lack of filial piety in not mourning the death of his father by the customary rite of spending three years in the mourning hut; and furthermore not even burying him but carrying his corpse into battle with him against the Shang.

The death of King Wen is shrouded in mystery. I have been able to find out very little about it. Confucius doesn't mention it. Mencius says he died in a place called Bi Ying and that he was a 100 years old.[22] Fung Yu-lan quotes Yang Xiong as saying 'death and decay' came to King Wen at Bi.[23] The 'Jijie' commentary on the *Shi Ji* of Sima Qian claims Bi was the place King Wen was buried.[24] The character Bi, which, incidentally, is not in the *Zhouyi*, is also used to refer to the Hyades star-cluster near Aldebaran in Taurus, known to the Chinese as 'The Net', which 'Jijie' asserts was emblazoned on King Wu's battle pennons.[25] There is no record in the *Documents* or the *Odes* concerning the timing or manner of King Wen's death, or his funeral.

The ancient plateau of Bi lies north-west of modern-day Xi'an, north of the Wei River. In 1936 H G Creel wrote in *The Birth of China* that the tombs of King Wen, King Wu, and the Duke of Zhou were located here, about four miles north of Xian Yang, but excavations had not at that time begun. He described the tumuli as flat-topped earthen pyramids, and regretted that he had not measured them on his visit there; he had supposed that this information would be easy to come by, which proved not to be the case. He estimated that the pyramids ranged from 25 to 40 feet in height and probably twice this dimension at the base. He described the tombs of Kings Wen and Wu as being very close together, and that King Wen's tomb was considerably larger, adding that these two tombs were fronted by a temple, in excellent repair, that had become a shrine for pilgrims.[26]

Creel wrote nothing about these tombs in *The Origins of Statecraft in China* (1970). Strange as it may seem, I have come across no other reference to these tumuli and their supposed occupants, despite trawling through innumerable archaeological journals and books, nor any mention of the excavation of early Zhou royal tombs. When he was 81 Creel gave a speech at the

Society for the Study of Early China Roundtable, on the 50th anniversary of the publication of *The Birth of China*, in which he said: 'The only proper thing to do about *The Birth of China* is what I did 50 years ago: forget it.' He admitted it was full of the kind of errors it is hard to avoid in a pioneer work.[27] Presumably Creel was mistaken about the pyramids. Nonetheless, it remains a real possibility that King Wen's tomb will indeed be discovered in this area one day.

The most fascinating statement concerning King Wen's death is in the fourth century BC *Tian Wen, Ask Heaven*, an important section of the *Chu Ci*, the *Songs of Chu*, that is the *locus classicus* for a number of early Chinese myths and fragments of history. The poet Qu Yuan poses the riddle: 'When Wu set out to kill Yin, why was he grieved? He went into battle carrying his father's corpse: why was he in such a hurry?'[28] David Hawkes, who translated the *Chu Ci* as *The Songs of the South*, offers a succinct explanation that deserves to be quoted in full:

> The Han historian Sima Qian twice tells us that it was the wooden 'spirit tablet' of his dead father that King Wu carried into battle, but that is because he was trying to make sense of two irreconcilable traditions. The first time he asserts it, in his 'Annals of the Royal House of Zhou', he says that these events took place in King Wu's eleventh year, *i.e.* eleven years after King Wen's death; the second time, in the 'Biography of Bo Yi', he says that Bo Yi and his brother travelled to the Zhou court intending to offer their services to King Wen, but were shocked to find that King Wen had just died and that his son was preparing to lead an army against the Shang king. What shocked them was not merely that the new Zhou ruler was planning to lead an armed insurrection against his overlord, but that he was planning to do it *before his father was in his grave*. I suspect that in the original version of the story which Qu Yuan is here referring to it was a dead body, as in El Cid's last battle, which led the troops to victory.[29]

Mencius twice mentions Bo Yi fleeing from the Shang tyrant Zhou Xin to settle on the edge of the North Sea, but on hearing of the rise of King Wen he stirred and said: 'Why not go back?

I hear that Xibo takes good care of the aged.'[30] Mencius, however, does not record their arrival. Sima Qian also mentions in the 'Biography of Bo Yi' that it was because the brothers had heard that Chang, the Earl of the West, knew well how to look after the old that they wished to travel to become his followers.

This strange set of circumstances casts the most illuminating ray of explanation upon the mysterious phrase *yu shi* in the third and fifth lines of hexagram 7: literally translated it means a 'sedan-chair corpse' or 'carted corpse', or even 'a corpse carried on the shoulders', following Karlgren's definition of the usage of *yu* in the *Zuozhuan*.[31] There being no distinction between singular and plural in classical Chinese, *shi* is usually translated as 'corpses'. Wilhelm-Baynes renders the third line as 'Perchance the army carries corpses in the wagon', which I had always assumed meant that the army was bringing home its war-dead or clearing a battle-ground. From his commentary Wilhelm himself appears to be struggling to understand the meaning of this line. I have to thank Richard Rutt, the former Bishop of Leicester, for pointing out the sense of translating *shi* in the singular by relating it to Qu Yuan's riddle.[32] I was trying to work out the significance of the character *huo*, 'perchance, perhaps', when it clicked that the third line reads like a record of another oracle-bone divination, the Zhou seeking an oracle for carrying King Wen's dead body with them against the Shang: 'The army perhaps carting the corpse.'[33] But what is one to make of the 'disastrous' prognostication after this statement? And, indeed, is attached to the first and fifth lines as well. Richard Rutt has drawn attention to a story told in the first century AD by the sceptic Wang Chong in his *Lunheng*, or *Doctrines Evaluated*, as a possible explanation. Anne Birrell translated it as follows:

> When King Wu of the [Zhou] was about to attack King [Zhou] of the Shang, he had divination made using stalks, but the result was negative, and the diviner declared, 'Very bad luck'. The Great Lord pushed aside the milfoil stalks and trod on the tortoises and said, 'What do withered bones and dead plants know about good luck or bad luck!'[34]

Hellmut Wilhelm cites another tradition that the tortoise oracle advised against the battle, but the yarrow-stalk oracle was in favour of it.[35] (Note that these traditions are anachronistic. Though yarrow stalks may have been used for divination at the time of the Conquest without an associated text, it is extremely unlikely that this method could have seriously competed with the tortoise oracle.) *Shi Ji* 32 states that King Wu wished to attack King Zhou and performed a tortoise divination, but the results were not auspicious, and violent wind and rain arose as additional bad omens. The assembled dukes were afraid, but Taigong, the king's great commander and military strategist, 'stiffened them to support King Wu'. King Wu then marched on the Shang.[36]

The fifth line of hexagram 7 reads: 'The elder brother leads the army, the younger brother carts the corpse.' Or possibly: 'The elder brother leads the army, the younger brother carries the corpse on his shoulders.' The elder would undoubtedly be King Wu, the younger probably the Marquis of Kang. The motif contrasting the respective duties of elder brother and younger brother is also used in the *Kang Gao*, 'The Announcement to Kang', a chapter of the *Book of Documents* in which King Wu, personifying himself as the elder brother, addresses Feng,[37] known as Kangshu, as the younger brother. For this reason I believe the younger brother mentioned in hexagram 7/5 is likely to be Kangshu, who appears in the judgment of hexagram 35 as Kanghou, the Marquis of Kang.[38] The top line also supports the interpretation linking hexagram 7 with King Wu's army marching on the Shang: 'The great prince has the Mandate to found a state and inherit the House.'[39] The Mandate is *ming* of *tianming*, the Mandate of Heaven. 'Inherit the House' refers to the replacement of the House of Shang by the House of Zhou.[40]

The character *yu* takes 'sedan-chair' as one of its meanings, but it has to be borne in mind that, just as the chair did not make its appearance in China until very late, after the Tang, a sedan-chair would in ancient times have been called a litter, which is more like a stretcher.[41] Marcel Granet mentions that it was a common practice in ancient China for an image of the deity to be carried on a litter and 'tossed about' (*balloter le Dieu*) in order to invoke the awesome powers of Heaven.[42] King Wen was known to have been in communion with Heaven as he had received its Mandate, and, as Granet further points out, the bodies of prophets were known to be 'withered and drained' (*desséché*) as a result of offering their life-force to the deity: he cites, as an example, the hemiplegia of Yu the Great.[43] So the act of carrying King Wen's *desséché* corpse into battle against the Shang has perhaps a far greater significance than is generally supposed. It can be compared to the Israelites carrying the Ark of the Covenant into battle against the Philistines 'that they might be too hard for their enemies', as Josephus put it in *Antiquities of the Jews*.[44] Bernhard Karlgren and Eduard Erkes had an amazing exchange of views over the question whether it was King Wen's corpse or merely his spirit tablet that King Wu took into battle.[45] Karlgren argues in favour of a wooden tablet, while Erkes believes the *Tian Wen* is referring to the custom of taking an actual corpse into battle, which later evolved into taking a human-shaped wooden image of the deceased, the 'wooden lord'.[46]

Shi, 'corpse', also means 'an impersonator of the dead'. Impersonators of the dead were living people who took the role of dead ancestors that the king played host to at a sacrificial banquet, known as the *bin* rite in Shang oracle-bone inscriptions. So far as I know, impersonators of the dead were never used in battle, and in any case would not have needed 'carting', as they impersonated the dead as if they were still alive, receiving the spirit of the dead ancestor in a trance-state much as the *loa* descends to 'ride' its human horse in Haitian voudoun, though without the frenzy.[47]

In trying to makes sense of the contradictions and varying accounts of the timing of King Wen's death in the *Shi Ji* of Sima Qian, which he ceased work on circa 99BC, I have come to agree with David Hawkes; the tradition that King Wen died just before the final invasion, and that King Wu took his corpse into battle with him against the Shang, does indeed appear to be the original version of the story. This is the earliest narrative by three centuries in that it is mentioned in the *Tian Wen*, and it is in the form of an eye-witness account, whereas the version in which King Wen dies 11 years before the Conquest exists merely as a statement to this effect by Sima Qian, which he himself contradicts.

Bo Yi and his brother Shu Qi were said to have been so appalled by King Wu's lack of filial piety, the break of hereditary rule, and regicide, that they refused 'to eat the corn of Zhou' and voluntarily starved themselves to death on Mount Shouyang in protest. To Confucius and Mencius in the mid-4th and early 3rd centuries BC they became praiseworthy as exemplars of non-violent political idealism.[48] Their story is told almost completely in Sima Qian's biography,[49] which describes how the brothers clutched at the reigns of King Wu's horses and reprimanded him, saying: 'The mourning for your father is not yet completed and yet you take up shield and spear. Can this be called filial? As a subject you seek to assassinate your lord. Is this what is called righteousness?'[50] The king's attendants moved to strike them down but their lives were saved by the intercession of the king's counsellor, Taigong, who said they were 'men of principle' and sent them away unharmed. Their time on the mountain where they starved themselves to death is also alluded to by Qu Yuan in *Ask Heaven*,[51] and referred to by Confucius.[52]

The impact of Bo Yi and Shu Qi on classical history cannot be ignored, yet this is precisely what a number of contemporary scholars have done in a vain attempt to defend their own chronological theories, preferring to regard the Bo Yi account as 'ahistorical' without ever acknowledging that this is a more apt description of Sima Qian's seemingly precise account of 11 years. If one takes this latter alternative history seriously it has to be asked what King Wu was doing during the 11 years he is supposed to have reigned between the death of his father and his attack on the Shang.

In Sima Qian's *Historical Records* this period is marked only by an unlikely account in the ninth year of an abortive foray to the Fords of Meng, two years before the actual crossing, the equivalent of the Rubicon for King Wu. Eight hundred feudal lords apparently converged without any pre-arrangement to offer their support, yet King Wu is supposed to have withdrawn his troops, after marching for almost a month from Feng, and returned home, telling them: 'You do not know the Mandate of Heaven.' This is hardly credible, particularly given that when King Wu made the crossing before the Battle of Muye, by Sima Qian's account two years later, he was joined by the lords of just *eight* other tribes, as is recorded in the *Mu Shi*, a chapter of the *Documents*, which says nothing of an earlier attempt to stage the Conquest. This ninth-year account is in addition characterised as apocryphal by folkloric elements, which usually originate from story-tellers as opposed to historians, such as the omens of a white fish jumping into King Wu's boat as he was crossing the Yellow River and heavenly fire transforming itself into a red crow. There is no extant source mentioning these details before Sima Qian, whereas the story of Bo Yi and his brother is deeply ingrained in prior literature. And is it conceivable that King Wu could have displayed his hostile intentions so visibly a mere 140 miles from the Shang capital without incurring repercussions? Yet the following two years of his reign apparently passed without incident.

Some scholars, being irretrievably sold on the idea that King Wen died 11 years before the Conquest, even take it upon themselves to presume that Bo Yi and Shu Qi arrived in the Zhou capital in this ninth year, and attempt to provide plausible explanations as to why King Wen's body had been lying around unburied for nine years and King Wu in all that time had not yet undergone the mourning rites. This is comical. The reason this version of events should be rejected is quite simple: how could Bo Yi and Shu Qi, having heard of the rise of the Earl of the West and that he took good care of the aged, not have heard that he died nine years ago?

In Chapter 13 of the *Huainanzi*, compiled circa 139BC, 40 years before Sima Qian completed his *Shi Ji*, King Wen was clearly thought to have been alive a year before the Conquest: 'When Yin was about to be overthrown, Huang and Yi, ministers, went over to Wen Wang, just a year before the death of [Zhou].'[53]

Returning to the top line of hexagram 55 in which a mourning hut is described, the sense of it now becomes apparent. The city of Feng has been plunged into sadness: King Wen has just died. A mourning hut has been erected for King Wu in which he will be expected to spend the next three years alone, seeing and speaking to no-one, just peering through the door for his glimpses of the outside world. Suddenly there are cries of alarm in the city as the sky darkens towards noon. A solar eclipse occurs, the omen of the fall of the ruling dynasty. King Wu realises he cannot spend the next three years withdrawn from the world, for this is a sign from Heaven. He rushes to perform the *yi* sacrifice, and cracks a tortoise shell to see whether he ought to remain in the mourning hut, or abandon the mourning rites. I suggest that over the crack obtained for 'perhaps mourning' he pronounced the ominous prognostication *xiong*, 'disastrous',[54] and that this became attached to the description of the mourning hut in the top line of hexagram 55, while 'not mourning' became part of the judgment, the decided course of action upon reading the crack that was made for the alternative charge, 'not perhaps mourning'.[55] I propose that these divination records, and the sighting of the Dipper over Feng at noon, were the raw materials that were used to construct hexagram 55.

This is the answer to Qu Yuan's riddle. When Wu set out to conquer Yin he was grieved because his father had just died, but the answer to the second half of the question has not been clear until now: he was in such a hurry because of the omen of the total eclipse of the sun combined with divination. Bo Yi and Shu Qi must have arrived shortly afterwards to find King Wu in the midst of making preparations for war, to complete the Conquest planned by his father. That they had not heard that King Wen had just died implies that the Shang would not have known either, giving even greater urgency once the decision to attack had been reached.

There remains one important matter. It was King Wen who had received the Mandate of Heaven, not his son. King Wu would not have attacked the Shang unless he had the Mandate, so how did he receive it? The eclipse was a sign that he had it, and divination corroborated it, but can we suppose these events also constituted the conferment of the Mandate itself? The answer to that was dug out of the ground in 1963. An inscribed bronze vessel known as the He *zun*, a vase-shaped goblet used for holding a wine libation, was unearthed at Baoji in Shaanxi, He being the name of the maker.[56] It is dated to the fifth year of the reign of King Wu's son, King Cheng. One sentence of the inscription on it hangs together well with the interpretation thus far developed, adding an extra detail: 'We repeat the Feng Ceremony in which King Wu requested blessings from Heaven.' Feng in this inscription is the same character as the title of hexagram 55.

What perplexed me the most during the piecing together of this reconstruction was why King Wu was not referred to specifically by name in hexagram 55. I was considering this problem when my eyes alighted on a single character in the second line of the Feng hexagram, *fa*, which is usually translated as 'to issue, to send forth', probably with the original sense of loosing off an arrow. The character looked vaguely familiar from another place. I quickly consulted the handy glossary of names from Nienhauser's *The Grand Scribe's Records*, Vol. I, hardly daring to believe I was right. Yet, there it was, undeniably present: the *personal* name of King Wu lying in full view, having awaited discovery for the past three thousand years.

In the *Mu Shi*, 'The Harangue at Mu', King Wu refers to himself as Fa in a rousing speech to his army at daybreak before the Battle of Mu. Sima Qian states King Wu proclaimed himself 'The Heir Fa' on departing the city of Feng, 'meaning he had received orders from King Wen to attack and would not have ventured to conceive these ideas on his own'.[57] With this most elusive piece of the jigsaw in its rightful place the picture was complete, the second line making perfect sense in a remarkably literal translation: 'The city of Feng was so obscured at noon the Big Dipper was seen. Though able to depart, the urgency was doubted. Having verification, Fa complied. (Prognostication:) Auspicious.'[58]

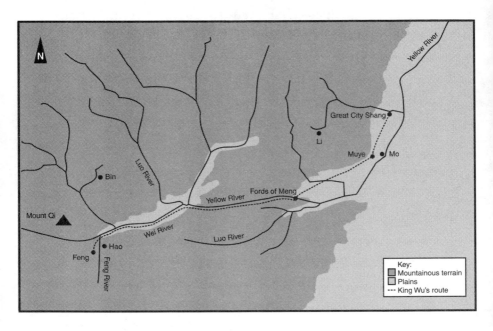

Map 1: *King Wu's march on the Shang, 1070BC.*

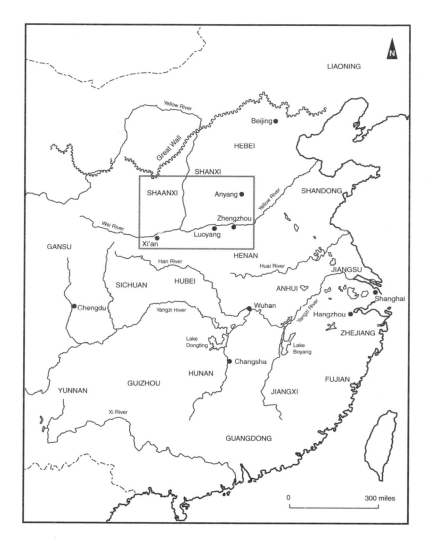

Map 2: *Area of modern China occupied by Map 1 (note that the course of the Yellow River has changed since the eleventh century BC).*

Chapter VII

Battling in the Wilds

Wu Wang asked Taigong whether the world would liken his punishing of Zhou to a servant murdering his master, and whether he was justified in fearing that his example might be too eagerly followed in later times, giving rise to endless strife.

Taigong praised the king's question and responded by way of an illustration: 'Archers hunting game-birds are anxious before they take the prey lest the hit is too slight; but once they have the bag their fear is lest the flesh is torn too much.'[1]

Given the mountainous terrain of the Zhou homeland, it is clear that King Wu and his army must have travelled from Feng to Mengjin, the Fords of Meng, following the valley alongside the south bank of the Wei and Yellow Rivers, a distance of roughly 240 miles. Mengjin, which still has this name today, is known to be the place at which King Wu 'crossed the great water'.[2] He was already well into Shang territory by this time, which began at the confluence of the Wei with the Yellow River. Most early literature agrees that an army is capable of travelling 30 *li* in a day, about ten miles, which means that if King Wu marched without any rest days the journey to Mengjin would have taken almost a month. At Mengjin the plains open out, giving King Wu a march of 90 miles as the crow flies to Muye, the Wilds of Mu, where the decisive battle of the Conquest took place, 50 miles away from the Shang capital. These distances are approximate, as scholars disagree on the exact location of Muye (see maps 1 and 2).

According to Sima Qian,[3] King Wu left Feng leading an army of 45,000 troops, with 3,000 'tiger braves' and 300 chariots.[4] By the time he reached the Wilds of Mu he had been joined by men from eight other states: Yong, Shu, Qiang, Mao, Wei, Lu, Peng, and Pu. These new allies were able to muster 4,000 chariots. The *Mu Shi*, 'The Harangue at Mu', a chapter of the *Book of Documents*, provided Sima Qian with his information for the next stage of the story.

It was a grey dawn on the day *jiazi*, the first day of the sixty-day cycle. King Wu came in the morning to address his men in the Wilds of Mu. In his left hand he wielded the yellow battle-axe; in his right he held the white ox-tail ensign, which he waved aloft to signal he was about to speak: 'Far you have come, you men of the western regions!' The king then began his harangue:

Ah! you great princes of my friendly states, you managers of affairs, director of the multitude, director of the horse, director of work and your subordinate officers, commanders, captains of thousands and captains of hundreds. And you, men of Yong, Shu, Qiang, Mao, Wei, Lu, Peng, and Pu. Lift up your halberds, join together your shields, raise your lances, I have a declaration to make.

The ancients had a saying: 'The hen does not announce the morning.' If the hen calls the morning it means the house will be ransacked.

Now Shou,[5] the king of Shang, follows only the words of a woman.[6] He forsakes his own ancestors' sacrificial rites and refuses to requite them. He casts aside his uncles and brothers and does not employ them. Yet the vagabonds of the four quarters, those exiled from their own states, these he honours, these he respects. These he entrusts with office, making them into dignitaries and ministers, empowering them to oppress the people and commit villainy and treachery in the city of Shang.

Now I, Fa, am about to administer Heaven's punishment. In today's action, we will not advance more than six or seven paces before halting to regroup. My brave men, exert yourselves! We will not attack in more than four, five, six, or seven sallies, before again halting to adjust our ranks.[7] Exert yourselves, officers!

May you be warlike! Be like tigers, like leopards, like bears, like brown bears![8] On the outskirts of Shang, do not rush on those who fly to us in submission; they can work for us in the western land. Exert yourselves, officers! If you do not exert yourselves, we will have a massacre.

Although Bernhard Karlgren considered the *Mu Shi* authentic, Herrlee Creel expressed reservations about relying on it as a genuine Western Zhou document, mainly on the basis that King Wu appears to allude to King Zhou's concubine Da Ji. Creel found it strange that no other text of the period mentioned that Zhou Xin had been under the influence of a woman, yet here King Wu felt it sufficiently important to begin his harangue to the troops with.[9] Six years after he expressed this view, however, an important archaeological discovery was made that corroborates a distinctive detail of the *Mu Shi*. In 1976 an inscribed bronze known as the Li *gui*, a vessel shaped like a tureen,[10] was excavated at Lintong in Shaanxi. Its inscription has immense historical value, because it confirms that the Battle of Muye took place on the day *jiazi*, in the morning, precisely as stated in the *Mu Shi*, and was over very quickly. The inscription says that at dusk of the same day the Zhou triumphantly occupied Shang, agreeing with a statement to this effect in ode 236. The text adds that metal, probably the bronze used to cast the vessel, was conferred as a blessing on the caster Li by King Wu himself on the day *xinwei*, which presumably is in the same sexagenary cycle and so on the seventh day after the battle.[11]

The emphasis on the day *jiazi*, neither the Li *gui* nor the *Mu Shi* giving any indication of year or season, suggests an auspicious day for the battle may have been chosen by divination. In the late third century BC *Liu Tao*, literally meaning 'Six Scabbards' but taken by Ralph D Sawyer to mean 'Six Secret Teachings', the military strategist Taigong, to whom the book is attributed, advises King Wu to command the Grand

Scribe to crack the sacred tortoise shell to divine an auspicious day for appointing the commanding general. The *Liu Tao* states that to prepare for the chosen day a vegetarian regime should be observed for three days before.[12] Compare the judgment of hexagram 18, which is remarkably similar to an oracle-bone inscription: 'Advantageous to cross the great water. Before *jia*, three days. After *jia*, three days.' *Jia* is the first day of the ancient ten-day week.[13] The 'week' or *xun* consisted of the following days:

1. *jia*   甲
2. *yi*   乙
3. *bing* 丙
4. *ding* 丁
5. *wu*   戊
6. *ji*   己
7. *geng* 庚
8. *xin*   辛
9. *ren*   壬
10. *gui* 癸

These are called the 'Ten Heavenly Stems'. When they are combined with the 'Twelve Earthly Branches' a cycle of 60 days results. A detailed discussion of the stems and branches is beyond the scope of this book.[14] For the purposes of the argument it is sufficient to understand stem-branch (*ganzhi*) combinations as simply a system for naming the days. In each sexagenary cycle there are thus six *jia* days, of which *jiazi* is day 1, *jiaxu* day 11, *jiashen* day 21, *jiawu* day 31, *jiachen* day 41, and *jiayin* day 51, before cycling around again to *jiazi* at the start of the next 60-day cycle. The first day of the cycle would have been regarded as the most auspicious *jia* day.

I cannot prove from the text of hexagram 18 itself that the judgment refers specifically to a tortoise divination to determine the most auspicious time to cross the great water at the Fords of Meng on the Yellow River, but circumstantial evidence suggests this. According to the *Shi Ji* King Wu's army crossed the Fords of Meng on *wuwu* (day 55).[15] Allowing for three whole days to pass after the *jia* day, *jiayin* (day 51), *wuwu* is the following day. This is fully consistent, given the distance involved, with King Wu's army drawing up on the battle-field at Muye on *jiazi* (day 1 of the next 60-day cycle). In addition, Hellmut Wilhelm observed that the judgment of hexagram 18 quoted in the *Zuozhuan* for the year 645BC does not say *li she da chuan*, 'Advantageous to cross the great water', but simply *she he*, 'Cross the He', *i.e.* 'Cross the Yellow River'. Hellmut Wilhelm believed that the more concrete 'He' was the original wording, which was later replaced by the generic *da chuan*, 'great water'.[16] (The only specific mention of 'the He' in the received text of the *Zhouyi* is in the second line of hexagram 11, all other references to river crossings seem suspiciously standardised as 'great water'. I have retained Richard Wilhelm's attractive translation, but *da chuan* is actually 'great stream'.)

If the above method of counting 'three days' is adhered to— *i.e.* implying three whole days before and three whole days after the divined and specified day, as in three whole days of a vegetarian regime before the chosen day, and waiting three whole days after the divined day and *then* crossing the great water (as opposed to crossing on the third day)—a veil is lifted on hexagram 57. In the first line of this hexagram a 'military man', *wuren*, the character *wu* being the same as King Wu, appears to be divining whether to advance or retreat. In the fifth line he receives an oracle in which he is told that his troubles will disappear and that it will be auspicious, presumably to advance, followed by a similar statement to the judgment of hexagram 18 concerning the timing: 'Before *geng*, three days. After *geng*, three days.'[17] *Geng* is the seventh day of the ancient ten-day week. The day following three whole days after *gengshen* (day 57) is *jiazi*, the day of the Battle of Mu.[18] That specific *geng* and *jia* days in the sexagenary cycle should appear in hexagrams 57 and 18 as general *geng* and *jia* days of the ten-day week is in keeping with the idea already discussed that the text was probably generalised by an editor, possibly working several centuries later. Notice that when the fifth line of hexagram 57 moves hexagram 18 results:

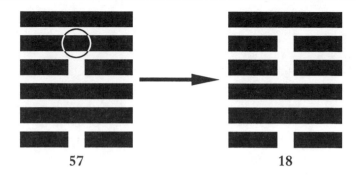

57   18

This provides strong evidence of a deliberate linking of these two hexagram texts via the changing line, and hence of editorial control.[19] Further supporting this interpretation of hexagram 57 is the fourth line, referring to a hunt in which three kinds of game are caught. In ancient China it was customary for the victor in a battle to hunt herds of game shortly afterwards to provide for the great celebration feasts and as offerings to the ancestors.[20]

After the harangue, King Wu arrayed his men at Muye, the Wilds of Mu. The character *ye* refers to an uncultivated wilderness area far outside a city. It appears twice in the *Zhouyi*, and in both instances I believe it may refer specifically to the Wilds of Mu. In the judgment of hexagram 13: 'Fellow-countrymen proceed to the Wilds.'[21] A sacrifice is offered and a divination is performed: 'Advantageous to cross the great water.' In the top line of hexagram 2 the identification of 'the Wilds' with the Battle of Muye is even more strongly indicated: 'Dragons battling in the Wilds. Their blood is black and yellow.' The motif 'black and yellow', *xuanhuang*, is conspicuous in another reference to the Conquest, in the *Wu Cheng* chapter of the *Documents*, 'Military Completion'.[22] Here it is said that when King Wu conquered the Shang state its people came out to show their gratitude by offering him baskets full of black and yellow silks. Although the original *Wu Cheng* chapter was lost, and the chapter by this name in the present text of the *Documents* is regarded as spurious, luckily this particular fragment that was incorporated into the forged material was quoted and commented upon by Mencius in the fourth century BC, who said it originated from the *Shujing*, though he didn't specify which chapter.[23]

Hexagram 53 may tell the story of what happened to the wife of a young soldier who went away to fight against the Shang with King Wu. In the judgment the signs are auspicious for their marriage, but soon he is called away, presumably 'those bamboo slips' arrived containing orders to depart.[24] Following a common practice of the time, she tries to read signs from the flight of the returning wild geese. When the geese reach the bank of the river in the first line everyone fears for the safety of the young men of the village. When they reach a rock in the second line this is seen as an omen that the young men are out of danger. *Pan*, 'a rock', also means 'firm, stable', which is possibly why it was regarded as a good omen. The villagers eat and drink together to celebrate. In the third line, the young woman's husband has not returned from the campaign and the wild geese are reaching dry land.[25] His wife was pregnant when he left, but now she miscarries after fending off ruffians who try to rob her, perhaps deserters returning early. Still she watches the behaviour of the wild geese, desperately missing her husband and looking for signs. In the fourth line the wild geese reach the trees. Geese have webbed feet, unsuited to perching, but the geese find a wide flat branch.

My reason for connecting this poignant story to the Conquest is because there is a similar ode in the *Shijing*, ode 181. Arthur Waley mentioned this three-stanza ode, in passing, as providing illustrative material for his insight that omens are being read from the flight of wild geese in hexagram 53, but there is more to it than that.[26] Waley focused his attention on ode 159, wishing simply to bring out the principle of reading omens from the flight of geese, but ode 181 fits the narrative of hexagram 53 much more closely. The first stanza describes the wild geese flying overhead while the army is on the march,[27] but then it says, in Waley's translation: 'Painfully they struggle through the wilds. In dire extremity are the strong men; sad are their wives, left all alone.' The character *ye* is used here, 'the Wilds', suggesting the ode refers to marching to the battle in the Wilds of Mu. The ode has a parallel structure to hexagram 53, even down to mentioning, in the third stanza where the wild geese cry woefully, that some foolish men urged their fellows to make trouble and rebel. It is tempting to think that those I have characterised as deserters in the third line of hexagram 53, who seem to have been responsible for the young woman losing her unborn child, were just these men whose heart was not in the Conquest and who returned early to the husbandless villages in the western land.

In the second stanza of the ode the wild geese alight in the middle of a marsh as the soldiers are erecting an encampment nearby. I can imagine some of these men lifted their heads and thought of their wives when they saw this. Ode 181 matches hexagram 53 like the other half of a tally, or the two halves of a 'broken mirror'.[28] The fifth line of hexagram 53 is not done justice in Wilhelm-Baynes, which says 'the wild goose draws near the summit'. Actually the returning wild geese head for the *ling*, 'burial mounds', the grave tumuli of the village cemetery. The meaning is plain. The young girl, who has been holding out hope and not wishing to read the worst into her husband's failure to return, now stands up to her fate. The sight of the wild geese settling on the burial mounds, in simple terms, is an omen informing her of his death, but, in the deeper significance of an omen, it catalyses an inner knowing not yet faced up to. 'Only geese return.' It's a beautiful sad story, a small portrayal of the lives and concerns of ordinary people caught up in the changing of the Mandate of Heaven, without which the story would have been strangely incomplete as we now turn our attention to the actual Battle of Muye.

When Zhou Xin heard that King Wu had brought an army to Shang territory, he raised a force of 700,000 men to oppose him. According to the *Wu Cheng*, King Zhou led forward his troops on the morning of *jiazi*; they massed themselves in the Wilds of Mu as dense as a forest.[29] But they offered no opposition to King Wu's far smaller army.[30] As soon as King Wu advanced on the Shang those in the front-line of King Zhou's army turned their lances and attacked those behind them till they fled. It was said that 'the blood flowed till it floated the pestles of the mortars'. Again, Mencius quotes this fragment of the *Documents*, substantiating its authenticity. Even so, this shocking image from the original *Wu Cheng* appears to have taxed his credulity, for he could not believe that a battle sanctioned by Heaven could possibly have led to so much bloodshed. Mencius said:

> It would be better to be without the *Book of Documents* than to give entire credence to it. In the *Wu Cheng* chapter I accept only two or three strips.[31] A benevolent man has no match in the Empire. How could it be that the blood flowed till it floated the pestles of the mortars, when the most benevolent waged war against the most cruel?[32]

When one realises that at the time of the Conquest a mortar was a rounded depression hollowed in the earth, and that the pestles were invariably made of wood, facts which were first recorded in the *Great Treatise* of the *Yijing*,[33] the poetic realism of this small detail attains a chilling ring of truth.[34] The more pragmatic Wang Chong (AD27–ca97) felt Mencius was indulging in romanticism. He too quotes this fragment of the *Wu Cheng*, adding that it also says that over a thousand *li* the earth was red. Both statements he found to contain verisimilitude by comparison with more recent observations of the battlefield aftermath of the war between the Han and Qin dynasties. He said that those who claimed the Conquest of Yin was so easy that the swords were unstained by blood intended a compliment to the virtue of King Wu, but that it was obviously an exaggeration of the truth.[35]

The detail about the pestles is realistic in still another way. If it is accepted that King Wu's army began preparations for war shortly after the total solar eclipse of June 20, as pieced together from hexagram 55, then by the time they reached Muye it would have been the autumn. This time of year, just after the harvest had been gathered in, was regarded as the ideal time to conduct military campaigns in ancient China because then one did not needlessly expose the common people to starvation. Here in the uncultivated ground of the Wilds of Mu it appears that farmers have been pounding rice to remove the husks, their work virtually completed when the opposing armies arrive to do battle. The pestles have been left lying in the mortars from the day before. The blood of the battle collects in these bowls pounded in the earth, the wooden pestles eventually floating in them.[36]

Sima Qian misses out of his account this extraordinary description, simply saying that King Zhou's army had not the will to fight, that they all desired King Wu to enter the capital quickly and so they turned their weapons around to open a way for King Wu. King Zhou's army collapsed upon itself and rebelled against the tyrant, who fled back to the capital. There he put on his jade suit, climbed to the top of the Deer Pavilion, and threw himself into the flames of his palace.[37]

King Wu's army swarmed into the city in search of the tyrant, seizing it as easily as one might shake down a dry leaf. King Wu held a large white banner to show that he meant no harm to the Shang people, white being the colour of the Shang. The third century BC *Xunzi* states that punishing King Zhou became no more difficult that punishing 'a lone commoner'.[38] The feudal lords welcomed King Wu, who saluted them. He announced: 'Heaven above has blessed you!' The people of Shang knelt before him and bowed their heads twice, King Wu returned the gesture. Mencius records that King Wu said: 'Do not be afraid. I come to bring you peace, not to wage war on the people.'[39] Mencius adds that the sound of the people suddenly prostrating themselves on the ground in gratitude was like a mountain crashing down. Entering the smouldering palace courtyard in his chariot King Wu saw the burnt corpse of King Zhou and personally shot three arrows into it. He dismounted and cut off Zhou's head with his precious sword.[40] He skewered it on the pole carrying the large white banner and erected it for all to see. The third century BC *Xunzi* said that Zhou's head dangled from a red pennant.[41] The fourth century BC *Mozi* said Zhou's head was hung from a red ring mounted on a white banner.[42] In his 'Basic Annals of the Yin' Sima Qian says King Wu then killed Da Ji,[43] but in his 'Basic Annals of the Zhou' he says King Zhou's two favourite concubines, neither of whom are named, had hung themselves and King Wu fired three arrows into each, beheaded them, and hung their heads on poles carrying small white banners.[44]

The next day the roads were cleared and the altars were repaired for a ceremony. The Duke of Zhou and the Duke of Bi, both holding halberds, stood either side of King Wu. An ox was sacrificed and the scribe read aloud the supplication:

> Zhou, the last descendant of the House of Yin, abandoned the virtues of the ancestors, defied the spirits, neglected the sacrifices, and thought nothing of inflicting cruelty upon the 100 honourable families of the city of Shang. May his deeds be known by Shangdi.

King Wu then knelt twice and bowed his head, saying: 'I have been given the Mandate of Heaven to replace the Yin dynasty.' He knelt twice more, bowed his head, and left.

King Wu had the Viscount of Ji released from prison, and raised a tumulus over Bi Gan's grave. He distributed grain to the people, and the wealth of the Deer Pavilion. He enfeoffed the feudal lords and established Zhou Xin's son Wu Geng to continue the sacrifices to the Yin ancestors. Then he returned to the west, leaving at least two of his brothers, Guanshu and Caishu, to oversee the Shang scion. Following the death of King Wu, which was seven years after the Conquest according to Legge,[45] these two brothers rose up in rebellion with Wu Geng, necessitating a punitive expedition by the Duke of Zhou, acting as regent for King Wu's young son, King Cheng. The Duke of Zhou executed Wu Geng and his own elder brother Guanshu. Tradition holds that Guanshu and Caishu had suspected the Duke of Zhou of attempting to usurp the throne of the young King Cheng.[46]

The story of how the Duke of Zhou's name was cleared is told in the chapter of the *Book of Documents* entitled *Jin Teng*, 'The Metal-Bound Coffer'. This states that in the second year after the Conquest King Wu fell seriously ill. The Duke of Zhou, without King Wu's knowledge, offered his own life to the ancestors, the former kings Tai, Ji, and Wen, asking them to spare King Wu and take him in his stead. The Duke of Zhou then sought the ancestors' decision by divining three times by the tortoise, and an unnamed book of oracles. On reading the answer he went to see the king and said: 'According to the indications of the oracle, you will suffer no harm.' King Wu recovered.[47] The Duke of Zhou, who was also spared, placed the records of his supplication in a chest bound with metal straps where important archives were kept.

After King Wu died, Guanshu and one or two of his brothers in the east overseeing the Shang scion spread rumours insinuating that the Duke of Zhou intended harm to the young King Cheng so that he could become ruler himself. The Duke of Zhou led a force east, spending two years capturing the slanderers. King Cheng did not dare to cast aspersions on the Duke. In the autumn, Heaven sent a tremendous storm that flattened the crops and uprooted giant trees. The people were afraid. King Cheng set out to perform a divination about these events and had occasion to open the metal-bound coffer. And so he learnt the truth about the Duke of Zhou offering his own life in place of King Wu. King Cheng wept as he read it, realising that the suspicions he had harboured were unfounded: 'There is no need to divine. Formerly the Duke of Zhou toiled diligently for the royal house, but I, the young one, had no way of knowing it. Now Heaven has set its terror in motion to vindicate the Duke of Zhou.' Heaven then sent a wind in the opposite direction to raise up the grain, and there was a bountiful harvest.

As Creel has pointed out, the *Jin Teng* treats history carelessly in that the Duke of Zhou makes his expedition east to silence slanderous reports, not mentioning that his brothers had conspired with Zhou Xin's son Wu Geng to raise an insurrection and destabilise the new dynasty. Creel suggests that the text has more merit as the first Chinese short story.[48]

To conclude this chapter, I would just like to mention a few further details that link in with the *Book of Changes*. Two years after the Conquest King Wu offered the Viscount of Ji a fief in Korea and requested that he return from voluntary exile to explain to him the reason why Yin had been destroyed.[49] On his way to pay homage to King Wu,[50] before travelling with his followers (historical legend mentions about 5,000 people) to settle at Pyong-yang in north-west Korea,[51] Jizi passed by the old Shang capital and was moved to see that the palaces and dwellings were already in ruins and that grain and millet had grown all over them.[52] Jizi was saddened; he would have liked to openly lament, but it was impossible. He would have liked to weep, but he thought it was womanish; so he composed the poem 'The Ears of Wheat' to express his feelings:

> The ears of wheat droop down;
> The grain and millet shimmers;
> The deceitful boy—has not been good for me.

Sima Qian explains that the one Jizi calls 'the deceitful boy' was King Zhou. When the people of Yin heard this poem they burst into tears.[53] There is possibly a pun operating in the poem, in that 'boy' is *tong* and millet is *liang* but *tongliang* is a grass that does not produce grain, resembling millet, corresponding to the injurious weeds or tares of the Bible that were maliciously sown amidst the wheat.[54]

This is a deceptively simple poem: at first sight it might not be thought that it provides a piece of information that enables a bold reconstruction of history to be made that casts light on the enigmatic judgment of hexagram 4. The most common meaning of the character that serves as the title of this hexagram, *meng*, is 'to cover; to conceal'. It is often used in the *Odes* to describe the way creepers cover over and conceal brambles, which may account for the fact that the character takes the 'grass' radical, indicating a connection with plants. Another one of its meanings is 'dull; stupid; an untutored child', which, in combination with *tong*, 'boy, youth', gave rise to 'the young fool' in the Wilhelm-Baynes translation. But in the *Zuozhuan* Karlgren defines the usage of *meng* as 'deceive',[55] also one of its definitions today, hence the *tongmeng* of hexagram 4 can actually be translated as 'the deceitful boy', revealing a more intelligent level of meaning. The judgment says: 'It was not I who sought the deceitful boy; the deceitful boy sought me.' The oracle explains that it has given its pronouncement and that persisting a second and third time merely serves to annoy it and it will not co-operate.

The implication is that the judgment of hexagram 4 may allude to the response of the tortoise oracle just before the Shang dynasty fell, when the 'divine tortoise' abandoned the Shang and they could learn nothing auspicious from it, described in Chapter III. Though this reference to divining a second or third time has been taken to mean that one should not ask the same question of the oracle twice, it is a fact that it was standard practice for the Shang to divine by the tortoise oracle five times on the same issue (*i.e.* making ten cracks on a single topic in five paired positive and negative charges).[56] In 'The Metal-Bound Coffer' the Duke of Zhou repeats his enquiry of the tortoise oracle three times and all three responses are auspicious. Hexagram 4 must therefore refer to a much more serious withdrawal of co-operation by the oracle, and for a far more substantial reason than simply repeating a question. By postulating that the judgment of hexagram 4 refers to the specific moment when Heaven withdrew its Mandate from the Shang, on the grounds of what appears to be an allusion to King Zhou as 'the deceitful boy', it is rendered intelligible as an oracular response. At the first divination the oracle informed them (that the Mandate had been withdrawn, and hence the right to the divine tortoise); when the Shang divined again, and again, the oracle gave no further information. King Zhou believed that because Heaven had given the Mandate to his House he personally could do no wrong, and that his excesses were by definition Heaven's will. Heaven disabused him of this notion, dealing an absolutely crushing blow to the Shang that was later alluded to in the *Zhouyi* in the form of a scathing rebuke: 'It was not I who sought the deceitful boy, the deceitful boy sought me.'[57]

This interpretation of hexagram 4 is corroborated by statements in the *Book of Documents*. In the *Da Gao*, or 'Great Announcement' chapter, it is said that the precious tortoise oracle handed down by the serene (*i.e.* dead) kings effectively gives voice to the Mandate of Heaven. When a suggestion is mooted that King Cheng countermand a pronouncement of the oracle it is looked upon as opposing the command of Heaven. 'As Heaven has helped the people how much more we should follow the oracle now.' It is stated that King Wu received the Mandate of Heaven because he followed only the oracle. In the judgment of hexagram 4, therefore, the original connotation of the oracle's refusal to co-operate must have been the withdrawal of the Mandate of Heaven.

These ideas are clearly important for our understanding of the *Yijing*, given that the yarrow-stalk oracle is the continuation and refinement of the tortoise oracle. Thus the *Yi* too transmits the Mandate of Heaven. This is not an irrelevant tradition; to consult the *Yijing* is literally 'to enquire of Wen Wang'. Not continuing the work of the dead kings is likened in the *Da Gao* to a son who is not willing to sow the seed after his deceased father has broken the soil: 'How much the less will he be willing to reap the crop?'

Chapter VIII

A few concluding remarks

Whether by chance or design, the *Book of Changes* contains a hidden history of the Conquest. The traditional understanding that King Wen 'doubled the trigrams' when he was imprisoned at Youli, and wrote the judgments of the hexagrams, is simplistic; nevertheless the association between King Wen and the *Zhouyi* has withstood critical analysis.

King Wu and the people of Feng were mourning King Wen's death when the midday sun itself died. Chang, the personal name of King Wen, means 'the light of the sun'. King Wu regarded the solar eclipse as an omen for the fall of the Shang dynasty and as a sign that he had the Mandate of Heaven to launch the invasion that King Wen had planned. Because King Wu was in mourning for his father at the time, he consulted the tortoise oracle to see whether he should complete the customary three years in the mourning hut. The cracks made in the tortoise shell convinced King Wu to abandon the mourning rites and attack the Shang immediately. This apparent disregard of filial piety was thought sufficiently disgraceful at the time for Bo Yi and his brother to starve themselves to death in protest against the Zhou Conquest.

King Wu consulted the oracle not because he doubted that he had the Mandate of Heaven, but because he doubted the urgency of attacking the Shang. Initially, King Wu himself cannot have been certain whether it was right to pursue this course while his father still lay unburied; it was the eclipse omen that led him to question his mourning plans. Records of the divinations that sealed King Wu's decision survived in the *Yi*, as did a record of the solar eclipse itself, but they went unrecognised because the historical content of the *Changes* was overlaid by symbolic interpretations that disguised the original meaning. According to the *Tian Wen* King Wu took his father's corpse into battle with him. Although this was clearly referred to in the *Yi* seven centuries earlier, the reference was misunderstood and only in retrospect does it now appear obvious.

The sequence of events following the death of King Wen, as revealed by the *Changes*, cries out to be understood, yet it has remained an untold story for three millennia. Only a kind of faith, existing alongside the *Yi* as 'tradition', has preserved an association between King Wen and the *Book of Changes*. The text itself has been silent, perhaps because, until the modernist challenge to tradition, there has been no need to speak. But now the oracle has spoken with great force, and has effectively refuted modern scepticism of its origins. At the same time, the simple traditional story, for so long taken on trust, has been replaced by a complex and dynamic historical scenario supported by a wealth of evidence.

Let us for a moment look at two decisive elements of the reconstruction. The title of hexagram 55, Feng, understood today as 'Abundance', is the name of the city King Wen built and from which King Wu launched his invasion. But I had consulted the *Book of Changes* for many years without realising this. I was reading an archaeology book that reproduced the character for the name of the city of Feng, which I suddenly saw was the title of hexagram 55. Had I not at the time been looking for clues to date the solar eclipse in that hexagram I might not have made the connection. And it was only after I had become thoroughly familiar with the Conquest story that I found King Wu's personal name, Fa, staring me in the face in the second line. It had been there for 3,000 years and no-one had noticed. It is conceivable, therefore, that those who edited the *Changes* to generalise it, circa 800BC, did not themselves read Feng and Fa as names, and so left in these pointers to the original context by accident. That said, we must remember that the *Changes* is not simply an ancient text, it is an oracle reputed to be capable of answering any question, so why then should it not be able to answer the question of its own origin? Here, perhaps, I have had some slight advantage over many modern scholars, in that I have never doubted the book's powers.

During my study of the *Changes* over the years I have gradually moved from a symbolic appreciation to a literal one, in an effort to discover the original concrete imagery buried beneath the layers of abstraction through which we know the hexagrams today. Further examples of the use of this technique follow in Section II. On the surface the phrases of the *Yi* appear to contain little of substance, yet, upon examination, one can find exact detail, verifiable allusions, hidden names and places, vivid imagery. The more one examines the text the more its fragments link together, yet the mystery of this extraordinary book, far from being solved, only deepens.

Section II

Further mysteries of the *Changes*

Chapter IX

The *mingyi* bird

It is worth explaining why the title of hexagram 36, Mingyi, translated as 'Darkening of the Light' in Wilhelm-Baynes, is now translated as a 'crowing pheasant'. The earliest extant interpretation of *mingyi* appears in the late Zhou *Zuozhuan*. In a recorded consultation of the *Changes* by yarrow stalks, which supposedly took place in 537BC, the diviner says *mingyi* relates to the sun, while also adducing a connection to a bird.[1] He expands on neither of these statements. In more recent times, Arthur Waley gave the modernist bird interpretation its first airing in the west in his 1933 essay 'The Book of Changes', drawing on Li Jingchi's work published in 1931. Waley pointed out that 'there is not the slightest doubt' that *mingyi* must be the lost name of a bird, because of the reference to wings and flying in the first line. Waley simply called it 'the *mingyi* bird', wisely refusing to venture a positive identification.[2]

Literally, the characters *mingyi* mean 'brilliance injured' or 'wounding of the bright', which Wilhelm rendered as 'darkening of the light' and justified on the grounds that the component trigrams picture the sun sinking under the earth, *li* beneath *kun*. This suggests a darkening due to a sunset, but Wilhelm doesn't specifically say so: he talks about the light being 'damaged'. Hexagram 36 arises by the change of the fourth line of hexagram 55, which contains a solar eclipse record. Curiously, Liu Dajun and Lin Zhongjun, in the first and fourth lines of hexagram 36, translate the compound as 'the sacred bird Ming Yi', only to translate it as 'solar eclipse' in lines 3, 5, and 6 (*mingyi* doesn't occur in the sixth line, *ming* appears on its own).[3]

Yi has other dictionary definitions besides 'injured' such as 'squatting on the heels; peaceful; level; even; just; common; ordinary; grades; classes; flying animals; to kill; to exterminate'. The character is a pictograph of an archer, formed of the elements 'man' and 'bow'. *Yi* is also the name of the autumn wind. In early Zhou China it was primarily the name of the Yi tribe of barbarians on the east coast, from which it came to mean barbarians and foreigners of any description.

Retaining *ming* as 'brightness' (the character is a composite of the sun and the moon), Greg Whincup translates *mingyi* as 'the bright pheasant' by replacing *yi* with *zhi*, 'pheasant'. Whincup explains that the Manchurian scholar Gao Heng suggested that these two characters 'were once quite similar in pronunciation'.[4] Gao himself also replaced *ming* with a homophone meaning 'the cry of a bird or animal', giving rise to 'the calling pheasant', a reading followed by Richard Kunst, Kerson Huang, and Richard Rutt. Li Jingchi proposed a substitution giving rise to 'the calling pelican'. Richard Wilhelm noted that hexagram 36/1 refers to flying and pointed out as early as 1924 that the animal symbol corresponding to the lower trigram *li* is the pheasant.[5]

As for 'Jizi's crowing pheasant' in the fifth line, as it has now become in Modern School readings, I have been unable to find any reference linking a calling pheasant or *mingyi* bird with the Viscount of Ji. William de Fancourt in *Warp and Weft* asserts Jizi heard a *mingyi* bird cry as the tyrant Zhou Xin was about to offer a sacrifice, which was an ill-omen portending the fall of the Shang dynasty.[6] But he has since acknowledged that he misremembered a story told in the *Book of Documents*, confusing Jizi for Zu Ji, who heard a crowing pheasant on the day of Gaozong's second-day sacrifice and took the bad omen as an opportunity to lecture the king. Sima Qian says that the pheasant flew onto one of the handles of the sacrificial caldron, which was considered extremely ominous. Jiao Xun

(1763–1820) suggested that the Viscount of Ji need not even be mentioned in hexagram 36, proposing a small emendation that would render his name as 'that fellow' or 'his son'.[7] Richard Wilhelm in Book III of his translation records the late tradition associating historical figures from the Conquest story with all six lines of hexagram 36:

1. Bo Yi[8]
2. King Wen
3. King Wu
4. Weizi[9]
5. Jizi
6. Zhou Xin

In ancient China, pheasants were said to call when a meteorite fell to earth,[10] which may have some bearing on the enigmatic top line where something 'not very bright at night first ascends in the sky; afterwards enters into the earth', which otherwise seems out-of-place in hexagram 36.[11] The devotees of the pheasant-god 'the Precious One of Chen', referred to by Sima Qian, formed a meteorite-worship cult. The Precious One of Chen caused all the female pheasants to call when he arrived on earth in the night, and in the morning the still-hot meteorite became a recipient of sacrifices. According to the *Jin Shu*, some meteorites fall to earth with a sound like the cry of pheasants and are regarded as auspicious for the state in which they land (other meteorites are bad omens). When the Xia dynasty fell, cranes had shrieked for ten nights beforehand.[12] The *Mozi* records that heavenly fire struck the north-west corner of the Xia capital, which must have been a meteorite.[13] Tang the Completer, the 'first good king' of the Shang, took the city in the ensuing panic.

One traditional interpretation of *mingyi* mentioned by Waley in his 1933 paper is 'injury to the eye'. This is supported both by the notion of a 'brightness injury' and by the trigram correspondences of *li*, which include brightness, the sun, and also the eye (because the trigram, like the eye, is hollow in the middle). In the *Zuozhuan* there is a quotation of the judgment of hexagram 24, Fu, that differs from that found in the received text: 'The Southern Kingdom is routed; shoot at its king and hit one of his eyes.' Hexagram 24 arises by the change of the third line of hexagram 36, which reads: '*Mingyi* during the hunt in the south, taking their great leader.' If *mingyi* is an injury to the eye there is a remarkable correlation between the two texts.[14]

If *yi* is the name of the Yi tribe of barbarians, *mingyi* may be read as *meng yi*, 'Alliance with the Yi tribe' or 'Allied Yi'. Simply by adding the 'bowl' radical beneath the character *ming*, 'brightness', one obtains *meng*, 'alliance, covenant, oath' (see the glossary of Chinese characters at the end of the book). Several sinologists have made this substitution in translations of other works.[15] This reading of the text proves fruitful because the character *yi* also appears in the fourth line of hexagram 55, which by its change yields hexagram 36. In Chapter IV it was mentioned that in hexagram 55 there was a meeting with another lord, probably to form an alliance. The fourth line of hexagram 55, as well as containing the record of a total solar eclipse, specifically refers to a meeting with the Lord of the Yi tribe. Possibly it is the record of an oracle-bone divination by King Wu before he met the Lord of the Yi, the 'auspicious' prognostication assuring him of a welcome from a potentially unpredictable war-lord.[16]

Before King Wu launched the invasion from the west, the Yi tribe did actually help to weaken the Shang state by revolts along their eastern borders.[17] Although the Shang succeeded in putting down the insurgency, the Yi tribe would have been a powerful ally for the Zhou when the Conquest came. In the third century AD forgery of the *Tai Shi* chapter of the *Book of Documents*, which has been shown to contain genuine ancient fragments, King Wu states in an harangue to his men at the Fords of Meng:

> It would seem that Heaven is going to rule the people by means of me. My dreams are in agreement with my divinations; the omen is doubly auspicious. My attack on Shang must succeed. Shou has control over hundreds of thousands of the Yi tribe— but their loyalties are divided.[18]

There is otherwise no historical record of King Wu having made an alliance with the Yi tribe, unless one regards hexagram 55/4 changing to hexagram 36 as a record of it. The fact that after the Conquest the Yi tribe became as troublesome to the Zhou as they had been to the Shang, which we know from bronze inscriptions, might be thought by some to cast doubt on this interpretation. The very nature of an alliance, however, is that it depends upon a mutual objective. After the Conquest the alliance would have served its purpose. (The character *meng* in Mengjin, the Fords of Meng, is commonly written in two ways in ancient texts, one of which is 'alliance'.[19] Mengjin has thus sometimes been translated as the 'Fords of Sworn Alliance'.)

But what is the connection between the Yi tribe, the character *yi* being a pictograph of an archer, and a pheasant, or, in the absence of a cast-iron identification, a *mingyi* bird, and its association with the sun, a solar eclipse, and 'darkening of the light' or 'brilliance extinguished'?

Nebulous though it may be, the solar-bird myth of Yi the Archer must suggest itself. Though Yi the Archer is written with a different character to the Yi tribe, Yi the Archer was known as the 'East Barbarian', and Yi-Yi, 'East Barbarian Yi'. The 'East Barbarians' are the Yi tribe.[20] The popular version of the myth of Yi the Archer consists of a number of originally discrete elements. A three-legged crow was said to live in the sun. There were ten suns, one for each day of the ancient ten-day week. They would traverse the sky one at a time, resting at the end of the day in the branches of the 100-mile-high 'Leaning Mulberry' or Fu Sang tree, which had leaves no bigger than mustard seeds. In the morning a fresh sun would make the journey after bathing in a pool.[21] One day all ten suns came out at once and threatened to incinerate the earth, but, on the orders of Emperor Yao, Yi shot down nine of them, which fell to earth as crows, scattering their feathers. These separate mythic strands were combined to form the neo-myth of Yi the Archer, the ten suns, and the crows falling to earth, in the early Han dynasty. The earliest reference to Yi shooting ten suns, for instance, does not mention the crows.

This appears in the *Huainanzi*, compiled 139BC.[22] Chapter 2 of the fourth century BC *Zhuangzi* mentions the ten suns coming out all at once, but without the crows or Yi the Archer.

Professor Anne Birrell emphasised to me that the earliest reference to the Yi the Archer sun-bird myth complex is *non-numerological*, but at first I did not grasp the profound significance this remark had for my own research.[23] The *locus classicus* is *l*.56 of the fourth century BC *Tian Wen, Ask Heaven*, a book of riddles by Qu Yuan that is part of the early poetry anthology *Chu Ci*. There is no distinction between single and plural in classical Chinese, but, because of the later version of the myth involving ten suns, most commentators interpret this line in the plural. Stephen Field translated it as: 'Why did Yi shoot down the suns? How did the crow feathers scatter?'[24] David Hawkes has: 'When Yi shot down the suns, why did the ravens shed their feathers?'[25] Both authors follow the earliest commentary on the *Chu Ci*, made by its compiler Wang Yi. Anne Birrell pointed out to me, in her letter (Wade-Giles romanisation retained):

> The earliest commentary on the *Ch'u Tz'u*'s non-numerological sun-bird myth is by Wang Yi (dates: AD89–158); and it comes as no surprise that his exegesis of the *Ch'u Tz'u* text cites the *Huai Nan Tzu*, 139BC text (Birrell, *Chinese Mythology*, p 79), but also incorporates *another* mythic strand, to the effect that when Yi shot the nine suns on Yao's orders, the nine birds, defined as *wu*-ravens/crows, all died, dropping their feathers. This may well constitute the earliest expression of the numerological sun-raven-feathers-death neo-myth. For it is clear that Wang Yi (as with Wang Ch'ung in *Lun Heng* vis-à-vis the Kung Kung and Nu Kua flood myth<u>s</u>) created a neo-myth, or mythopoeia, by conjoining two separate mythic narratives, to provide a cause-and-effect sequence. The story gets developed by Ch'eng Hsuan-ying (fl. AD630–660) in his commentary on *Chuang Tzu*, (also cited by Kuo Ch'ing-jan, 1844–1896, see Birrell, *id.*, p 140).

> As you will appreciate, these are complex problems.

Mulling over this enigma staring at the eight characters of *l*.56 of the *Tian Wen* in Chinese, I suddenly realised that something important had been missed since the time of Wang Yi. Bernhard Karlgren, who was aware that the explanation of *l*.56 in terms of the 'ten suns' motif was a product of the Han dynasty, translated the riddle in the singular: 'Why did Yi shoot at the sun, why did the raven shed its feathers.'[26] This begs a question Karlgren never seriously addressed: why *indeed* did Yi shoot at the sun, if there was not the risk of ten suns incinerating the earth? Karlgren interpreted it merely as 'a sacrilegious act', in line with other texts that depict Yi as arrogant and prone to displays of hubris. In actual fact, there can be only one satisfactory answer why Yi would shoot at the sun: because there was a total solar eclipse.

It was a common practice to fire arrows at the sun during a total solar eclipse, I have already mentioned 'the bow that comes to the aid of the sun' in Chapter VI. According to Chapter 55 of the *Guanzi*, which is thought to date to the third century BC, solar eclipses were caused because the three-legged crow that inhabited the sun was eating it.[27] Even in later times, though Chinese astronomers understood the real reason for solar eclipses, ordinary Chinese went on believing that a celestial dog was eating the sun and so fired arrows into the sky, beat wooden clappers, and crashed gongs in the hope of scaring it away.[28]

In *l*.56 of the *Tian Wen* the character *wu*, which means both 'crow' and 'raven', also means 'black' and is clearly used for its value as a pun, ensuring that a hidden double-meaning can be read. This is revealed by translating the riddle another way: 'When Yi shot at the black sun why did feathers scatter?'

Yi the Archer shot at the sun because it was totally eclipsed, killing the *wu*-crow that lives there and was eating it, and this is why feathers scattered. Then the eclipse was over. It's as simple as that. Clever though the riddle is, one surmises it would not have been too difficult to solve at the time it was written; it was only when the 'ten suns' myth was grafted onto it in the Han that it became truly perplexing. By the creation of a neo-myth Wang Yi ensured that the knowledge was lost for 2,000 years that Yi the Archer had originally saved the sun from being extinguished, not the earth from being incinerated.

Thus, we come full circle and find that 'darkening of the light' is, after all, a justifiable interpretation of hexagram 36. I am left, however, with a niggling question. Fabulous legendary Chinese birds and beasts usually have names. I have yet to come across any mention of the solar crow ever being called anything. *Mingyi* is believed to be the lost name of a bird. Could the name of the crow that lives in the sun be *mingyi*?

Chapter X

Melons, willows, hoarfrost, and creepers

Marriage customs inform a number of otherwise enigmatic images in the *Zhouyi*,[1] such as the second and fourth lines of hexagram 44, 'Fish in the wrapping' and 'No fish in the wrapping', respectively. The *Book of Odes* has several songs in which fish caught in nets or traps are an indication of the blessings Heaven will bestow on newly-weds. Ode 104 associates a wicker fish-trap with a girl going to be married. Karlgren comments on this ode: 'The fishes were so plentiful as to burst the wicker fishing baskets in the water to catch them; so numerous will be the offspring of the bride.'[2]

Fish-traps were made from the pliant twigs of the willow, a craft known as osiery or wickerwork. The willow is mentioned in the fifth line of hexagram 44: 'A melon wrapped with willow.' Here the character *bao*, 'wrapping', is used, just as it is in the second and fourth lines, thus suggesting that the 'wrapping' is in these cases also willow, which in turn implies a wicker fish-trap. A further meaning of *bao* is 'container', but I have translated it as 'wrapping' in all three lines so that the connection between them becomes obvious, as it is in the Chinese.[3] The melon may be visualised in a wickerwork basket, or more crudely wrapped around with willow to which the leaves are still attached. The melon is a fecundity symbol in the *Odes*, as indeed are fish. And the character *bao* is thought to have originally depicted a foetus in the womb.[4]

The melon features as an offering made to the Celestial Weaver Girl, the star Vega and patroness of brides, on the seventh day of the seventh moon, known as the 'Feast of Women'.[5] Then the Herdboy or Draught Ox, the star Altair, crosses the Milky Way, or 'River Han', over a bridge of magpies linking wings to lie with her for a single night in the classic Chinese tale of star-crossed lovers 'coming to meet'. This tale is at least 2,000 years old.[6] The two stars are mentioned in ode 203, which dates from the Western Zhou. Though it is uncertain whether the story linking the two lovers had been developed then, the ode is set in the autumn and mentions the number seven.

The 'melon wrapped with willow' might have been an offering to the river goddess.[7] Possibly it was inspected the next day for marriage portents. In the second line there is 'no fish in the wrapping', which is an ominous sign, the beginning of trouble. But in the fourth line one or more fish has got trapped, though still this is interpreted cautiously: it is not yet time for the groom to introduce his bride to his family's ancestors, there will still be a period during which she can be sent back to her own family. The line reads: 'Fish in the wrapping. No fault. Not beneficial to perform the *bin* rite.' The character *bin*, ordinarily translated as 'guests', is in this context a reference to the ceremony where a new wife is introduced to her husband's ancestors and formally accepted into the household. Before the *bin* rite is performed there is a trial period of three months; after this time has passed the new wife can be returned to her own family, the marriage being annulled merely by this action without it being seen as repudiation. During these three months, the husband's family keep the horses of the cart that brought the girl to their home, so that they can take her back if necessary.[8] If she died during her probation period she would not be regarded as a wife and could not be buried at her husband's side. Only after the sacrifice to the ancestors was she his lawful wife. These images fit together well with the judgment of hexagram 44, which counsels against marriage to a 'strong' woman. The title of hexagram 44, Gou, translated in Wilhelm-Baynes as 'Coming to Meet', literally means 'copulation' or 'pairing off'.

Favourable omens for marriage can change. Ode 226 describes a case where a young girl, about to be married, goes to gather plants from which to extract green and blue dyes for her trousseau-dresses. But she fails to fill her basket, a bad omen that proves itself when the man does not show on her wedding day. She dwells on the happy days of their courtship, when the omens were still good; such as the day she reeled his line and he caught a great haul of bream and tench, which she strung together. She was joyous then, for it meant they would be married and have many children.

The willow too has sexual connotations. The willow is the symbol of spring, 'season of erotic awakenings', and features in traditional Chinese innuendo. 'Willow feelings and flower wishes' means sexual desire; 'looking for flowers and buying willows' means visiting a prostitute. A young girl is a 'tender willow and fresh flower'; a woman long past her prime is a 'withered willow and faded flower'. Many erotic Chinese paintings are set on the river bank underneath the willow. Hexagram 28, the only other hexagram that mentions the willow besides hexagram 44, thus begins to make more sense.[9] 'A withered willow sprouting new shoots' is likened in the second line to an old man taking a young bride; in the fifth line 'a withered willow bearing flowers' is compared to an old woman gaining a young husband. In Arthur Waley's opinion these are willow omens. If an old man sees a withered willow sprouting shoots then he reads this as a sign that he will find a young wife, and similarly for the other line. Waley translated the text as follows: 'When the rotten willow bears sprouts, the old husband will get a lady wife; when the rotten willow flowers, the old wife will get a lord and husband.'[10] I am inclined to think this is overdoing the omen-text interpretation, and that these expressions are simply examples of the poetic parallelism so characteristic of the Chinese classical language.[11]

Fornication outdoors is a great taboo in China. It was euphemistically referred to as 'stepping on green' when lovers who had 'come to meet' at the spring love festival[12] withdrew from prying eyes and went into the hills to sample the new spring grass.[13] In the *Book of Odes* the parallel expression

relating to the autumn, 'stepping on hoarfrost', is associated
with marriage. This phrase occurs in the first line of hexagram
2, which appears to have originally meant that the time for
marriage was fast approaching.[14] A widow, who since Song
times was not expected to re-marry, is called to this day a
'hoarfrost woman' as a permanent reminder of her marriage. In
ode 34, 'The gourd has bitter leaves', a young lady waits
impatiently at the ford for her sweetheart to come and bring her
home as his wife. She turns down the boatman's offer of a
crossing, explaining she is waiting for her friend.[15] He says the
ford is too deep to wade, but she replies that if it is deep there
are still stepping-stones and if it is shallow she can tuck up her
skirts. He says the ford is in full flood, but she replies that the
ford is not yet deep enough to wet the axles of a carriage. She
hears the female pheasant cry, seeking her mate. As the
cloudless dawn breaks she hears wild geese call, and mulls over
an old saying: 'If a gentleman is to bring home his bride, he
must do so before the ice melts.' This means that a gentleman
cannot keep a young lady waiting indefinitely. As it says in the
Yijing: 'Stepping on hoarfrost, solid ice is not far off.' What this
means is that by the time hoarfrost is underfoot one should be
thinking about getting married, or the seasons will inevitably
roll on and before one knows it there will be solid ice. By the
time the ice has melted the traditional time for marriage will
have been lost, the couple will not have had a winter shut up in
their house together.[16] The Neo-Confucian interpretation of
hexagram 2/1, that hoarfrost underfoot indicates encroaching
danger (a slippery path ahead?), is specious.

Hexagram 47/6 has marriage connotations: 'Distressed by the
ge-creeper and brambles.' Sandals made from the fibres of the
ge-creeper, which is sometimes called the 'cloth-plant', dolichos,
or kudzu from the Japanese pronunciation *kuzu*, are said in odes
107 and 203 to be 'good for stepping on hoarfrost'. In ode 101 a
girl is taking five pairs of *ge*-creeper sandals on her way to be
married. In ode 2 a girl notices how much the *ge*-creeper has
spread since she came to live in her husband's home, already it
has reached the middle of the valley. She presumably walked
through this valley on her way there, when the *ge*-creeper was

still confined to the slopes—the passage of time must have suddenly struck her. She decides to make her first visit to see her parents.

Creeping vines are symbolic of the entwining marriage bond in traditional Chinese poetry, particularly the *ge*-creeper. Ode 124 contains an image very similar to hexagram 47/6: 'The *ge*-creeper grew till it covered the brambles.' In the ode a woman sitting and lying alone, day in day out, summer passing into winter, year after year, pledges her intention to remain loyal to her absent husband, presumed dead, until her days are over; meanwhile, the *ge*-creeper spreads, covering over the thorny brambles. This is in stark contrast with the image in the third line of hexagram 47: 'Distressed by rocks, taking thorns in the hands, entering his dwelling, doesn't see his wife. Sorrow.'[17] For many years I couldn't see what was depicted here, until I started to reflect on the similarity of ode 124 and then asked myself the key question: for what reason would a man take thorns in his hands before entering his dwelling? The rather shocking image suddenly clicked. A man returns home after a long absence;[18] he is hoping to be greeted by his wife but instead he comes upon a scene of ruin. He is sick with dread to the pit of his stomach when he sees that there have been rockfalls onto the path from the mountain slopes that have not been cleared away, and creepers have grown over the door of their dwelling. Frantically he tears them away, ripping his hands, the creeper having covered over brambles, not knowing whether his wife is dead inside. When he gets the door open he doesn't see her. She has gone, leaving another kind of sorrow for her husband to find. She was not like the woman of ode 124.

Chapter XI

King Wen is fed his own son

I have not wanted to dwell too much on late fictionalised accounts of the Conquest story in the first section of the book, preferring to concentrate on the earliest historical sources. But the account would be incomplete without some mention of the tradition that the Shang tyrant Zhou Xin, while he had King Wen imprisoned, secretly fed him his own son, Yi Kao, in the form of meat pies. This was regarded as a test of King Wen's divinatory powers, to gauge whether he would be a threat in the future if released from Youli. This episode was imaginatively elaborated in Chapters 19 and 20 of the Ming dynasty novel *Feng Shen Yan Yi*, the *Investiture of the Gods*, an anachronistic tale of 100 chapters packed with supernatural happenings, Daoist immortals, gods in disguise, magical weapons, germ warfare, and a mass inoculation programme organised by the spirit of Shen Nong, patron of herbalists. King Wen's octogenarian minister and military strategist Jiang Ziya, also known as Taigong and Lu Shang, becomes the central character, upstaging Kings Wen and Wu. In Chapter 99 Jiang Ziya deifies all the participants in the drama, both good and bad: hence the title. It is not the best Chinese novel ever written, being both repetitive and long-winded, and it cannot bear comparison with such classics as *Shuihuzhuan* or *Hongloumeng*,[1] but nonetheless it does have some entertaining set-pieces, such as the 'Banquet of the Spectres' in Chapter 25.

Because of the popularity of the *Feng Shen Yan Yi*, published sometime between AD1621 and 1627, the motif of King Wen eating his own son is often repeated as a part of the Conquest story. This idea does have a reasonable antiquity, being first mentioned in the reconstructed fragments of the *Di Wang Shi Ji*, the *Genealogical Records of Emperors and Kings*, compiled by Huangfu Mi (AD215–282), where it appears in a commentary on Sima Qian's 'Basic Annals of the Yin', Chapter 3 of his *Shi Ji*.[2] Three centuries before the *Feng Shen Yan Yi* the Yi Kao episode appeared in a Yuan dynasty 'prompt-book' (*huaben*) entitled *Wu Wang Fa Zhou Binghua*, or *King Wu's Expedition Against King Zhou*, published between AD1321 and 1323. Long lost in China but preserved in Japan, this narrative, like other tales in the prompt-book genre, was used by story-tellers as an outline from which they extemporised to village audiences. The prompt-book also served as the plan for the *Feng Shen*. In both versions King Zhou's malevolent and bewitching concubine Da Ji is a nine-tailed fox; she is the one who suggests to King Zhou that he feed King Wen his own son, but in the *Feng Shen* the reason she does this is vastly elaborated and personally motivated. She tries to seduce Yi Kao, but he spurns her advances. The following is Chapter 19 and the start of Chapter 20, slightly abridged, of the *Feng Shen Yan Yi*:

> It was the seventh year of King Wen's imprisonment at Youli. His eldest son Yi Kao wished to visit him, despite the fact that King Wen had expressly warned against anyone journeying to see him. King Wen had previously prophesied that he would not be executed by the tyrant Zhou but would instead be jailed, and released seven years later.[3] Yi Kao grew anxious, however, and wished to take a tribute to King Zhou in the hope of securing his father's release. When he arrived at the Shang palace, no-one was about, and he dared not enter uninvited. He waited for five days before he saw King Zhou's minister Bi Gan approaching the gate. Yi Kao told Bi Gan he had brought a tribute of precious family heirlooms for King Zhou, that he might be persuaded to release his father Chang.
>
> 'What tribute are you offering?' enquired Bi Gan.
>
> 'The seven-fragrance carriage, a sobriety carpet, a white-faced monkey, and ten beautiful maids,' said Yi Kao.

Bi Gan asked Yi Kao why these items were so precious. 'The carriage,' answered Yi Kao, 'needs neither driver nor horses, responding freely to the will of its occupant, the sobriety carpet sobers up anyone who has had too much to drink merely by lying on it. As for the white-faced monkey, he is a marvellous musician, knowing 3,000 classical pieces and 800 folk-songs.'

Bi Gan warned Yi Kao that the king had lost all virtue and may possibly be made even worse by such gifts, but, not wishing to thwart Yi Kao's filial intentions, took him to see King Zhou. Bi Gan announced Yi Kao at court, the king ordered he be admitted. Yi Kao immediately fell down to his knees, shuffling forward to face the throne.

'The son of the criminal Chang ventures to seek an audience with his majesty,' said Yi Kao.

King Zhou was deeply impressed by Yi Kao's filial piety and courteous manners. He ordered that he rise to his feet and stand behind the rail of the court. King Zhou's concubine Da Ji, the nine-tailed fox, peeped out from behind the curtain at Yi Kao and was captivated by his handsome appearance and evident refinement. King Zhou called her out, saying:

'Yi Kao, son of the Earl of the West, has brought fine gifts to atone for his father's crime. Wouldn't you say he is rather pitiful?'

'I have heard,' said Da Ji, 'that Yi Kao is a wonderful musician. His skill on the zither is unrivalled.'[4]

'How do you know that, my dear?'

'When I was at my parent's home they constantly praised Yi Kao's musical abilities, time and time again mentioning his talent on the zither.'

King Zhou believed every word of it and ordered that a zither be brought in. Da Ji asked sweetly: 'I've heard you're excellent on the zither, would you play a tune for me?'

'Your Majesty,' said Yi Kao, 'it is said that when one's parents are in ill health, the son should undergo austerities. My father has been suffering for seven years, I fear I dare not take pleasure in music, my heart is broken, I doubt if I could play in tune.'

'Yi Kao,' said King Zhou, 'if you play us a tune, and your skill is outstanding, I'll set both you and your father free.'

Yi Kao's spirits were immediately lifted, knowing well his skill on the zither, and he was not at all perturbed by King Zhou's implied threat against his own liberty. He played a delightful tune, 'The Wind in the Pines'. The notes fell like pouring pearls, everyone was overcome with emotion, as if they had visited paradise.

King Zhou ordered that the table be laid for a splendid banquet in Yi Kao's honour. Da Ji grew ever more infatuated with the lad, contrasting his youthful good looks with King Zhou's wrinkles. She thought to herself: 'I must keep him here at the palace on the pretext of teaching me to play the zither. I shall take him to the bedchamber and have my way with him.'

Da Ji made her suggestion to King Zhou: 'Set Earl Chang free, but keep Yi Kao here so that he can teach me the zither, then you can enjoy his beautiful music every day.' King Zhou thought it the perfect solution.

Da Ji got Zhou so drunk he collapsed into bed, safely out of the way. She instructed the maids to bring two zithers and asked Yi Kao to begin her lessons.

Yi Kao first taught her the pentatonic scale, describing how the fingers of the left hand should assume the shape of a dragon's eye, and those of the right should resemble the eye of a phoenix. He taught her the eight types of fingering, and added that there were six frames of mind in which one should never attempt to play.

'What are those?' asked Da Ji.

'When affected by the wailing of mourners, when one is tearful, when one's mind is heavy, when one is angry, when one is sexually aroused, and when one is frightened.' Yi Kao continued the lesson with great formality, finally moving his fingers across the strings to illustrate the theory with a breathtaking crescendo of notes.

Da Ji did not have her mind on the zither; she sought only to seduce Yi Kao with charming smiles, amorous peeks, and flattering words. Never far from Yi Kao's mind, however, was the reason he had visited the palace; his heart he kept immobile to Da Ji's advances. He fended off her ploys most graciously when she asked him to sit closer, but when Da Ji's manoeuvres became ever more forward he decided to admonish her even at the risk of losing his life, rather than live with dishonour.

'If I did as you suggest, I would be a loathsome brute. It is most indecorous that under the pretext of learning the zither you should lower yourself to this extent. Were this matter to reach the ears of those beyond the palace walls, your chastity would be in doubt for generations. If you insist on being so indiscreet, people will hold you in contempt.'

Da Ji blushed at the humiliation. The pretence was finally broken. Da Ji gave up the object of her lust and her infatuation turned to hate. She ordered Yi Kao back to his room, inwardly swearing that she would have her revenge.

In the morning, King Zhou enquired: 'Did Yi Kao teach you well last night?'

Da Ji seized her opportunity: 'If Yi Kao had had his mind on teaching me the zither I might have learned, but he wanted nothing better than to seduce me. He is most uncouth, he intended to violate me.'

King Zhou was furious and ordered Yi Kao to the court. He couched his question tactfully: 'Why is it that Da Ji made so little progress on the zither last night?'

'Patience and sincerity are required for learning the zither, it cannot be learned in a single night.'

Da Ji, sitting beside King Zhou, interrupted: 'You weren't sufficiently diligent in teaching me, you explained nothing clearly. If you had I could have mastered it easily, playing the zither isn't that hard.'

King Zhou still didn't mention Da Ji's accusation, but instead asked Yi Kao to play the zither once more. Yi Kao played a song full of loyal and patriotic sentiments. King Zhou was at a loss to find fault with it. Da Ji, with a second trick up her sleeve, requested that the white-faced monkey be brought to the court: 'I have heard that the white-faced monkey is also a skilled musician, shall we hear it?'

The white-faced monkey was let out of its cage and began to beat wooden clappers and sing in a most soothing manner. King

Zhou immediately forgot his anger, and Da Ji was mesmerised—
but she became so enchanted by the haunting music that she
forgot herself and her true fox spirit form flew out.

To King Zhou and Yi Kao this essence was invisible, but the
white-faced monkey, who had cultivated himself for a thousand
years, instantly spotted it and lunged at Da Ji, attempting to
scratch her to pieces. King Zhou struck a blow to the monkey,
knocking it dead to the floor.

'This is clearly a plot,' said Da Ji, 'Yi Kao brings a monkey to
court pretending to amuse your majesty, but secretly he has
trained it to murder me!'

The king was outraged and ordered that Yi Kao be dragged to
the serpent pit. Yi Kao protested his innocence: 'Your majesty,
monkeys are wild animals, this one is unused to people, he is not
yet fully tamed. The monkey had no knife, how could he have
murdered Da Ji? I have received your hospitality, I would never
throw it back in your face. If you will consider this matter,
though I may be cut into a thousand pieces, I will die with my
spirit requited.'

King Zhou mulled it over, and agreed that it was a far-fetched
idea. He pardoned Yi Kao.

'Since you've forgiven him,' said Da Ji, 'let him play the zither
again. If his playing is full of loyalty it will confirm your
judgment. But if there's any hint of a plot, you must reconsider.'

'A brilliant idea!' said King Zhou.

Yi Kao saw there was no escape, his mind was on the honour
of his family. He sat on the floor and began to play:

A noble king is full of virtue,
Never will he resort to cruel torture.
Roasting pillars burn flesh to ashes,
Writhing snakes devour intestines.
The Wine Lake is brimming with blood,
Corpses hang in the Meat Forest.
The women's looms are empty,
Yet the Happy Pavilion is full.
Men's ploughs are broken,
While royal granaries rot.

> *May the king expel his minions,*
> *And restore peace to the land.*

King Zhou could not see the meaning of Yi Kao's lyrics, but Da Ji cried: 'How dare you insult his majesty with your insidious slander! You deserve death!'[5]

King Zhou flew into a rage, yelling at the palace guards to seize him. Yi Kao said: 'I have one more verse, be so kind as to indulge me.'

> *May the king abandon his lust*
> *And get rid of that queen,*
> *For the sake of the state.*
> *When the evil is gone,*
> *The nobles will gladly submit.*
> *When lust is cleansed,*
> *The kingdom can live in peace.*
> *I do not fear a cruel death,*
> *But wipe out Da Ji*
> *To clear your name.*

When he had finished, he hurled the zither at Da Ji.

King Zhou was sent into a frenzy: 'Attempting to kill her majesty with a zither is an unpardonable capital offence. Guards! Throw him into the serpent pit at once!'

But Da Ji's revenge was not complete. 'I have an idea,' she said, 'let me deal with him.'

Da Ji had Yi Kao removed to the dungeons where she ordered the executioners to nail his hands and feet to a board. She sliced the flesh off him alive, Yi Kao swearing at her until he expired. After Yi Kao's body had been minced up, King Zhou was about to feed it to the serpents, when Da Ji said:

'Let's test Earl Chang. They say he is a man possessed of extraordinary powers of divination. Let's make pies of his son's flesh. If he eats them then there is nothing extraordinary about him. Then you may set him free and your kindness will be recognised. If he refuses to eat them, he is clearly a danger and must be put to death to avoid trouble in the future.'

◆◆◆

King Wen sat in his cell at Youli, it was close to the time he had predicted he would be released. He picked up his zither and idly began to play. Suddenly the thickest string began to resonate with an undertone of melancholy and death. He stopped playing and performed a divination with three gold coins.[6] Seeing the result, he began to weep.

'Ah! My poor son, you failed to observe my strict instructions, and now if I refuse to eat your flesh I will not be able to avoid death either. But how can I eat my own son's flesh? I feel as if my heart is pierced by a sword, but I must conceal my feelings, and not show any signs of mourning.'

Soon an envoy from the Shang palace arrived.

'The king shot deer on the hunt today. As you've been here for so long, Earl Chang, the king has ordered that these pies be made and brought to you.'

Chang, who had not yet got up from his knees after tossing the gold coins, opened the basket. 'His majesty is doubtless exhausted from his day's hunting, yet still he finds the energy to order that his convict minister should taste the fruits of his labour. How kind!'

He took the first pie and ate it, then the second. Licking his lips, he ate the third. He said to the envoy: 'I regret I cannot offer my gratitude in person to his majesty, would you be so kind as to pass on my warmest regards.'

The envoy looked down his nose at Earl Chang, realising he was not the prophet everyone supposed he was. He returned to the capital and reported the matter to King Zhou, conveying Chang's deepest good wishes.

'Ah! Chang is known for his virtue and the accuracy of his predictions,' said King Zhou, 'but today he has eaten his own son without even realising it. His reputation is clearly a sham.' He turned to his minister Fei Zhong and said: 'He's been imprisoned seven years now, I think I'll forgive him and let him go, what do you say?'

'Chang never makes mistakes in his divinations,' cautioned Fei Zhong, 'I'm sure he knew it was his son he was eating. He forced himself to eat those pies, knowing that if he didn't he would have lost his life. He expects you to be generous enough to set him free, but take care, don't be deceived by him.'

King Zhou could hardly believe it: 'Chang would never have eaten the pies had he known the truth. . .'

◆◆◆

In the *Feng Shen Yan Yi* Fei Zhong remonstrates with the king and persuades him to change his mind. Chang is finally released, however, after his second son, Fa, bribes Fei Zhong and another minister to speak out in favour of letting him go, which is an elaboration on the ransom account of Sima Qian. In the *Wu Wang Fa Zhou Binghua*, as soon as King Zhou hears that Chang has eaten his own son he immediately orders that he be released, confident that he will pose no threat. The ransom does not form a part of the story. In Chapter 22 of the *Feng Shen Yan Yi* King Wen vomits three times the flesh of Yi Kao. On each occasion the lump of half-digested meat sprouts four legs and two long ears, turning into a rabbit that scurries away. This is a somewhat mysterious idea, until one realises that *tuzi*, 'vomit son', and *tuzi*, 'rabbit', are homophones in Chinese.

Liu Ts'un-yan extensively researched the Daoist and Buddhist influences on the *Feng Shen Yan Yi*, and determined its likely author. He also translated the *Wu Wang Fa Zhou Binghua*. Both his research and the translation were published in a single volume in 1962. The *Feng Shen Yan Yi* itself was translated in 1992 by Gu Zhizhong. See the bibliography for publication details of both works.

Chapter XII

The curse of the ancestors

Hexagram 18, Gu, contains some of the most archaic remnants of oracle-bone divination in the whole of the *Zhouyi*, as we shall see shortly. In later times, however, the character *gu* that forms the title of this hexagram became associated with a virulent black magic that was carried out by placing in a covered bowl the 'five poisonous animals', the snake, scorpion, centipede, gecko, and toad.[1] They were left there until one, which became the *gu*, had killed or eaten all the others. The toxin extracted from this sole survivor was then administered to the human victim, who became ill and died. This is not a straightforward case of poisoning, it took place in a supernatural context; the *gu* was a spirit capable of securing the victim's possessions and wealth for the perpetrator of the heinous deed. This practice is well-documented in bizarre tales from the Tang dynasty and later, which were extensively studied by Feng and Shryock in 1935 and so will not be repeated here.[2] Besides which, this is not what I want to emphasise in this essay. The earliest clear account of *gu* magic involving the five poisonous animals appears about AD600, but it is uncertain whether the practice existed in this form in the Shang and early Zhou dynasties. Though the character *gu* is a pictograph showing three insects, worms, or snakes in a bowl, with the original Shang oracle-bone graph being similar, showing two worms or snakes in a vessel, it cannot be ruled out that *gu* magic as practised in the Tang could have been inspired by the character itself. What is not in doubt, however, is that the character *gu* has always been associated with injurious magic.

The slant I wish to take in these notes is the notion of *gu* as an *ancestral* curse. Discussing hexagram 18, Arthur Waley pointed out that the character *gan*, occurring in lines 1, 2, 3, and 5, is merely a fuller form of the generic term for the ten 'celestial stems'. The ancestors were named after stem-name days, such as Father Ding, Brother Bing, Mother Yi. *Ding*, *bing*, and *yi* are the fourth, third, and second 'stems', respectively, which are used to name the corresponding days of the ancient ten-day week. In three lines *gan*, 'stem', appears as 'stem-father's *gu*', while in the second line it is 'stem-mother's *gu*'. Waley translated these phrases as 'stem-father's maggots' and 'stem-mother's maggots', regarding it as 'surely obvious that the maggots referred to are those which appeared in the flesh of animals sacrificed to the spirits of dead parents'.[3] Waley's concentration on maggots got away from the point, but his identification of the terms stem-father and stem-mother is an insight that allows the true sense to emerge. Clearly then we need to understand what is meant by *gu*. I propose that it is best translated as 'curse' in hexagram 18.

The most archaic graph of *gu* shows two snakes or worms in a high-sided vessel:[4]

This appears to be a drinking vessel, implying (to me) poisoning by snake venom. That the original graph:

is a snake and not a worm is suggested by the fact that the oracle-bone graph of *long*, 'dragon', shows a snake with horns:[5]

It is clear from the Shang oracle-bone inscriptions that *gu* is a curse of the ancestors. The oracle-bone character of *gu* is used to refer to the evil power of the ancestors to cause illness in the living. Another common oracle-bone character used to refer to ancestral cursing depicts a snake striking out at the foot of a person about to step on it.[6]

Particular ancestors were believed by the Shang to be responsible for causing certain sicknesses (and also for providing meaningful dreams). Divinations were performed to discover precisely which ancestor was involved so that a sacrifice could be offered to propitiate his or her spirit, persuading the ancestor to lift the curse, which had been placed only because the sacrifice had been forgotten. For example, one oracle-bone tests the proposition: 'The king's bellyache, it is Grandmother Ji who is cursing.'[7] *Ji* is the sixth day of the ancient ten-day week, the sixth of the ten 'celestial stems'. Grandmother Ji is thus a particular named 'stem-grandmother'.

David Keightley pointed out that the power of an ancestor was directly proportional to the length of time he or she had been dead, and furthermore:

> It should also be stressed that the increased power of the senior generations was exercised in increasingly impersonal ways; that is, recently dead ancestors might plague living individuals (who would perhaps have known them when they were alive), but the dead of more distant generations affected the state as a whole by influencing harvests, droughts, and enemy invasions.[8]

I have already adduced, in Chapter III, the connection between the Shang idea that an ancestral curse could adversely affect the state, and the Zhou concept of the transfer of the Mandate of

Heaven. The last Shang king Zhou Xin, in particular, was said to have greatly angered the ancestors by disregarding their sacrifices. It seems, then, that ancestral *gu* must have played a part in the downfall of the Shang. King Wu himself is reported as saying that the reason the Zhou were able to bring about the Conquest was because Heaven had not received sacrifices from the Yin for 60 years, traditionally regarded as the length of Zhou Xin's reign.[9]

Bearing in mind that the *Zhouyi* appears to have been subjected to editing to remove specifics, we should not be surprised to see in three lines the generic term 'stem-father' as opposed to, say, Father Ding, Father Jia, and Father Geng (the names of the fourth, first, and seventh days, respectively). 'Stem-father' is, in fact, an obvious generalisation, telling us that the actual ancestors involved in the original tortoise divinations from which the general idea was abstracted are not particularly important in this instance. Rather, it is the practice itself, that of divining to discover which particular ancestor is cursing the king or state, that is the subject of hexagram 18. This knowledge appears to have been lost early on in the Zhou dynasty, it being solely a Shang custom to classify dead relatives according to stem-days. This implies that hexagram 18 contains remnants of *Shang* tortoise divinations. In other words, oracle-bones captured in the Shang capital and brought back to the Zhou homeland after the Conquest might have inspired hexagram 18. Not only this, there is another factor to take into consideration: archaeological excavations suggest that Shang oracle-bones were buried as a ritual act in refuse pits soon after they were cracked and inscribed, and were not intended to be stored for any length of time on the surface as a working temple archive, or as a record preserved for posterity.[10] Thus, one can speculate that the divinations to discover which ancestor was responsible for a *gu* curse that appear in hexagram 18 had been freshly made just before the Conquest by the tyrant Zhou Xin in a last desperate attempt to avert the calamity. Such a conjecture would explain why these distinctively Shang fragments should have been included in the *Zhouyi*.

There is powerful circumstantial evidence that this theory may actually be correct. This style of divination—*i.e.* divining to discover the identity of a cursing ancestor—was no longer used after the reign of Wu Ding (1324–1266BC, according to the traditional chronology).[11] A fixed ritual schedule came into being to cater for the sacrificial needs of the ancestors, who were sacrificed to in a regular order on their stem-name day, and there were no longer any attempts to discover the chain of cause and effect between a specific ancestor and a particular calamity. Towards the end of the Shang dynasty it had become a routine practice simply to divine the generalised charge: 'In the next ten days there will be no calamity.' As we saw in Chapter VI, an almost identical formula is used in the first line of hexagram 55 (another dating criterion, incidentally). Hexagram 18, on the other hand, contains fragments of tortoise divination in a style discontinued two centuries before the Conquest. If the Shang buried their oracle-bones soon after they were cracked and inscribed, how can we account for such archaic inscriptions being in the possession of the Zhou at the beginning of the new dynasty? Perhaps Zhou Xin, who had wantonly disregarded his duty to provide the routine sacrifices to the ancestors, had to fall back upon the old method. Hexagram 18 might contain fragments of the last divinations of Zhou Xin to discover which ancestors were bringing the dynasty to an end by means of a *gu* curse, just before the tortoise oracle abandoned him—'the deceitful boy'[12]—and the Mandate of Heaven was transferred to the Zhou. We thus have a Shang perspective on these events preserved in the *Zhouyi*. This I believe is what was originally intended, but, as with many other parts of the *Changes*, this knowledge slipped from view and was supplanted by other interpretations.

The earliest extant explanation of *gu* after hexagram 18 comes from a discussion in the *Zuozhuan* between a feudal marquis and a physician, said to have taken place in 541BC. The doctor describes the 'disease' his patient is suffering from, saying it 'resembles' *gu*, in terms more applicable to syphilis, and appears to negate the aspect of cursing:

The disease cannot be cured. It is said that when women are approached [too frequently] the result is a disease resembling [*gu*]. It is not caused by a spirit, nor by food (the methods of magic); it is a delusion which has destroyed the mind.[13]

When the minister of the marquis asked what was meant by *gu*, the doctor replied:

That which is produced when one sinks into delusion through debauch. In terms of the graph, a vessel (*min*) and insects (*chong*) make up *gu*. The flying away of grain is also *gu* [*i.e.*, the insects that appear as if spontaneously generated in rotting grain]. In the *Zhouyi* a woman deluding a man and the wind blowing down a mountain are called *gu*. These are all the same thing.[14]

The *Shuowen*, a Han dictionary, adds that *gu* is 'worms in the belly' (intestinal parasites) or 'the spectres of those who have been executed and had their heads publicly exposed spitted on the point of a stake' (which was the fate of Zhou Xin). It expands slightly on the *Zuozhuan* definition of 'a man's bewilderment caused by a woman' by saying that this 'is generated by nocturnal sensuality'.

In the Han and late Zhou dynasties 'stem-father's *gu*' was not read in this way. The character *gan*, 'stem', was understood to mean 'carry out, perform'. Wilhelm-Baynes translates *gan* as 'setting right'. The phrase 'stem-father's *gu*' is translated: 'Setting right what has been spoiled by the father.' *Gu* becomes 'what has been spoiled'.

The real clue to how hexagram 18 might have originated came when I noticed the close correlation in structure with the oracle-bone sequence known as *Bingbian* 11–20, which shows how King Wu Ding made a series of divinations in an attempt to discover who among the ancestors had placed a curse on him.

The king has toothache on the eve of his departure on a military campaign. In the oracle-bone inscriptions toothache is represented by the worm or snake graph depicted between the teeth, showing that it was caused by a curse.[15] Wu Ding presumably wishes to trace the origin of the curse not only to relieve himself of toothache but also to ensure his military venture is not adversely affected by a sacrificial oversight, of which the toothache is a sign. Four 'stem-fathers' are to be tested to assess their culpability. Following Shang practice each of the four ancestors will be divined about five times. Five prepared tortoise shells lie ready and waiting. Thrusting a brand of flaming thorn into a hollow on the right-hand side of the first shell, the diviner calls aloud: 'The sick tooth is not due to Father Jia!' The red-hot tip of the brand is fanned to keep it bright. Eventually there is the sharp sound of a tiny splitting hairline crack in the shell. The tortoise has spoken. Now a red-hot brand is thrust into a hollow on the left-hand side of the shell for the paired alternative charge: 'It is due to Father Jia!' The shell cracks. This process is repeated on the other four shells and the results are examined.[16] The living sons of the dead fathers look on, in the knowledge that one or more of their ancestors will be blamed for the king's toothache. For Father Jia there has been no sign. Two more cracks are made for Father Jia in each of the five shells, but again there is no indication this ancestor is responsible for the curse. The 'tortoise's ten pairs' has cleared his name. The process continues for the second stem-father to be tested:

> 'The sick tooth is not due to Father Geng!'
> 'It is due to Father Geng!'

The divinatory pair is again repeated on the other four shells. Discussion ensues between the diviners and the king to assess the cracks. This time the signs are quite decisive with just the five pairs. Father Geng, the king's senior uncle, is deemed responsible for the curse. His sons are the king's elder cousins. But cracks are made for two further ancestors to see if Father Geng is solely responsible:

> 'It is not due to Father Xin!'
> 'It is due to Father Xin!'
>
> 'It is not due to Father Yi!'
> 'It is due to Father Yi!'

In both cases, there is no sign with the first five pairs of cracks, so the process is repeated, as for Father Jia. Both ancestors are found to be without blame. Thus, after 70 cracks have been made, Father Geng is held to be the only ancestor cursing. Following a further 20 cracks to decide whether or not to offer Father Geng a sacrifice, the king kills a dog and dismembers a sheep to propitiate him and remove the curse.[17]

Compare these lines of hexagram 18:

> Line 1: 'Stem-father's *gu*.'
> Line 2: 'Stem-mother's *gu*.'
> Line 3: 'Stem-father's *gu*.'
> Line 5: 'Stem-father's *gu*.'

Imagine if specific stem-names were substituted for these generalisations:

> 'Father Jia's *gu*.'
> 'Mother Yi's *gu*.'
> 'Father Geng's *gu*.'
> 'Father Xin's *gu*.'

Now imagine if they were presented in typical divinatory pairs:

> 'It is not Father Jia's *gu*!'
> 'It is Father Jia's *gu*!'

> 'It is not Mother Yi's *gu*!'
> 'It is Mother Yi's *gu*!'

> 'It is not Father Geng's *gu*!'
> 'It is Father Geng's *gu*!'

> 'It is not Father Xin's *gu*!'
> 'It is Father Xin's *gu*!'

Hexagram 18 appears to have been constructed from such original divinatory materials. I have already demonstrated in Chapter VII that the judgment of this hexagram is likely to be derived from a tortoise divination by King Wu to determine the most auspicious day to cross the Yellow River at the Fords of

Meng, on the way to the Wilds of Mu where the decisive battle of the Conquest took place. It might therefore have seemed apt to the redactor of these source materials to juxtapose a divination by King Wu that led him to victory with captured Shang divinations concerning an ancestral *gu* curse that brought the dynasty to an end.

Chapter XIII

Clouds follow
the dragon

The importance of returning to the concrete images of the *Book of Changes* is emphasised when it can be shown that the accepted symbolism of a hexagram has strayed from the original idea. Hexagram 1 is a case in point.

'Clouds follow the dragon, winds follow the tiger.' This expression commenting on the fifth line of hexagram 1 comes from the oldest section of the *Wenyan* treatise, the seventh of the Ten Wings, possibly dating from the fourth century BC.[1] 'Clouds follow the dragon' is one of a handful of phrases that survive in the *Yijing* that hint that the original meaning of hexagram 1 is to do with rain magic. Two other phrases appended to the first hexagram corroborate this interpretation. Part I of the *Tuanzhuan*, the First Wing, simply notes: 'The clouds gather and the rain pours down.'[2] Another section of the *Wenyan* comments: 'In accord with the time, when the six dragons are ridden through the sky the clouds gather, the rain pours down, and all under Heaven is at peace.'[3]

Wang Bi, whose commentary on the *Yijing* defined the work for 700 years after his death in AD249 at the age of 23, passes over these remarks about rain as if they meant nothing to him. To Wang Bi the dragon was solely a metaphor for a great man blessed by Heaven. Six centuries earlier, the anonymous 'Master' of the *Wenyan* treatise, from whom Wang Bi took his lead, had already understood the dragon of hexagram 1 to refer to a man who had the character of a dragon, but he shows by the two quotations given above that he also knew exactly what the specific character of a dragon actually was, beyond generalities such as 'virtuous'.

Wang Bi sets out his philosophical position clearly in his commentary on hexagram 1:

> The *Changes* consists of images, which are produced from concepts. One first has a concept, which one brings to light with a concrete image. Thus a dragon is used to express the idea of hexagram 1.[4]

In his essay on the *Changes*, the *Zhouyi lueli*, Wang Bi goes on to say: 'Only by forgetting the images can one grasp the concept.'[5]

The mistake Wang Bi made was to be so concerned with the abstract concept that he did not fully fathom the depths of the concrete image before pronouncing upon its meaning. Thus he grasped the concept expressed by hexagram 1 only nominally. Presumably he either wasn't familiar with the natural history of the Chinese dragon, or considered it too folkloric and 'low culture' to possibly contain within it a deeper meaning than he supposed. In fairness, he may simply have thought it was no longer relevant.[6] Wang Bi regarded the dragon as synonymous with heavenly virtue, but does not mention the reason: the dragon had since Shang times brought the life-giving spring rain for the crops, and so, similarly, the great man, and later the Emperor or 'Son of Heaven', was seen as dispensing blessings on the people from above. Wang Bi appears not to have believed in real dragons. The official history of the period contains several dragon sightings, but the literati were anxious to distance themselves from peasant superstitions and belief in magic in order to develop a higher philosophy.

Yet it is by investigating the manner in which the dragon is 'awakened' from winter hibernation, and persuaded by sympathetic magic to ascend to Heaven to attract the rain clouds, that it becomes clear the primary interpretation of hexagram 1 resides in just these details. It is not enough merely to exchange the dragon for the concept 'heavenly'; the literal image must be reinstated to bring out the ramifications.

Without the literal aspect, Wang Bi's symbolic counterpart was cut loose from its empirical anchorage and drifted, with the result that today hardly anyone grasps the true meaning of hexagram 1. There is an old Chinese saying: 'Off by a fraction in the beginning, far off the mark at the end.'

Hexagram 1 contains the earliest appearance of the dragon in Chinese literature, which is represented by the character *long*, a miraculous creature about which there is a rich folkloric record. The habitat of the *long* is typically a whirlpool in a mountain gorge, a prime spot for a 'dragon's lair' in later *fengshui*. The *long* spends the winter hibernating at the bottom of its pool, and is aroused by sympathetic magic in the spring. When the first thunder clouds of the year gather, peasants rush from their fields to the local dragon pool in the mountains to throw into the water all manner of items the *long* is supposed to loathe and detest, such as 'dirty objects', the shoe of an old woman, poisonous plants, a muddy sucking pig, and lumps of iron. Dragons are said to fear iron, either because it stings their eyes or because it has the power, in the popular imagination, to dissolve pearls. All dragons are known to jealously guard a hoard of pearls. The *long* is commonly depicted in Chinese paintings frolicking through the clouds chasing a pearl, a feat it performs without the aid of wings.[7] The muddy sucking pig is intended not only as a sacrifice to the dragon but also to anger the thunder god, who has a pig's head and bat's wings. It is typically Chinese to arouse the gods to action by infuriating them.

When the dragon rises from the depths of its pool and ascends to the heavens with the first lightning it is immediately enshrouded in rain clouds, because 'clouds follow the dragon'.[8] As clouds descend low in the mountains it is perhaps easy to enter into the spirit of the occasion, particularly as the dragon is said to possess the power of making itself invisible when it leaves the water to make its ascent. Those intoxicated by wine may swear they saw a claw, or the tip of the tail, entering a cloud. That the rite is not performed until rain looks certain is the essence of sympathetic magic, in that the participant is simply helping along the forces of nature, not commanding them. Agricultural concerns lie at the heart of many early magical rites. If the rain did not come at the right time then the crops would fail. The late Tang poet Bai Juyi (AD772–846) wrote a satire on these practices entitled 'The Dragon of the Black Pool', illustrating not only that such peasant superstitions were ridiculed by the literati of his time, but also, and perhaps more importantly, that this dragon rite was still actively practised then.

Bai Juyi describes a deep pool, its waters looking like black ink. People believe a sacred dragon lives at the bottom of the pool, though no-one has ever seen it. Next to the pool a shrine has been built, and an established ritual for raising the dragon has been passed down. Bai Juyi comments that 'a dragon will always be a dragon, but men can make it a god'. The people of the village regard prosperity and disaster, rain and drought, plague and pestilence as all the sacred dragon's doing. And so they make offerings of sucking pig and pour wine libations, depending on a shaman's advice. When the dragon comes all that happens, according to Bai Juyi, is that the wind whips up a little, and the villagers throw their paper money sacrifices into the air and wave their silk parasols. When the dragon goes, the wind dies down, the air is still. Eventually the incense burns itself out and the cups and vessels grow cold. The people depart leaving meats stacked high on the rocks around the pool. Wine flows into the grass in front of the shrine. Bai Juyi says: 'I have no idea how much of these offerings the dragon eats, but I do know that the mice of the woods and the foxes from the hills are always drunk and eat their fill. Why should the foxes be so lucky, what have the sucking pigs done that they should be killed year after year just to lay a banquet for the foxes? Does the sacred dragon know the foxes are stealing his sucking pig? Deep down in his inky pool, does he know—or not?'[9]

Even as late as the 1930s local farmers ascended Hua Shan ('Flower Mountain') in times of drought to perform similar rites at the Black Dragon Pool on the summit.[10] Sacrifices on Hua Shan date back to the time of the legendary Emperor Shun, according to the *Book of Documents*.

There are many places in China that to this day retain in their names evidence of these former practices. The plant-hunter E H Wilson wrote of his arrival 'with camera, vasculum, and gun' at 'Small Dragon Pool' in Western China in the early years of the twentieth century:

> The hamlet of [*Xiaolongtang*] (Small Dragon Pool), alt. 7400 feet, consists of two dilapidated wooden huts pitched on opposite sides of a lovely burn, which flows through a narrow sloping valley lying almost due east and west. This valley is flanked by steep ridges clad only with grass and shrub. Odd patches of birch and silver fir attest to forests which have all been destroyed by fire. From the numerous old graves and abandoned fields it is evident that formerly more people dwelt in this valley than do so today. Tiny patches of cabbage and Irish potato occur around the huts; and also plantations of ['Dong Quai'] (*Angelica polymorpha*, var. *sinensis*), a valued Chinese medicine.[11]

Wilson further describes the place as a dirty hovel housing pigs in no more luxurious accommodation than the owners, in places a foot deep in mud. Though he does not mention the use of dragon pools in sacrificial rites for rain he notes that the miserable surroundings of this place were less in evidence on his third visit, it being the only occasion on which he enjoyed fine weather: 'Twice previously I had been marooned here for days, and either stayed in bed or shivered by the doorway watching the rain.' This, incidentally, is a perfect illustration of what is meant by 'Waiting' in hexagram 5, Xu, the title of which is literally 'Stopped by the rain'. This is the original concrete image that later gave rise to the extended conceptual meaning of 'waiting' generally. The rain radical can be seen at the top of the character.[12]

Being more aware of the habits and habitat of the Chinese *long* dragon, we may now turn to hexagram 1 to find the correlation. In the first line the character translated as 'hidden' in Wilhelm-Baynes takes the water radical and specifically refers to things hidden under water, hence both Kunst and Lynn translated it not as a 'hidden dragon' but as a 'submerged dragon', while Whincup has 'the dragon remains underwater'. This line thus refers to winter, when the dragon is still hibernating at the bottom of its pool. The time is not yet ripe for its ascent to the heavens. In later times 'a dragon hidden in the depths' was an Emperor who had not yet ascended the throne.[13]

The 'dragon appearing in the field', in the second place, possibly refers to gathering storm clouds over the crop fields at the time of the spring rain rite. An alternative astronomical explanation also links this line with the spring. The star Spica, the bright star of the pair making up *Jiao*, the 'Horn' asterism in Virgo, starts rising above the horizon at dusk in the spring.[14] This star, sometimes simply called the 'dragon star' in that it signals the rising of the Azure Dragon, has been used as an agricultural marker since Babylonian times, its western name Spica meaning 'ear of wheat'. The character *tian*, 'field', has 'to sow grain' among its definitions in the first century AD dictionary, the *Shuowen*. Thus the second line of hexagram 1 could conceivably mean that when the dragon star appears it is time to sow the crops.[15]

The dragon is not mentioned in the third line. Nor is it in the fourth line, though it is implied. The translation in Wilhelm-Baynes gives the impression that the dragon is already out of the water and in shaky flight: 'Wavering flight over the depths.' The character *yuan*, 'depths', again takes the water radical and features in names of gorges. A more literal translation is: 'Something leaping up from the depths.' Notice that when this line changes hexagram 9 results, which mentions rain in the judgment: 'Dense clouds, no rain from our western region.'[16]

The dragon does not leave its pool until the fifth line: 'Flying dragon in the heavens.'[17] Some think that the 'flying dragon in the heavens' is the Azure Dragon constellation fully risen above the horizon and emblazoned on the night sky in the summer. This may well be an important secondary interpretation, but confirmation that hexagram 1 is primarily about rain magic comes from a little-known paper published in 1931 by Lionel Hopkins, who was a British diplomat in China and one of the first oracle-bone collectors. Oracle-bone inscriptions linking the dragon with rain are rare. Creel in 1937 said he could find no inscription linking any of the early forms of the character *long*, in excess of 40, with water or rain, though he added that there was every reason to suppose the dragon's association with rain magic went back even to the Shang period.[18] Florence Waterbury in 1942 selectively quoted Creel's research to lend weight to her theory that the dragon was originally associated with thunder and lightning, and not water.[19] Peter Glum in his 1982 article 'Rain Magic at Anyang?', in which he speculated that the function of two Shang bronze vessels filled with revolving dragons was to induce rain, could offer no oracle-bone inscription to show the Shang regarded the dragon as a rain-bringer, he had to rely on much later sources to fuel his conjectures. Indeed, at the time he was writing most scholars thought that dragon images on Shang ritual bronze vessels were purely decorative. Even today, it is hard to find this question being addressed.

Yet as early as 1931, in an almost completely overlooked paper, 'The Dragon Terrestrial and the Dragon Celestial', Lionel Hopkins pointed out that there are in existence a handful of inscribed carved miniatures of dragons among the Henan relics of the Shang, photographs of which he provides. Hopkins did not make any connection to the *Yijing*, but the inscriptions on these miniatures provide crucial fragments of knowledge that achieve a close fit with the text of hexagram 1. One in the British Museum records the taking of an omen by the tortoise oracle, the result of which was regarded as meaning: 'If the dragon comes then a rain sacrifice should be performed.' This correlates well with the second line, where the dragon 'appears'. A miniature in Hopkins' own collection remarks on 'the dragon in motion' in the sixth moon, omens being announced for which days rain was expected to fall.[20] Hopkins notes that the expression 'the dragon in motion' or 'the moving dragon', *xing long*, 'we may suppose more or less equivalent to the much commoner *fei* [*long*], the flying dragon'. *Fei long* is the term used in the fifth line of hexagram 1. The inscriptions establish that the provision of rain is the essential concern of hexagram 1, the title of which, *Qian*, beyond its circular dictionary definition of 'the title of hexagram 1, Heaven', in any other context means 'dry' as in the dry season and drought. The character appears to be a pictograph of the sun bearing down intensely and vapour rising from the ground.

The top line, usually translated as 'arrogant dragon', may also be translated as 'Dragon's Gullet', *kang long*. *Kang* is the name of a constellation, the second mansion of the Azure Dragon, rising after *Jiao*. In the autumn the 'Gullet' or 'Neck' constellation starts to disappear below the eastern horizon at nightfall. Similarly in folklore autumn is when the dragon descends back to its pool to hibernate for the winter again, rain no longer being necessary because the crops are being gathered in. As it says in the *Great Treatise*, II, V, 3: 'Dragons and snakes hibernate in order to preserve life.'

The astronomical interpretation is indeed persuasive; a number of commentators have written versions of it that give the impression it is in fact what hexagram 1 'means'.[21] In my opinion, particularly with the evidence of Hopkins' inscribed miniatures, hexagram 1 is first and foremost a reliquary of ancient magical practices for arousing the dragon to provide rain.

Chapter XIV

No skin on his thighs

The historical detail we have found in the *Yi* required a close examination of the text before it became obvious. Previously, few historical allusions had been identified. Similarly, no reference to a mythological theme in the *Changes* has ever been conclusively proved. I have, however, discovered one mythological allusion for which the evidence is solid and convincing.[1]

Regarding the fourth line of hexagram 43 Richard Wilhelm explains, following commentaries traditional since the Song dynasty, that 'There is no skin on his thighs, and walking comes hard' means that 'a man is suffering from inner restlessness and cannot abide in his place', and thus the line refers to obstinacy in enforcing the will. Wang Bi in the third century AD explained that the phrase meant 'He loses the means to keep himself secure'.[2] In the third line of hexagram 44, which in the Chinese repeats the phrase from 43/4, Wang Bi further notes that it 'represents someone who is out of step with the moment and so is subject to danger'.[3] Wilhelm says it 'leads to painful indecision in behaviour'. Yet none of this wise exegesis provides a satisfactory answer to the simplest of questions, the question a child might ask: why doesn't he have any skin on his thighs?

I wondered about this for many years before coming across a single illuminating sentence in Wolfram Eberhard's *The Local Cultures of South and East China*. Eberhard says, in passing, making no reference at all to the *Yi*: 'Because of his many labors, Yu had torn the skin on his thighs.'[4] Suddenly I realised there was far more to the expression than met the eye, that it probably alluded to the flood hero Yu the Great, the demi-god who founded the Xia dynasty, the dynasty before the Shang, which is regarded by many as mythical in the absence of archaeological evidence to prove its existence. Yu reigned 2205–2197BC, according to the traditional chronology. Allusions to Yu's great task appear in literature contemporaneous with the *Zhouyi*, featuring in four odes in the *Shijing*, 210, 244, 261, and 304; Yu's flood work is also found in the early chapters of the *Shujing*, and by 541BC it had become the subject of a joke in the *Zuozhuan*, when a noble quips: 'Were it not for Yu, we would just be fishes!' In later literature there are numerous references to Yu and the flood.[5]

Strictly speaking, Yu did not actually *tear* the skin on his thighs; he appears to have suffered from a wasting disease contracted by wading through water for many years as he laboured to form channels to clear the flood that had ravaged China. Marcel Granet, followed by Edward Schafer, diagnosed the condition as hemiplegia.[6]

Mencius mentions that in the time of the Emperor Yao the flood still raged unchecked and in an effort to drain the land by cutting canals 'Yu spent eight years abroad and passed the door of his own house three times without entering'.[7] In later sources the story is developed further, so that Yu passes his door three times without entering even though he can hear his son crying inside, indicating his self-sacrifice in serving the Empire rather than his own kin. The third century BC *Spring and Autumn Annals of Master Lu* states that as a result of the arduousness of Yu's great task: 'His bodily orifices and his vital organs did not function properly, his steps were faltering.'[8] Chapter 49 of the *Han Feizi* says that Yu worked until there was no more hair left on his thighs and shins; Chapter 50 adds that in spite of Yu working to benefit the people they gathered tiles and stones to throw at him.[9]

A recurring image in ancient Chinese mythological literature is the cutting off of the hair and the fingernails as a mimesis of animal sacrifice, which is undoubtedly what Han Feizi is echoing by saying Yu wore away the hair on his thighs. The *Shizi* echoes it even more strongly by saying that no nails grew on Yu's hands and no hair grew on his shanks. In this regard, Mencius reports the famous doctrine of Yang Zhu: 'The principle of Master Yang is "Each one for himself". Though he might have benefited the whole world by plucking out a single hair, he would not have done it.'[10] In the fourth century AD 'Yang Zhu' chapter of the *Liezi*, the example of Yu the Great suffering paralysis to one side of his body to benefit the Empire is brought into the discussion to counterpoint Yang Zhu's opposition to the principle. Here it is explained that though a hair is insignificant compared with the skin, nonetheless the accumulation of single hairs forms the skin.[11] From this we can deduce that no hair on the thighs is the equivalent of no skin on the thighs.

The most informative account, describing the specific nature of Yu's difficulty in walking, is contained in the *Shizi*:

> For ten years he did not see his home, on his hands there grew no nails, on his shanks there grew no hair, he contracted a sickness which made him shrivel in half the body, so that in walking he could not carry the one leg past the other, people called this 'the walk of Yu'.[12]

If Yu could not lift one leg past the other then this must have necessitated bringing up one foot to meet the other before taking the next step. The phrase in the *Zhouyi* translated in Wilhelm-Baynes as 'walking comes hard' is literally 'he walks haltingly' or 'walking by halting-places'.

In Chapter 8 of *Chinese Mythology* Anne Birrell collects together many of the myths of Yu the Great. I wrote to Professor Birrell at Cambridge University asking if she agreed with my characterisation of this passage, to which she replied: 'On the face of it, it would appear to allude to the "Walk of Yu" myth (*cf.* Granet, 'Pas de Yu', *Danses*, 549, 610, 611). *Caveat* dating chronology.'[13] The *Shizi* dates from the fourth century BC, the *Han Feizi* a century later, and Eberhard has shown that the dance performed by female shamans on one leg known as the 'Dance of Yu', which has survived to the present day in South China, is likely to have an extremely ancient origin.[14]

The reference in the *Zhouyi* appears to be the earliest literary allusion to the 'Walk of Yu' myth. The 'footsteps of Yu' is also mentioned in passing, without detail, in the *Li Zheng* chapter of the *Book of Documents*.[15]

The name of Yu the Great has been associated with the *Yijing* before, in that it was he who was said to have received the *Luoshu*, the 'Luo Writing', which was supposed to have been borne out of the Luo River on the back of a tortoise/turtle while Yu was draining off the great flood. Yu apparently used the *Luoshu* to create the *Hong Fan*, the 'Great Plan' chapter of the *Documents*. The existence of the *Luoshu* is well attested to in late Zhou literature, though its original form is unknown. It may have been an inscribed tortoise plastron or carapace, *i.e.* an oracle-bone, washed up from the Luo. But in the Song dynasty, when the *Luoshu* as it is known today was attached to the *Yijing* by Chen Tuan (ca AD906–989),[16] the 'writing' became a diagram or 'map' of nine groups of 45 black and white dots that form a magic square of three.[17]

Some sources also link Yu the Great with the similar *Hetu*, or 'He River Map' of 55 black and white dots in ten groups, which was also first attached to the *Yi* by Chen Tuan, its original form again unknown.[18] The most repeated version of the story is that the *Hetu* was seen on the back of a 'dragon-horse' that emerged from the Yellow River, the He.[19] In Han dynasty lore the *Hetu* was received by Fuxi, who used it to invent the eight trigrams. But the late Zhou *Shizi* states that the *Hetu* was given to Yu the Great by a tall white-faced man with a fish body who came out of the He.[20] The fourth century AD *Shi Yi Ji, Researches into Lost Records,* says that a god with a human face and a serpent's body showed Yu a chart of the eight trigrams spread out on top of a bench of gold, adding that this god was Fuxi.[21] Both the *Luoshu* and the *Hetu* are mentioned by name in the third century BC *Dazhuan*, the *Great Treatise* of the *Yijing*.[22] Confucius sighs that 'the He does not bring forth any chart', meaning that there has been no auspicious omen for his teaching in his day and age.[23] The earliest mention of the *Hetu* is in a chapter of the *Book of Documents* called *Gu Ming*, 'The Deathbed Commands', where the chart is displayed as an ancient relic on the eastern wall during the funeral rites for King Cheng.

The contemporary Chinese commentator Gao Heng has suggested that the judgment of hexagram 8—translated in Wilhelm-Baynes as 'Whoever comes too late meets with misfortune'—may allude to the myth of Yu the Great holding an assembly of the gods on a mountain, which is mentioned in the fifth century BC *Guoyu*, the *Discourses of the States*. The title of hexagram 8, Bi, means 'assembly'. Fangfeng arrived too late, so Yu killed him and beheaded his corpse. The top line of the hexagram—translated in Wilhelm-Baynes as 'He finds no head for holding together. Misfortune'—could refer to a beheading. Gao understands it as: 'Giving counsel to the king and losing one's head for it.'[24] This legend became the precedent for feudal chiefs to execute laggards, as when the Duke of Song in 641BC offered up as a sacrifice the Viscount of Zeng, who had arrived late for a meeting.

Returning to Yu having no skin on his thighs as a result of his labours in draining the flood, one final piece of evidence suggests that 'the walk of Yu' is indeed alluded to in lines 43/4 and 44/3. According to the third century BC *Tuanzhuan*, the title of hexagram 43, Guai, meaning 'to fork', should be read with the water radical, making it Jue, which refers both to the bursting of dikes and to clearing a flood by opening up waterways.[25]

Section III

Appendices

附
录

Appendix I

The sinological maze of Wilhelm-Baynes

Joseph Needham was harshly critical of the organisation of the Wilhelm-Baynes translation of the *Yijing*, saying that it constituted a 'sinological maze' and belonged to 'the Department of Utter Confusion'.[1] In Wilhelm's translation the Ten Wings, circa third century BC, were dismembered and distributed throughout the work under numerous headings alongside the original eleventh century BC *Zhouyi*, with a commentary from undifferentiated sources. Wilhelm's arrangement of the translation into three books, with much repetition in Book III, continues to confuse many readers. Richard Wilhelm's explanation of the structure of his translation is incomplete and has been misunderstood by even experienced users of the *Changes*. Hellmut Wilhelm cleared away a little of the confusion in his 'Preface to the Third Edition', but it was still not fully explained.

I have already differentiated the *Zhouyi* in Chapter I, and pointed out that the slightly smaller unindented text attached to it is a collation of primarily Song commentaries made by Wilhelm. As a rule, the unindented smaller text throughout all three books of the Wilhelm-Baynes translation is Wilhelm's own encapsulation of commentaries. The origin of the remaining larger indented text is outlined below, with headings used in Wilhelm-Baynes rendered in small capitals.

The text of the First and Second Wings, Parts 1 and 2 of the *Tuanzhuan*, respectively, becomes the COMMENTARY ON THE

DECISION in Book III. The *Tuanzhuan* comments briefly on all 64 hexagrams: Part 1 deals with hexagrams 1 to 30; Part 2 with hexagrams 31 to 64. The text has been sub-divided accordingly between the hexagrams.

The text of the Third and Fourth Wings is collectively known as the *Xiangzhuan*, the *Commentary on the Images*, and has a rather complex distribution. It actually consists of two completely different texts, the *Great Images* and the *Small Images*, having nothing to do with each other. Gerald Swanson has stated, incorrectly, that the *Great Images* constitutes the Third Wing and the *Small Images* the Fourth Wing,[2] but in actual fact both texts have been split so that the Third Wing applies only to hexagrams 1–30, and the Fourth Wing to hexagrams 31–64, after the fashion of the first two Wings. The Third Wing thus contains both the *Great Images*, Part 1, and the *Small Images*, Part 1. Wilhelm then divides these sections as follows: *Great Images*, Part 1, becomes THE IMAGE for hexagrams 1–30; *Small Images*, Part 1, becomes line text (b) for hexagrams 1–30 in Book III. Similarly for the Fourth Wing: *Great Images*, Part 2, becomes THE IMAGE for hexagrams 31–64; *Small Images*, Part 2, becomes line text (b) in Book III for hexagrams 31–64. The *Great Images* commentary expands on the general theme of the hexagram and discusses the constituent trigrams, whereas the *Small Images* forms a long poem of 386 lines when its two parts are restored to its original whole.[3] Note that line text (a) in Book III is the original *Zhouyi* repeated from Book I. It is this that line text (b) is commenting upon. Ritsema and Karcher have incorrectly stated that line text (a) in Wilhelm-Baynes derives from the First and Second Wings, the *Tuanzhuan*.[4]

The Fifth and Sixth Wings make up the first and second parts, respectively, of the *Dazhuan* or GREAT TREATISE. This consists of the larger indented text under that title in Book II. The *Dazhuan* is also known as the *Xicizhuan*, the *Commentary on the Appended Judgments*.[5] Part of the text that comments on a selection of hexagrams has been repeated in Book III; it has been split up and apportioned to 19 hexagrams under the title APPENDED JUDGMENTS. This text is found in the following hexagrams: 10; 15; 16; 17; 21; 24; 28; 30; 32; 34; 38; 41; 42; 43; 47; 48; 57; 59; 62. Many of these citations come from the 'History of Civilization' chapter of the *Dazhuan* (Part II, Chapter II). Others come from 'The Relation of Certain Hexagrams to Character Formation' (Part II, Chapter VII). The chapters of the original *Dazhuan* do not have titles, those appearing in Book II were invented by Wilhelm.

Wilhelm repeats a further 18 sections of the *Dazhuan*, pertaining to the line statements, in his own commentary in both Books I and III, preceded by the formula 'Confucius says of this line'. These extracts, with one exception, come from the chapters entitled 'On the Use of the Appended Judgments' (Part I, Chapter VIII), and 'Explanation of Certain Lines' (Part II, Chapter V). They appear in the following lines in Book I: 12/5; 13/5; 14/6;[6] 16/2; 21/1; 21/6;[7] 40/3; 40/6; 42/6; 47/3; 50/4; 60/1; 61/2.[8] And in Book III: 15/3;[9] 24/1;[10] 28/1; 31/4; 41/3. In the *Dazhuan* itself Confucius is not named, the words are actually attributed to an anonymous 'Master'. Few scholars today believe these statements were made by Confucius; it was Sima Qian who first attributed the *Dazhuan* to Confucius, 389 years after his death.[11] The *Dazhuan* contains one of the earliest technical definitions of *yin* and *yang*: 'One *yin* and one *yang*: that is Dao.' (Part I, Chapter V.)

The Seventh Wing, the *Wenyan*, applies only to the first two hexagrams; it appears in Book III as COMMENTARY ON THE WORDS OF THE TEXT, which is further sub-divided under the headings ON THE HEXAGRAM AS A WHOLE and ON THE LINES for hexagrams 1 and 2. The contents of the *Wenyan* applying to hexagram 1 come from four sources, a fact that Wilhelm attempts to communicate through the use of letters a, b, c, and d. But unless one is already aware of what he is talking about one is none the wiser after reading his explanation. Richard Rutt elucidates the structure of the *Wenyan* with great clarity, so this need not be repeated here.[12] The oldest section of the *Wenyan* may be fourth century BC. The *Wenyan* commentary on hexagram 2/6 contains a further early explanation of *yin* and *yang* (translated as the dark and the light principle in Wilhelm-Baynes).

The Eighth Wing appears in Book II. This is the *Shuogua*, the DISCUSSION OF THE TRIGRAMS. The essay 'The Structure of the Hexagrams', which also appears in Book II, was written by Wilhelm.

Finally, the Ninth Wing, the *Xugua*, is split up and allocated to each hexagram as THE SEQUENCE in Book III, while the Tenth Wing, the *Zagua*, is similarly sub-divided under the heading MISCELLANEOUS NOTES, again in Book III. The *Xugua* may not be as old as the other Wings; it has been suggested that it dates from the Later Han.[13]

Richard Rutt has translated the Ten Wings in their original undivided form.[14] If Rutt's translation is compared with the corresponding sections of Wilhelm-Baynes, each extract located according to the arrangement described above, Wilhelm's complicated structure becomes a lot clearer.

Wilhelm's division of the *Yijing* into three books can be summarised as follows:

- Book I, which Wilhelm called THE TEXT, is essentially the *Zhouyi* (THE JUDGMENTS and THE LINES), with the addition of THE IMAGE, which belongs to the Wings. Wilhelm also provides an abridgment in smaller type of Neo-Confucianist Song dynasty commentaries.
- Book II, THE MATERIAL, consists of philosophical material from the Ten Wings that is explanatory of the underlying principles of the system of the *Yijing* as a whole, annotated in smaller type by Wilhelm.
- Book III, THE COMMENTARIES, repeats the translation of the *Zhouyi* and THE IMAGE from Book I. The remaining Wings are distributed throughout the 64 hexagrams. Again, Wilhelm provides a commentary in smaller type based on Song dynasty ideas.

Appendix II

Genealogical matters

The ten sons of King Wen

King Wen, by most accounts, had ten sons. As already stated in Chapter VI, Kangshu was the ninth son and King Wu the second, *shu* meaning 'younger of brothers'. The eldest son, Yi Kao, is supposed to have predeceased King Wen. In one tradition Zhou Xin is said to have fed King Wen meat pies made of this first son when he was imprisoned at Youli, and because he ate them he remained unharmed by the tyrant, as mentioned in Chapter XI. Book II of the *Li Ji*, the *Record of Rites*, however, states Yi Kao was passed over as heir to the throne in favour of King Wu.[1] Chapter 13 of the *Huainanzi* says the same, finding it a constitutional irregularity.[2]

The third son of King Wen was Xian, known as Guanshu, who conspired against the new dynasty after the Conquest with two younger brothers, Du, known as Caishu, and Chu, known as Huoshu. *Shi Ji* 35 says Caishu was the fifth son and Huoshu the eighth son.[3] The rebellion was led by Wu Geng, Zhou Xin's son, also known as Lu Fu. Most authorities name only Guanshu and Caishu as the disloyal sons of King Wen who joined forces with Wu Geng. But in 'The Charge to Zhong of Cai', a chapter of the *Documents* the authenticity of which has been contested, the Duke of Zhou, the fourth son, is said to have put to death Guanshu for his treason, confined the movements of Caishu, and reduced Huoshu to the rank of private citizen.[4] The *Shi Ji*, however, says that King Cheng, King Wu's son, ordered the Duke of Zhou to put to death both Guanshu and Caishu, Huoshu not being mentioned.[5] *Mencius* 2B/9 says that the Duke of Zhou was the younger brother of Guanshu.

As for the other three sons, details are sparse, but their names are recorded in *Shi Ji* 35. The sixth was Caoshu Zhenduo; the seventh Chengshu Wu; the tenth Danji Zai.[6] Shi, the Duke of Shao, is thought to have been a secondary son of King Wen by a concubine.[7] This suggests that Gao, the Duke of Bi, the third of the 'three dukes', may also have been a secondary son, though I have been unable to find a reference to substantiate this idea. Bi is the place where King Wen was buried.

In the Ming dynasty novel *Feng Shen Yan Yi*, the *Investiture of the Gods*, King Wen has a hundred sons. And a reference in the *Zuozhuan* is at odds with the generally accepted ten sons: 'Formerly, when Wu Wang subdued the Shang, he broadly possessed the empire. Fifteen of his brothers received states. . .'[8] In summary, the ten sons of King Wen were:

1. Yi Kao
2. Fa, King Wu
3. Guanshu Xian
4. Dan, Duke of Zhou
5. Caishu Du
6. Caoshu Zhenduo
7. Chengshu Wu
8. Huoshu Chu
9. Kangshu Feng
10. Danji Zai

King Wen's wife and mother

The fourth stanza of ode 236 says that Heaven made a mate for King Wen, and that she lived on the banks of the Wei River. The fifth stanza says King Wen fixed a lucky day and went in person to meet his bride. She lived on the other side of the Wei, so King Wen made a bridge by tying rafts together. This woman is generally assumed to be Taisi, who is named in ode 240 as bearing a multitude of sons. Yet ode 236 also appears to be saying, in the sixth stanza, that Heaven then commanded King Wen to give the succession to a girl from Shen, and that 'she staunchly bore King Wu'. The stanza concludes: 'Heaven's protection and help are allotted to you to march and attack the great Shang.'

Most commentators assume that Taisi and the girl from Shen are one and the same person, but they interpret the reference to succession unconvincingly, saying King Wen's wife 'succeeded' to the position of honour formerly held by his mother. It seems to me that King Wu, the second son of King Wen, had a different mother to the other nine brothers; that the girl from Shen was made King Wen's primary wife *by the Mandate of Heaven* to ensure that King Wu would accede to the throne and complete the Conquest. This reading of the ode in turn provides an explanation why Yi Kao, the eldest son, was passed over, as stated in the *Li Ji* and the *Huainanzi*, strongly corroborating the interpretation.

In the past few decades there has been a growing consensus that hexagrams 11/5 and 54/5 refer to King Wen's wife: 'Di Yi gave his younger sister in marriage.' Di Yi was the penultimate Shang king, the father of the tyrant Zhou Xin and the noble Weizi, who also had different mothers.[9] Gu Jiegang (1893–1980), in his study of five historical vignettes in the *Zhouyi*, suggested these two lines refer to King Wen's wife, an opinion he advanced in 1929. Gu's entire reconstruction of the marriage he himself characterised as a 'guess'.[10] Several commentators have since repeated his interpretation, and some have accorded it the status of a fully-fledged fact.[11] Gu felt that King Wen's bride in ode 236 was Shang solely because it is said she came from 'a great state'. Yet, more specifically, the ode actually says she lived on the banks of the Wei, which means it is unlikely she was Shang. The demarcation line between Zhou and Shang territory was at the confluence of the Wei and Yellow Rivers, with the Wei in Zhou territory (see map 1 on page 82). And the same may be said about the girl from Shen; Shen was not in Shang territory.

Far more plausible is the supposition that Di Yi gave his younger sister to King Ji, King Wen's father, as Hellmut

Wilhelm believed.[12] Odes 236 and 240 name King Wen's mother as Tairen. Ode 236 specifically states that Tairen came from Shang to marry King Ji in the Zhou capital; she 'became big with child' and bore King Wen. Pre-dynastic Zhou oracle-bones discovered at Mount Qi in 1977 show King Wen sacrificed to Shang ancestors as well as his own, including Di Yi, which suggests that Di Yi belonged to the previous generation.

Perhaps the reason some commentators follow Gu Jiegang's interpretation is because it gives them licence to explain the difficulties of hexagram 54 by concocting a scenario in which it is supposed that Di Yi's younger sister was barren and bore no son for King Wen, whereupon the secondary wife who accompanied her from Shang, who had 'finer sleeves', is then elevated to the rank of primary wife and gives birth to King Wu.[13] Even on its own terms this interpretation has not been thought through. If Di Yi's younger sister produced no son for King Wen, how is this to be reconciled with the fact that King Wu was the *second* son and Yi Kao was passed over?

Appendix III

Chinese text of hexagram 55

Below is the received text of hexagram 55 from *A Concordance to Yi Ching* (Harvard-Yenching edition, 1935). Only the characters of the *Zhouyi* are shown, *i.e.* the judgment and the six lines.

豐

Judgment:

豐　　亨。王假之。勿憂。宜日中。

Line texts:

初九　遇其配主。雖旬无咎。往有尚。

六二　豐其蔀。日中見斗。往得疑疾。有孚發若。吉。

九三　豐其沛。日中見沫。折其右肱。无咎。

九四　豐其蔀。日中見斗。遇其夷主。吉。

六五　來章。有慶譽吉。

上六　豐其屋。蔀其家。闚其戶。闃其无人。三歲不覿。凶。

Appendix IV

The sexagenary cycle

1	2	3	4	5	6	7	8	9	10
jia- zi	yi- chou	bing- yin	ting- mao	wu- chen	ji- si	geng- wu	xin- wei	ren- shen	gui- you
11	12	13	14	15	16	17	18	19	20
jia- xu	yi- hai	bing- zi	ting- chou	wu- yin	ji- mao	geng- chen	xin- si	ren- wu	gui- wei
21	22	23	24	25	26	27	28	29	30
jia- shen	yi- you	bing- xu	ting- hai	wu- zi	ji- chou	geng- yin	xin- mao	ren- chen	gui- si
31	32	33	34	35	36	37	38	39	40
jia- wu	yi- wei	bing- shen	ting- you	wu- xu	ji- hai	geng- zi	xin- chou	ren- yin	gui- mao
41	42	43	44	45	46	47	48	49	50
jia- chen	yi- si	bing- wu	ting- wei	wu- shen	ji- you	geng- xu	xin- hai	ren- zi	gui- chou
51	52	53	54	55	56	57	58	59	60
jia- yin	yi- mao	bing- chen	ting- si	wu- wu	ji- wei	geng- shen	xin- you	ren- xu	gui- hai

The 'Ten Heavenly Stems', also used to name the days of the ancient ten-day week, appear first, *jia, yi, bing* . . . forming the ten columns. These are combined with the 'Twelve Earthly Branches', *zi, chou, yin* . . . even with even and odd with odd, forming a cycle of sixty days. Thus the first branch, *zi*, appears in day 1, and reappears in days 13, 25, 37, 49. Odd and even combinations are not possible. The *wu* stem and the *wu* branch are written with different characters.

Appendix V

Simplified dynastic chronology

Xia dynasty	2205–1766BC (traditional)
Shang dynasty	1765–1123BC (traditional)
Western Zhou dynasty	1122–771BC (traditional)
Eastern Zhou dynasty	770–256BC
Spring and Autumn	722–481BC
Warring States	480–222BC
Qin dynasty	221–206BC
Former (Western) Han dynasty	206BC–AD8
Wang Mang usurpation	9–23
Later (Eastern) Han dynasty	25–220
Period of disunity	221–581
Sui dynasty	581–618
Tang dynasty	618–906
Five dynasties	907–960
Song dynasty	960–1279
Northern Song	960–1126
Southern Song	1127–1279
Yuan (Mongol) dynasty	1260–1368
Ming dynasty	1368–1644
Qing (Manchu) dynasty	1644–1911
Republic of China	1911–1949
People's Republic of China	1949–

Notes

Chapter I – The framework of the argument

1 Hexagram 11/6.
2 The dating is still under discussion, I shall come to this argument in due course.
3 My objective in this chapter is to differentiate the *Zhouyi* from the rest of the material. But I delineate all the sections of Wilhelm-Baynes, such as 'Commentary on the Decision', 'Miscellaneous Notes', and Line Texts (a) and (b), in Appendix I, 'The sinological maze of Wilhelm-Baynes'.
4 See Smith *et al.*, *Sung Dynasty Uses of the I Ching*, for an excellent treatment of the ideas of Zhu Xi, Cheng Yi, and other Song dynasty thinkers. Richard Lynn, in his translation of the Wang Bi interpretation of the *Changes*, includes numerous footnotes translating Zhu Xi and Cheng Yi, which are invaluable for directly comparing the statements of these philosophers with Wilhelm's encapsulations of their thought.
5 Carol Anthony, in her preface to the third edition of *A Guide to the I Ching*, attempts to correct other people's misapprehensions over who wrote what in Wilhelm-Baynes, but ends up misleading readers still further. Somewhat embarrassingly, she commits a fatal *faux pas* by saying that in the lines the slightly larger indented type was written by King Wen and the smaller unindented type was written by the Duke of Zhou. She cites Richard Wilhelm's own introduction as her authority, but has misread him. Hellmut Wilhelm explains it more clearly in his 'Preface to the Third Edition', *xviii–xx*, which appeared in the single volume Wilhelm-Baynes published in 1968.
6 There is no evidence that the philosophy of *yin* and *yang* was in existence when the *Yi* was conceived; the broken and unbroken lines

of the hexagrams were termed *yin* and *yang* lines much later. The first technical usage of the concept of *yin* and *yang* is in the fourth century BC *Mozi*. The character *yang* does not appear in the *Zhouyi*, but *yin* appears once, in hexagram 61/2: 'A crane calling in the shade.' Here *yin* has its original meaning of 'shade; the northern or shady side of a mountain'. Curiously, the crane was later regarded as a *yang* creature. Even in the *Daodejing*, *yin* and *yang* appear only once, in Chapter 42.

7 In the west *Rediscovering the I Ching* by Greg Whincup led the way in 1986. See also *Yi Jing* by Wu Jing-Nuan, and *I Ching: The Oracle* by Kerson Huang. The PhD dissertations of Edward Shaughnessy (1983) and Richard Kunst (1985) began to gain influence in the academic world. In 1996, *Zhouyi: The Book of Changes* by Richard Rutt was published, which is the most complete exposition of the modernist transformation to date. Hexagram 16, for example, is now thought to be about elephants, and hexagram 30 about the yellow oriole. I explain in Chapter IX, 'The *mingyi* bird', why hexagram 36 is interpreted as referring to a pheasant, and also include a few notes on the piglet.

8 Creel, *The Origins of Statecraft in China*, p 79.

9 Shaughnessy, 'The Composition of the *Zhouyi*', p 8.

10 The Shang divined by means of ox scapula in addition to tortoise/turtle shell; the term 'oracle-bone inscription' covers writings on both types of bone. Less and less use was made of scapula towards the end of the dynasty, by which time the tortoise had become regarded as sacred. It has been supposed that the use of bovine scapula waned because it was less available (cattle sacrifices involved fewer animals as time went on), but it seems to me that what was originally merely a means of forming meaningful cracks in bone became focused by a growing devotion to the 'magic tortoise'.

11 A photograph of the Kanghou *gui* and its inscription appears in Rawson, ed, *Mysteries of Ancient China*, p 20.

12 I am reminded of Wilfred Owen's preface to his First World War poetry as a reason why proper names were removed: 'If I thought the letter of this book would last, I might have used proper names; but if the spirit of it survives—survives Prussia—my ambition and those names will have achieved fresher fields than Flanders....'

13 *Caveat:* I point out in Chapter IV the difficulty of dating the *Zhouyi* in its entirety on the evidence of selected parts. Note that some commentators have suggested that because Kanghou is named in the judgment of hexagram 35 this means that the judgments cannot have been written by King Wen. Diao Bao (1603–1669) used a similar argument to disprove the idea that King Wen wrote both the judgment and the line texts, a theory widespread in his time. He cites the naming of the Viscount of Ji in the fifth line of hexagram 36 as

ruling King Wen out as the author of the lines, he himself being more inclined to ascribe them to the Duke of Zhou. (Shchutskii, *Researches on the I Ching*, pp 75–78.) The chronological basis of both ideas, however, is unsound, because there is an ancient contradiction over the timing of King Wen's death, to which I return in Chapter VI.

14 As for King Wu, the 'Martial King', King Wen's son who completed the Conquest after the death of his father, the character *wu* does appear twice in the *Zhouyi* as *wuren*, literally 'military man', in hexagrams 10/3 and 57/1, where Wilhelm-Baynes translates the term as 'warrior'. Incidentally, those who translate *Wen Wang* as 'the Civilised King' or 'King Civility' or even the 'Accomplished King', 'Cultured King', and 'King Writing', have missed the significance of the names *Wen Wang* and *Wu Wang* as a pair: the 'Civil King' and the 'Military King', respectively. Civil is used in the sense of non-military as opposed to polite, it being King Wu who actually launched the Conquest militarily. Note also that *wen* and *wu*, when each is combined with the character for 'fire', *huo*, means a 'slow fire' and a 'quick fire', respectively, reflecting the slow fuse-like build-up in the planning of King Wen and the quickfire response of King Wu when the time arrived.

15 *Great Treatise*, Part II, Chapter XI, Section 1 (the Sixth Wing). Translation by Wilhelm-Baynes, *I Ching*, 3rd edition, p 352. Yin is an alternative name for the Shang. The Yin period is often taken to be the last 273 years of the Shang dynasty, when it was based in what is today the Anyang region, in Henan. Note that it is a different character from *yin* of *yin* and *yang*.

16 Dan, meaning 'dawn', also does not appear in the *Zhouyi*.

17 Fung Yu-lan, *A History of Chinese Philosophy*, Vol. I, p 379, n4.

18 Watson, *Records of the Grand Historian of China*, Vol. 2, p 472.

19 King Wen.

20 Though Sima Qian is writing at a remove of 1,000 years, it should be noted that his list of the Shang kings was substantially validated when the inscribed oracle-bone records, first discovered in 1899, were deciphered. The Shang dynasty had previously been regarded as mythical. This shows Sima Qian was in receipt of accurately transmitted materials. Wang Bi (AD226–249) attributed the creation of the 64 hexagrams (the diagrams) to the legendary Emperor Fuxi, as well as the eight trigrams. It is unlikely, however, that the trigrams existed before the hexagrams. Hellmut Wilhelm wrote: 'I have not yet come across any evidence concerning the date when the concept of the trigrams arose and I do not believe that the traditional view that the complexes of the trigrams anteceded the hexagrams should be accepted without further proof.' (Wilhelm, 'I-Ching Oracles in the *Tso-Chuan* and the *Kuo-Yu*', pp 276–277.) Steve Moore, author of

The Trigrams of Han (1989), who has studied the question in great depth, is still of this opinion (personal communication, December 1997). The evidence for the so-called '*bagua* numerals', supposed references to hexagrams and trigrams on early Western Zhou oracle-bones and bronzes, is at present vague and unconvincing. See, for instance, the papers by Chang Cheng-lang and Zhang Yachu/Liu Yu.

21 Wilhelm-Baynes, *I Ching*, 3rd edition, p 353.
22 Legge, *I Ching*, 2nd edition, p 21.
23 The traditional Chinese scholar Wei Tat even plagiarised Legge's passage word-for-word, without crediting its source, omitting Legge's careful framing of these remarks as purely his own imagination ('I like to think...'). See Wei Tat, *An Exposition of the I-Ching*, p 72.

Chapter II – The title of the oracle

1 Fung Yu-lan, *A History of Chinese Philosophy*, Vol. I, p 380.
2 Though the excavated Shang oracle-bones are mostly turtle shells, in this book I refer primarily to tortoise shells because in early literature the character for 'tortoise' is used consistently to refer to this type of divination. It is never called the 'turtle oracle', always the tortoise oracle.
3 According to the first century AD *Bo Hu Tong*, the *Comprehensive Discussions in the White Tiger Hall*, a thorn-stick must be used (p 526 in Tjan Tjoe Som's translation).
4 See Keightley, *Sources of Shang History*, for a detailed account of Shang pyromancy.
5 Wieger, *Chinese Characters*, p 246.
6 See Waley, 'Notes on Chinese Alchemy', p 7.
7 Legge, *The I Ching*, 2nd edition, p 38.
8 Chang, *Shang Civilization*, pp 43–45.
9 See entries 850b–e in Karlgren's *Grammata Serica Recensa*. The American edition of Wilhelm-Baynes now has only the lower character *Yi* on the cover. Some UK impressions of Wilhelm-Baynes lack the Chinese title page.
10 For examples of such inscriptions, see: Chang, ed., *Studies of Shang Archaeology*, p 106 and p 116; entry 28 for *Yi* in Schuessler, *A Dictionary of Early Zhou Chinese*; Serruys, *Studies in the Language of Shang Oracle Inscriptions*, p 37 and p 68.
11 The character also appears in oracle-bone inscriptions in reversed form (mirror-imaged).
12 Serruys, *op. cit*, p 80.
13 See *Mathews' Chinese–English Dictionary*, entry 2952(c)–7, a usage listed under *yi*: 'to change the dynasty'. *Zhou*, besides being the name of the dynasty, also means 'to encircle' or 'complete, comprehensive'.

Some commentators suggest on the basis of this that *Zhouyi* does not mean *Change of the Zhou Dynasty* or *Zhou Change* but rather *Encompassing Change*. There is no evidence, however, to support this interpretation of the title. Because there is no distinction between single and plural in classical Chinese, *Yi* can mean either *Change* or *Changes*.

14 Watson, *Basic Writings of Mo Tzu*, p 44. The original *Tai Shi* was lost long ago. The chapter by this name extant in the *Documents* today is a 'forgery' of the third century AD, though it does contain a passage much like the one quoted by Modi in the *Mozi*, the inference being that the forger extracted it from the *Mozi* to lend credibility to his work.

15 Wilhelm, *A Short History of Chinese Civilization*, p 114.

Chapter III – Imprisoned for a sigh

1 The narrative developed in this chapter follows closely the account given in the *Shi Ji*, the *Historical Records* of Sima Qian, in particular Chapters 3 and 4, the 'Basic Annals' (*benji*) of the Yin and the Zhou. Though the *Shi Ji* was written nearly a millennium after the events it describes, it presents the most complete skeleton of the story, which I have fleshed out from other sources as indicated. Note that Zhou the tyrant and Zhou the dynasty are written with different characters, neither of which appear in the text of the *Zhouyi*. The tyrant Zhou's name means 'the crupper of a saddle'. Ezra Pound, in his charmingly vernacular version of the *Analects*, actually translated the character like a nickname, calling the Shang ruler 'Crupper' (*Analects* 19/20). Zhou Xin is also known as Di Xin. Xin, the eighth of the ten 'celestial stems' (*tiangan*) used to designate the ancient ten-day week, is conventionally believed to denote the day on which King Zhou was born, added after his death to make the compound title Zhou Xin, as happened with other Shang rulers. K C Chang, however, in '*T'ien Kan*: A Key to the History of the Shang', suggests that the assignment of stem-name titles cannot correspond to birthdays because a disproportionately large number of people had names of the even-numbered days of the week. His speculation is that stem-name titles represent a way of keeping track of multiple lines of a 'circulating succession'.

2 The 'Deer Pavilion' is *lutai*, which is literally a tower or a terrace. Other common translations are 'Stag Tower' and 'Deer Terrace'. I visualise it as a kind of pleasure palace with a pagoda-like tower as part of its structure. It was probably a separate building from the actual palace. It is an assumption on my part that its name derives from deer roaming the grounds, among other wild animals. 'Deer'

later became a pejorative term for fawning ministers.

3   Watson, *Basic Writings of Mo Tzu*, p 91. Mozi is quoting the *Tai Shi*, 'The Great Harangue'. The text appearing under this title in the present edition of the *Documents* is believed to be a third century AD compilation that was passed off as the original. It takes the form of a speech by King Wu just before the Conquest, and cleverly incorporates the same sentiments as the section quoted by Mozi.

4   The earliest naming of Da Ji is in the fifth century BC *Guoyu*, the *Discourses of the States* (7/2). In the *Mu Shi*, 'The Harangue at Mu', a chapter of the *Book of Documents*, King Wu possibly alludes to her, without naming her, on the eve of the Battle of Mu, the decisive battle of the Conquest; but there is no other mention of King Zhou having been under female influence in Western Zhou sources. This is surprising, as Da Ji became a dominant feature of the story in later times. The third century BC *Xunzi* simply says '[Zhou] was obsessed by his favourite concubine [Da Ji]' (Watson, *Basic Writings of Hsun Tzu*, p 122). But by the seventeenth century, in the famous Ming novel *Feng Shen Yan Yi*, the *Investiture of the Gods*, the innocent girl Da Ji has her soul sucked out of her nostrils by a thousand-year-old nine-tailed fox spirit, who then occupies her body as a sinister changeling, transforming her into the bewitching *femme fatale* known to history. A fox spirit is able to assume the form of a beguiling and sensuous young woman in order to lure men into debauchery, resulting in their eventual demise. The fall of the Ming dynasty itself illustrates the ancient Chinese saying that 'a beautiful woman can overthrow an Empire'. A quarrel over a concubine caused a rift between the two Ming generals who together might have staved off the impending Manchu conquest (see van Gulik, *Sexual Life in Ancient China*, p 334). At the end of the Western Zhou dynasty, King You continually lit the beacons that were intended to rally the feudal lords to his assistance in the event of invasion, solely because seeing them dash to the rescue was the only thing that made his favourite concubine, Bao Si, smile. When the invasion came he had cried wolf so many times no-one turned out to repel it. Ode 192 says that Bao Si has destroyed the Zhou. One ruler who wished to invade a remote kingdom sent its king the gift of a troupe of beautiful female musicians, knowing it would only be a matter of time before the king became enamoured of their charms and lax in affairs of state (Watson, *Basic Writings of Han Fei Tzu*, pp 62–65). Perhaps the archetypal case is that of Xi Shi, the beauty presented by King Goujian of Yue to his rival, King Fucha of Wu. Fucha became completely infatuated with her, and his kingdom was conquered by Yue in 472BC (Li Han and Hsu Tzu-kuang, *Meng Ch'iu*, trans: Burton Watson, Tokyo, Kodansha, 1979, p 102). The court commentaries from the Song

dynasty on hexagram 44, Gou, which literally means 'copulation' not 'coming to meet' as Wilhelm-Baynes coyly puts it, are so heavily laced with misogyny because ministers advising the Emperor continually feared their advice would be disregarded if an Imperial concubine could turn the Emperor's ear in the bedchamber. This explains why, in Wilhelm-Baynes, one should not 'come to meet' if the object of the enquiry is 'a bold girl who lightly surrenders herself', but it is legitimate for 'a prince and his official'. The problem was compounded by eunuchs. Having sole right of entry into the Imperial seraglio besides the Emperor they learnt the Emperor's secrets from the gossip of the concubines and were able to use this information to plot and inveigle ministerial favours. (See Chapter X for further notes on hexagram 44.)

5   The third century BC *Han Feizi* refers to 'the wild and licentious music' composed for the lute by Master Yan for King Zhou as 'the music of a doomed nation', pp 53–54 in Burton Watson's translation. Sima Qian contradicts himself, identifying the composer both as Music Master Yan and Music Master Zhuan in two separate places in the *Historical Records*.

6   Graham, *The Book of Lieh-tzu*, pp 151–152. As King Zhou's excesses were made worse by his drunkenness on black millet wine, after the Conquest King Wu introduced the death-penalty for those officials of the old House who persistently 'steeped themselves in wine', giving them a period of grace to be instructed in the ways of the new dynasty. This is described in the *Jiu Gao*, 'The Announcement about Wine', a chapter of the *Book of Documents*. King Wen is here said to have approved of drinking wine only when it was used as an offering at sacrifices to the ancestors.

7   Liao, *The Complete Works of Han Fei Tzu*, Vol. I, pp 239–240. At this time, in the final phase of the Shang dynasty, the sacrifices to the ancestors were offered on the cyclical days corresponding to their stem-names, according to a fixed ritual schedule, so if Zhou got so drunk he couldn't even remember what day it was then this implies disregard for the ancestors. Though it is unlikely Han Feizi intended such an implication, as the details of Shang practices had been lost by this time.

8   Forke's translation of the *Lunheng*, Vol. I, p 354. The story is doubtless apocryphal: ivory was not used to make chop-sticks until much later.

9   Liao, *op. cit*, Vol. I, pp 217–218. Han Feizi records this story to illustrate a line in Chapter 52 of the *Daodejing*: 'Seeing the small is said to be enlightenment.' Seeing the small means the same as 'knowing the seeds', which is associated with hexagram 16/2 in the *Great Treatise*, Part II, Chapter V, Verse 11. In the Wilhelm-Baynes

I Ching (3rd edition) see p 70 and p 342. Compare with the 'extraordinary salience of small things' in hexagram 62/6 (pp 243–244); 'pay especial attention to small and insignificant things' in 62/3 (p 242); 'discerning the seeds of coming events' in 3/3 (p 19). Chapter 64 of the *Daodejing* deals with similar ideas. Stephen Field has suggested that the story of the Viscount of Ji and the ivory chop-sticks explains *l*.95 of the *Tian Wen*, a fourth century BC book of riddles, which he translates as: 'The beginning of the end, how was it recognized?' (Field, *Tian Wen: A Chinese Book of Origins*.) David Hawkes translates the same line: 'Who foresaw it all in the beginning, when the first signs appeared?' (Hawkes, *The Songs of the South*, p 130.)

10 Watson, *The Basic Writings of Mo Tzu*, p 106. This is the earliest mention of Zhou cutting open pregnant women. It was made much of in later fiction. In the fourteenth century novella *Wu Wang Fa Zhou Binghua*, or *How King Wu Defeated the Tyrant Zhou*, the fox sprite concubine Da Ji claims she can tell whether a pregnant woman is carrying a boy or a girl. King Zhou, highly curious, accedes to her request to try an experiment on a hundred pregnant women. Da Ji pronounces her verdict on the first. King Zhou asks her how she knows, to which she replies: 'If my Lord does not believe it, rip up her belly and see.' Each day a hundred pregnant women are cut open to show Da Ji is right. This motif also appears in the forged third century AD *Tai Shi* chapter of the *Book of Documents*, which mentions another story that was also picked up on in later fiction. One winter's day King Zhou and Da Ji watch a young man and an old man wading an icy river. The old man takes it in his stride, but the young man appears afraid of the cold. Curious, and spurred on by Da Ji, King Zhou orders his guards to cut off the legs of both men so that he can examine their bone marrow. The earliest mention of Zhou cutting off the legs of waders is in the third century BC *Han Feizi* (Liao, *op. cit*, Vol. II, p 153).

11 Waley, *The Way and its Power*, pp 126–127.

12 *Analects* 19/20.

13 *Li Sao*, *ll*.159–160. Translation by David Hawkes.

14 Legge, *Chinese Classics*, Vol. V, p 567. Youli was a few miles south of the Shang capital, near the modern-day city of Anyang in Henan.

15 *Tian Wen*, *l*.148.

16 *Ibid.*, *l*.157. Translation by David Hawkes.

17 Birrell, *Chinese Mythology*, pp 111–112.

18 These ransom gifts may be mentioned in the *Zhouyi*. In hexagram 22/4, rendered in Wilhelm-Baynes as 'a white horse comes as if on wings', the character translated as 'wings', *han*, also means 'the red feathers of the pheasant'. The picture appears to be of a white horse

with its mane decked out with a plume of red pheasant's feathers. In addition to this, the character *bi*, featuring throughout hexagram 22 and its title, pictures a cowrie shell (money, valuables) decorated with flowers, hence its meaning of 'ornaments'. The fourth line also refers to the practice of 'bride abduction'. In ancient Chinese marital custom, when the groom came from a poor family he and his friends would disguise themselves as bandits and stage a mock abduction of the bride, so the bride's family could save face by not being seen to 'willingly' give their daughter to a poor man (see Eberhard, *Local Cultures*, p 277). In Wilhelm-Baynes the phrase is translated delightfully, if a little obscurely: 'He is not a robber, he will woo at the right time.' Wilhelm, although he doesn't explain in the *Changes* that this is what this curious expression is all about, which is also repeated in hexagrams 3/2 and 38/6, mentions the practice on p 75 of his 1929 *A Short History of Chinese Civilization*. My feeling is not necessarily that hexagram 22 alludes to King Wen's ransom gifts to King Zhou, but rather that Cai Yong may have been inspired by the *Yijing* when coming up with these distinctive items. Sima Qian had earlier stated that the ransom consisted of a beautiful girl, dappled horses, nine four-horse teams, and other unspecified unusual objects. Neither the *Documents* nor the *Odes* mention the ransom, or, for that matter, King Wen's imprisonment. Some commentators have suggested there are allusions to King Wen's imprisonment in the *Zhouyi*, such as in hexagrams 17/6, 29/4, and 29/6, but I am not convinced. The earliest reference to King Wen's imprisonment at Youli appears to be in the third century BC *Han Feizi* (Liao, *op. cit*, Vol. II, p 160).

19 See also Morgan, *Tao: The Great Luminant*, pp 125–126, for another version of this episode from Chapter 12 of the *Huainanzi*.

20 In late fictionalised accounts of the Conquest from the Yuan and Ming dynasties, before King Wen is released he is fed a meat dish made from his eldest son, Yi Kao. The earliest extant reference to this motif is third century AD, although Qu Yuan's remark, in the fourth century BC *Tian Wen*, that King Zhou bestowed flesh on the Earl of the West, may allude to the Yi Kao story rather than Mei Bo. Because of the influence of the Ming novel *Feng Shen Yan Yi*, the idea that King Wen was forced to eat his own son has entered the popular imagination and is often recounted as part of the legend without its sources being acknowledged. See Chapter XI, 'King Wen is fed his own son'.

21 Karlgren's translation of the *Shu*, p 39. In the same work, see also p 61 and p 78 for further examples of statements that Heaven gave King Wen the Mandate.

22 At this time the Earl of the West's capital was at Mount Qi.

23 This is the Luo River in present-day Shaanxi that flows south to join
    the Wei, not the Luo River near Luoyang in Henan. See map 1 on
    p 82.
24 Han Feizi mentions both of these details (Liao, *op. cit*, Vol. II, p 160).
25 Watson, *Basic Writings of Mo Tzu*, p 107.
26 Liao, *op. cit*, Vol. II, p 21.
27 *Ibid.*, Vol. I, p 227.
28 *Ibid.*, Vol. II, pp 74–75.
29 This is reminiscent of the third line of hexagram 1.
30 A *li* is about a third of a mile. In the judgment of hexagram 51 the
    phrase translated in Wilhelm-Baynes as 'The shock terrifies for a
    hundred miles' is literally 'Thunder terrifies for a hundred *li*'. (The
    significance of the judgment of hexagram 51, 'Thunder comes—oh,
    oh! Laughing words—ha, ha!', may be heightened by comparison
    with the story of Tang the Completer's act of self-sacrifice. The first
    seven years of the reign of Tang, the 'first good king' of the Shang
    dynasty, was blighted by severe drought. Tang decided to offer
    himself as a sacrifice, taking the blame upon his own shoulders. A
    woodpile was assembled at the altar at the Mulberry Forest and Tang
    lay down upon it. His body had been wrapped in dry white rushes so
    as to more readily catch fire. The kindling was lit at the bottom of the
    pyre. Tang remained composed as the flames began to lick around his
    body, not even flinching when suddenly there came a great clap of
    thunder. Everyone was terrified. Then the heavens opened and rain
    poured down, dousing the flames and saving Tang. Everyone cheered
    and laughed as they were drenched. Note that there is a good
    indication that the thunder in hexagram 51 was accompanied by
    heavy rainfall by the presence of mud in the fourth line. For
    translations of the original texts concerning Tang's sacrifice, see
    Birrell, *op. cit*, pp 85–87. Also see Allan, 'Drought, Human Sacrifice,
    and the Mandate of Heaven in a Lost Text from the *Shang Shu*'.)
31 Watson, *Basic Writings of Mo Tzu*, p 120.
32 *Analects* 8/20.
33 *Mencius* 2A/1.
34 Some have suggested they got their name because they used hunting
    dogs, others say it was a meant as an insult. The Dog Rong brought
    the Western Zhou dynasty to an end when they sacked the capital of
    Hao in 771BC, killing King You, who, it will be recalled, lit the
    warning beacons so many times to amuse his concubine that the
    feudal lords did not turn out to repel the invasion. The character *rong*
    appears three times in the *Zhouyi*: in hexagram 13/3, the judgment of
    hexagram 43, and 43/2. Wilhelm-Baynes translates it according to its
    meaning of 'arms, weapons', but the Rong tribe equally fits the
    context.

35   For these locations, see map 1 on p 82. Dayi Shang is how the Shang capital appears on the inscribed oracle-bones, *yi* meaning either 'city' or 'settlement'. It is uncertain whether it had any other name. The city of Zhao Ge, literally 'Dawn Song', was believed by some scholars to be the Shang capital just before the Conquest, but the oracle-bones offer no evidence to support this.

36   Morgan, *Tao: The Great Luminant*, p 126.

37   See *Analects* 19/21 and *Mencius* 2B/9 for a comparison of eclipses to the superior man's errors.

38   The translation is based on Ho Peng Yoke, *The Astronomical Chapters of the Chin Shu*, p 154.

39   There can be little doubt that in the case of the Athenian general Nicias it was his own reaction that caused one of the most appalling blood-baths ever associated with an eclipse. At a time when lunar eclipses were routinely recorded in Chinese annals as 'normal', in 431BC Syracuse was besieged by the Athenian fleet and army, both under the command of Nicias, who had delayed giving the order to attack. The night of the full moon had been selected, August 27, but just before the signal was given the moon entered into eclipse, lunar eclipses often being blood-red (*cf.* the *Book of Joel*, II, 31, in the *Old Testament*). The Athenian soldiers, and Nicias himself, were terrified. Nicias was advised by soothsayers to await the next full moon, but before that came the Syracusans were joined by reinforcements and the Athenians were cut to shreds, Nicias himself being executed for his blunder. On the question whether an omen is an unalterable pronouncement on events-to-be, there are number of examples in history of ill-omens being averted by quick thinking. When William the Conqueror leaped ashore at Bulverhythe he stumbled and fell on his face. A great cry went up from his army that it boded disaster, but the Conqueror, with remarkable presence of mind, quelled the panic and averted the ill-omen by shouting out: 'I have taken seisen of this land with both my hands.' ('Seisen' was a custom of medieval Europe whereby a new tenant took possession of land by taking a clod of earth in his hand.) The same is also told of Julius Caesar when he landed in Africa.

40   Li is thought to have been situated near the present-day city of Zhangzhi in Shanxi, approximately 100 miles north-north-east of Luoyang, just 80 miles west of the Shang capital. See map 1 on p 82.

41   This event illuminates the meaning of hexagrams 41/5 and 42/2: 'The tortoise's ten pairs cannot oppose it.' The Shang oracle-bone divination record shows that sometimes 20 cracks were made on the same topic as ten pairs in positive and negative mode, *e.g.* 'We will receive millet harvest' and 'We will not perhaps receive millet

harvest'. Keightley suggests that large sets of cracks on a single issue may have been made because the diviner, encouraged by early auspicious readings (it was a common practice to divine the same charge in five pairs), wished to pursue a 'lucky streak' in the hope of obtaining a 'jackpot' set (*Sources of Shang History*, p 38, n47). Hexagram 41/5 has the prognostication *yuanji*, 'most auspicious', the highest ranked prognostication of good fortune in the *Yi*, corresponding to *shangji*, 'highly auspicious', found in Shang divinations. The tortoise oracle's ten-pair set known as *Bingbian* 145.1–2 has three *shangji* prognostications (*ibid.*, p 38, n47). In the case of the vassal warning King Zhou, however, fortunes are reversed. It appears that desperation drove the diviner to make a large number of cracks hoping to find celestial partiality for the future of the House of Yin, but the tortoise oracle was not able to oppose with favourable readings, *dared* not oppose, the fate that was to befall the dynasty. In the *Shi Ji* version of the taking of Li, the vassal warns King Zhou: 'Heaven has ended Yin's Mandate and has given away the divine tortoise to others, we can learn nothing auspicious from it.' The 'divine tortoise' is the *linggui*, referred to in hexagram 27/1, where it is translated in Wilhelm-Baynes as 'magic tortoise'. Thus hexagram 27/1 may refer to the Shang's loss of the good auspices of their own tortoise oracle. Rather than 'You let your magic tortoise go', as it is translated in Wilhelm-Baynes, a more literal translation may be made that coheres well with the *Shi Ji*: 'The divine tortoise abandons you.' This would certainly explain the 'disastrous' prognostication attached to this line. (Note that in hexagrams 41/5 and 42/2 the character *peng*, 'pair', also referred to a set of stringed cowries, used as money. Some translators suppose the tortoise was worth ten of these. That may be so. But still the four characters *gui fu ke wei* appear together as an expression, literally: 'The tortoise is not able to oppose it.' Before this it might read: 'Someone profits ten *peng*.' Possibly a diviner's reward for a successful divination, if one were to go along with this translation. Those who follow the 'cowries' school of thought, however, such as Whincup, Kunst, and Rutt, do not interpret it this way. They suppose that the person cannot refuse either the ten *peng* offered for the tortoise or the offer of a tortoise that valuable, 'refuse' stretching the more common meaning of *wei*, 'oppose', and in the process they lose what I feel is the true idea, that the tortoise oracle is not able to oppose fate.)

42 Creel, *Origins*, pp 84–85. The 'Documents of the Shang' in the *Shujing* are merely so-called; they cannot be dated before the Zhou.

43 This belief informs hexagram 18. See Chapter XII, 'The curse of the ancestors'.

44 Boltz, 'Perspectives on Literacy in Ancient China'.

45 The Nationalist Revolution of 1911 set a precedent in China, being resolutely described as 'ending the Mandate'. Curiously, *wenge*, the 'Cultural Revolution', uses the character *wen* of King Wen's name for its meaning of 'culture'.

46 Tang the Completer.

47 Karlgren translated this sentence as: 'The old men of our house have withdrawn in senility.' He explains: '[Weizi] complains that the eldest of the house, who should be the pillars of the state and guides of the wicked king, are dotards.' ('Glosses on the Book of Documents', *BMFEA* 20 [1948], pp 223–224.)

48 For an impression of how seriously such a thing would have been regarded, see the *Spring and Autumn Annals* where, recorded alongside deaths and disasters, is the curious detail that fieldmice had nibbled the horns of a pure sacrificial bull, meaning it could not be used.

49 According to tradition, the Senior Master had recommended to the former king, Di Yi, that the Viscount of Wei should accede to the throne instead of Zhou. The *Shi Ji* explains that the reason the Viscount of Wei was unable to become heir, though he was the eldest brother, was because he had a lowly mother, whereas Zhou Xin's mother was the ruler's primary consort.

50 The Senior Master fears that Weizi will be ashamed of fleeing, so emphasises that by doing so he will be serving the spirits of the former kings. It was important that there be a remaining direct-line relation to make the sacrifices to the ancestors. A phrase that recurs in ancient Chinese annals is 'the sacrifices were discontinued', meaning that every last member of a ruling family was wiped out by a rival. Immediately after the Conquest Zhou Xin's son Wu Geng was graciously allowed to continue the Shang sacrifices after King Wu died, but he conspired against the new dynasty with the disloyal sons of King Wen and was subsequently executed by the Duke of Zhou. King Cheng, King Wu's son, then had the son of the previous Shang king, the Viscount of Wei, take over the Shang sacrifices at Song. So the Senior Master's advice showed great foresight. It was not simply a noble gesture for the Zhou to allow the Shang sacrifices to continue: by doing so they prevented a horde of angry ghosts from wreaking havoc. (For the disloyal sons of King Wen, see Appendix II.)

51 The translation is based on the versions of Legge and Karlgren.

52 Bi Gan is thought to have been King Zhou's paternal uncle. In Chapters 25 and 26 of the Ming fantasy novel of the Conquest, the *Feng Shen Yan Yi*, the fox sprite concubine Da Ji wishes to avenge the murder of her fox relatives by Bi Gan, so she fakes an illness that can only be cured by a soup made from a human heart with seven apertures. Bi Gan, when he hears of what is in store for him, burns a

magic charm and drinks the ashes mixed with water. After taking this precaution, when ordered to give up his heart he cuts it out himself with a sword and throws it down on the floor of the court, with not a drop of blood flowing from the wound, and walks out in disgust. He dies when the innocent remark of a street-vendor selling heartless cabbages, that a man would surely die if he had no heart, breaks the spell. The novel has been translated by Gu Zhizhong as *Creation of the Gods*.

53   Liao, *op. cit*, Vol. I, p 246.

54   The French 'authority' on the *Yijing*, Cyrille J-D Javary, in his imaginative but unsourced and inaccurate reconstruction of these events, 'Un meurtre familial fondateur: La germe historique du Yijing', muddles it up by placing these events just before the imprisonment of King Wen, saying King Wen sighed over the death of Bi Gan and the imprisonment of Jizi, missing out completely the earlier outrage when the Marquis of Jiu was made into meat stew and the Marquis of E was made into strips of dried meat. Admittedly it is a difficult task to sort out the various strands of the story into an unfolding narrative, and even Sima Qian has confused the timing of King Wen's death, an issue fraught with difficulty dealt with in Chapter VI.

55   Hexagram 36 is among the most perplexing in the *Yi*. I have written a few notes on it in Chapter IX, 'The *mingyi* bird'.

56   *Tian Wen*, l.148.

57   Watson, *Basic Writings of Hsun Tzu*, p 72.

58   Liao, *op. cit*, Vol. II, p 190.

59   *Mencius* 2A/1.

60   The translation is based on the versions of Arthur Waley and Bernhard Karlgren, using Karlgren's extensive glosses.

61   Shangdi is the deity of the Shang, as opposed to Tian, 'Heaven', the deity of the Zhou. Shang of Shangdi is not the same character as the name of the dynasty, it simply means 'above', Shangdi being 'The Lord on High'. The name is believed to be effectively synonymous with 'the ancestors'.

62   The Mandate of Heaven is not to be taken for granted as something that lasts forever, regardless. Heaven's grace is easily lost.

63   Guifang, literally the 'Demon's Territory' or 'Land of Ghosts', is referred to in the third line of hexagram 63 and the fourth line of hexagram 64. Wilhelm-Baynes translates it as the 'Devil's Country'. Hexagram 63/3 refers to the military campaign waged by 'Gaozong', the 'Illustrious Ancestor', the temple name of the Shang king Wu Ding, against Guifang, believed to be in the north-west (some think it may be Tibet). After three years he succeeded in subduing it. Wu Ding reigned towards the beginning of the Yin period at Anyang.

Fang is a Shang word for an 'alien state'; the Zhou state is referred to as Zhoufang in Shang oracle-bone inscriptions. For more details on *fang* states see Hsu and Linduff, *Western Chou Civilization*, pp 248–253. The 'wagon full of devils' in the top line of hexagram 38 may refer to a wagonload of men from Gui, possibly captives, or to the 'Ghost Carriage' constellation, the four stars in Cancer boxing Praesepe, the 'Beehive Cluster'. Praesepe, a misty patch of sky at the centre of the 'Ghost Carriage', is known to the Chinese by the wonderful name of 'Exhalation of Piled-up Corpses'. Eberhard showed that the expression 'ghost cart', *guiche*, has been used to refer to a large butterfly, a bat, and an evil phantom bird with ten heads and ten beaks (*Local Cultures*, pp 166–170). Regarding strange hard-to-fathom imagery in the *Zhouyi*, we cannot afford to overlook the possibility that it may actually derive from fragments recording divinations about the significance of dreams. The Shang certainly divined about dreams. King Wu Ding, according to the oracle-bone record, had a dream that he was tending a stone deer, and wished to know whether it was a good omen or a bad omen (Glum, 'Rain Magic at Anyang?', p 260). Hellmut Wilhelm briefly considers the dreamlike nature of some of the imagery in the *Yi* in *Heaven, Earth, and Man in the Book of Changes*, pp 201–202.

64 One struggles to translate this saying so as to draw out the true sense of it. I have followed Karlgren, who explains it this way: 'So "the root" of the state, the royal house, is disposed of, without the branches and leaves, *i.e.* the people, coming to harm.' Waley's translation is a trifle confused, but conveys the impression that an otherwise healthy-looking tree may one day fall down because its roots are rotten and decayed. There is a similar Neo-Confucian saying: 'Forgetting the root but preserving the branch.' Its meaning is different again: it was applied to those who lost sight of the essence of a teaching but upheld its form. It was often aimed at those who practised divination but lacked wisdom. Another saying after this fashion is satirical: 'When the tree falls the monkeys scatter.' It refers to hangers-on whose only power resides in fawning on an influential man, who become non-entities once he is toppled or dies.

65 The 'Xia king' is a reference to King Jie, the wicked last king of the Xia dynasty, the legendary dynasty before the Shang, for which no decisive archaeological evidence has yet been found. The *Mozi* also refers to him semi-anonymously as 'the man of Xia' (Watson, *Basic Writings of Mo Tzu*, p 122). King Jie is very much a mirror-image of the last Shang king Zhou Xin. Jie is also said to have been enchanted by a favourite concubine, Mo Xi, and to have made a lake of wine, on which they both sailed about in a barge amidst an orgy of inebriated naked men and women bathing and drinking. The *Han Shi Wai Zhuan*,

a second century BC commentary on the *Odes* that records tales of Jie's depravity, says the wine lake was big enough for 3,000 people to drink from like cattle (4/2). King Jie didn't build bridges, so he could amuse himself watching people trying to cross on the ice in winter; King Zhou cut off the legs of waders in the winter. The mirroring is too perfect to be entirely free of invention, suggesting that King Zhou's attributes have simply been transferred to King Jie as part of a Zhou propaganda campaign, or vice-versa, it being impossible to know for sure who served as the prototype. King Jie was overthrown by Tang the Completer, who, like King Wen, was also imprisoned then set free. According to the *Huainanzi* (13/10A), compiled 139BC, King Jie's only regret was that he didn't kill Tang when he had him incarcerated in the Tower of Xia, just as King Zhou's only regret was that he didn't execute King Wen when he was imprisoned at Youli. Sarah Allan discusses this and other parallels in her PhD dissertation, *The Heir and the Sage*. See also Xunzi's discussion of parallels in Watson, *Basic Writings of Hsun Tzu*, pp 122–123. Mozi mentions parallel ill-omens at the end of the Xia and Shang dynasties, Watson, *Basic Writings of Mo Tzu*, pp 57–58, and further parallels pp 105–107. In the *Documents*, both King Wu and the Duke of Zhou, after the Conquest, are emphatic that the Zhou must study the fate of their predecessors as a mirror (*i.e.* a warning) that reflects what will become of those who do not live up to the responsibilities they have assumed (p 45 and p 49 in Karlgren's translation). Mirrors at this time, incidentally, were made of polished bronze.

Chapter IV – An overlooked solar eclipse record

1 The Chinese text of hexagram 55 is reproduced in Appendix III.
2 Granet, *Festivals and Songs of Ancient China*, p 138.
3 *I Ching: The Classic Chinese Oracle of Change*, pp 591–592.
4 Edward Schafer in his *Pacing the Void: T'ang Approaches to the Stars*, p 46, has an excellent diagram showing how it was missed.
5 Conjee is starched water in which rice has been boiled.
6 The Chinese Azure Dragon constellation consists of the first seven of the 28 lunar mansions, forming the Eastern Palace. It stretches through the constellations Virgo, Libra, Scorpio, and Sagittarius, of the solar zodiac.
7 It is tempting to consider that this may not be a mere coincidence of names. According to Chapter 6 of the *Zhuangzi*, Fu Yue, the minister of the Shang king Wu Ding, turned into a star and may now be found deep in the south below Sagittarius, where he is Gamma Telescopii.
8 'Obscuration' is based on Nathan Sivin's gloss of this character from his *Cosmos and Computation in Early Chinese Mathematical Astronomy*,

a translation I favour in these two lines over Bernhard Karlgren's definition of 'screen' from his *Grammata Serica Recensa* (entry 999g). Wilhelm translated it as *der Vorhang*, 'curtain'. Wang Bi (AD226–249), oddly without any reference to an eclipse at all, says *bu* in hexagram 55 refers to 'a thing that covers over and darkens, that wards off the light' (Richard Lynn's translation).

9   Legge, *Chinese Classics*, Vol. V, p 170.

10 Wu Ding's reign (1324–1266BC, traditional chronology) was beneficial for the Shang, but not for those neighbouring states whose prisoners-of-war were routinely decapitated as sacrifices to the Shang ancestors. The Qiang tribe, in particular, were slaughtered *en masse*; the Qiang were later one of the eight tribes that joined King Wu's army against the Shang. King Wu Ding also dispatched troops to fight the pre-dynastic Zhou.

11 Watson, *Basic Writings of Mo Tzu*, p 68.

12 *Analects* 14/40.

13 Some contemporary scholars believe that there is no evidence that the custom of kings spending three years in the mourning hut goes back much before the time of Confucius. Hexagram 55 itself provides that evidence.

14 Smith, 'The Difficulty of the *Yijing*', p 3.

15 The Former Han scholar Dong Zhongshu made a similar point about the *Spring and Autumn Annals*: 'The [*Chunqiu*], as an object of study, describes the past so as to illumine the future. Its phrases, however, embody the inscrutableness of Heaven and therefore are difficult to understand. To him who is incapable of proper examination it seems as if they contain nothing. To him, however, who is capable of examining, there is nothing they do not contain. Thus he who concerns himself with the [*Chunqiu*], on finding one fact in it, links it to many others; on seeing one omission in it, broadly connects it (with others). In this way he gains complete (understanding) of the world.' (Fung Yu-lan, *A History of Chinese Philosophy*, Vol. II, p 75.) Dong believed that Confucius wrote the *Chunqiu* after receiving the Mandate of Heaven. It is now thought unlikely that Confucius was the author.

16 Creel, *The Birth of China*, p 268.

17 Maspero, *China in Antiquity*, p 447, n36, in the English translation.

18 Waley, *The Way and its Power*, p 101.

19 Smith, *op. cit*, p 3.

20 See Chapter XIII, 'Clouds follow the dragon', for an interpretation of the original meaning of hexagram 1.

21 Wylie, 'Eclipses recorded in Chinese works', in his *Chinese Researches*.

22 See Hartner, 'Das Datum der Shih-ching-Finsternis'.

23 Subsequently published under the title *Historical Eclipses*.
24 Chatley, 'Ancient Chinese Astronomy', p 4.
25 van Esbroeck, 'The So-Called Eclipse in the *Shu-King*'.
26 Cited by Joseph Needham, in his *Science and Civilisation in China*, Vol. III, p 412.
27 Since this chapter was written I have noticed that David Pankenier made the same point in the forum discussion in *Early China* 15 (1990), pp 128–130.
28 Creel, *The Origins of Statecraft in China*, p 484. The *Bamboo Annals* ('Current Text') has for the past two centuries been regarded as a fake. Since the early 1980s, however, it has attracted a small but influential following of scholars interested in establishing an absolute Zhou chronology, notably Nivison, Pankenier, and Shaughnessy, who have sought to prove its authenticity, as they have used it as the linchpin for their theories. Several potential dates for the Zhou Conquest have been derived by various interpretations of the *Bamboo Annals*, which are in a range about 25–30 years after the solar eclipse recorded in the *Zhouyi*. I show in Chapter VI that King Wu launched the Conquest in the same year as the eclipse.
29 *Ibid.*, pp 444–447.
30 Wilhelm thought Cheng Tang was the king referred to, though Baynes mentioned in a footnote that modern scholarship no longer accepted this identification. Di Yi was the penultimate Shang king and father of the tyrant Zhou Xin. In these two hexagram lines Di Yi gives his younger sister in marriage (not 'daughter' as in Wilhelm-Baynes). There is good evidence this woman was King Wen's mother, see Appendix II.
31 That the prognostication was made by the king, see, for instance, Keightley, *Sources of Shang History*, pp 40–42; Chang, *Shang Civilization*, pp 256–257.
32 For evidence of the existence of a written manual for the tortoise oracle in the late Zhou, see Hellmut Wilhelm, 'On the Oracle recorded in the *Tso-chuan*, Hsi 4 (656BC)', *JAOS* 91 (1971), pp 504–505. Hexagram 18, Gu, contains a high proportion of phrases characteristic of the tortoise oracle. See Chapters VII and XII.
33 Kunst, *The Original Yijing*, pp 3–4.
34 Shaughnessy, *The Composition of the Zhouyi*, p 49.
35 The author of the *Zuo* could of course have simply invented 'quotations' from the *Zhouyi*, though this appears less likely as more of his quotes agree with the received text than disagree. There is a growing consensus, following Kidder Smith, *HJAS* 49, that those 'quotations' that do not agree with the received text are not in fact quotations at all, but simply diviners' rhymes extemporised from a

text presumed to be much as we have it today. This may be so, but then the question arises: what about those quotations that *are* quotations, that agree with the received text? We cannot rule out, therefore, the possibility that those seemingly quoted passages that do not agree with the received text are indeed quotations from variant texts of the *Zhouyi* or a text still subject to change.

36 Shaughnessy, *op. cit*, p 39.

37 Take, for instance, the judgment of hexagram 24, Fu or 'Return'. Its quotation in the *Zuozhuan* reads: 'The southern kingdom is routed; shoot at its king and hit one of his eyes.' The received text, however, seems to use the character *dao*, 'a road, path, way', in its philosophical sense: 'Turning back *(fan)* returns to the Dao.' This phrase is almost identical to the first line of Chapter 40 of the third century BC *Daodejing*: 'Turning back *(fan)* moves to the Dao.' In the Western Zhou dynasty *dao* literally meant a path or way, it was not a philosophical concept, 'The Way', until the Warring States period. The similarity of the two sentences, particularly given that the *Zuozhuan* quotes a different sentence altogether, implies a substitution may have been made for the judgment of hexagram 24 at this later time. No-one would suggest this was proof that the *Zhouyi* was composed in the third century BC, yet this is precisely the quality of 'evidence' that Shaughnessy is proffering with his argument for *tianzi*.

38 Kunst, *op. cit*, p 7.

39 Creel, *Origins*, p 495, n5.

40 Allan, *BSOAS* 55, pp 585–587.

41 Its graph, according to Karlgren in his *Grammata Serica Recensa* (entry 1014a), is a drawing of a ritual vessel with something in it.

42 Mount Qi is referred to in hexagram 46/4: 'The king offers a sacrifice to Mount Qi.' It is also alluded to in hexagram 17/6: 'The king offers a sacrifice to the Western Mountain.' The sacrifice is offered to the spirit of the mountain, as opposed to it being a sacrifice offered on or at the mountain, though this reading is also possible. Kerson Huang, following Gao Heng, claims hexagram 17/6 refers to a sacrifice offered by King Wen upon his release from Youli. His translation, however, is forced: 'Imprisoned first, then set free. The King makes offerings at the West Mountain.' Personally, I cannot make the Chinese budge an inch in this direction.

43 The co-ordinates of Xi'an, which were used in the eclipse calculations in the next chapter, were supplied by *The Times Atlas of the World*, 9th edition.

44 Hsu and Linduff, *Western Chou Civilization*, p 92.

45 Classical Chinese has no tense. I have translated the sentence in the past tense as this is more in keeping with a historical record.

Chapter V – Darkness at noon, June 20, 1070BC

1 The Battle of Muye was probably just after the autumn harvest had been gathered in, following the solar eclipse in the summer. This is discussed further in Chapter VII.

2 Appendix 3 of his 1991 *Sources of Western Zhou History.*

3 1027BC was based on a historian's citation of the *Bamboo Annals* in the fifth century AD, which appears to have been a misquotation.

4 See, for instance, the individual papers relating to Zhou chronology by Nivison, Pankenier, and Shaughnessy, listed in the bibliography.

5 See the paper by Kevin Pang *et al.*, *Vistas in Astronomy* 31 (1988).

6 An annular solar eclipse occurs when the moon is in the most distant part of its elliptical orbit and so cannot manage to completely obscure the sun. An annular or ring eclipse is formed instead; the light diminution may be so slight as to be indistinguishable from an overcast day. Similarly, a partial solar eclipse would often not be noticed, unless the observer chanced to see the sun with a bite taken out of it through hazy cloud, or reflected in a puddle.

7 The variable in the equation is known as 'delta T' (ΔT), the accumulated clock drift. See the introduction to Stephenson's 1986 *Atlas* for further explanation. Stephenson notes on page xi: 'On the question of investigating hitherto unused records of large solar eclipses from the Far East to deduce ΔT more accurately, possibly the best prospects would seem to relate to the more ancient observations; the material since about 200BC has been extensively studied. At present, only three records of total solar eclipses are known before 200BC, all from the chronicle of a single small state— Lu, the home of Confucius. The dates of these events as recorded in the [*Chunqiu*] are as follows: 709, 601, and 549BC. If any additional observations from the Shang or [Zhou] dynasties were to come to light they might revolutionise present knowledge of the history of ΔT.'

F R Stephenson published a major new work after I wrote this chapter, *Historical Eclipses and Earth's Rotation* (1997). Although he has substantial material on ancient Chinese eclipses, the eclipse in the *Zhouyi* has still escaped attention, Stephenson concentrating his search on the Chinese annals and dynastic histories, as did those before him. Stephenson mentions a compilation of astronomical records in Chinese history published by Beijing Observatory in 1988, *Zhongguo Gudai Tianxiang Jilu Zongji* ('A Union Table of Ancient Chinese Records of Celestial Phenomena'), but this work also appears to have missed the *Zhouyi* eclipse. Note that Stephenson believes that the 'double dawn' eclipse in the *Bamboo Annals*, calculated using his program, is unlikely to have a real factual basis; he thinks it is probably legendary material (p 220).

 8 Pankenier, 'Reflections of the Lunar Aspect on Western Chou Chronology,' pp 58–67.
 9 *Ibid.*, pp 62–64.
10 Pankenier, 'Astronomical Dates in Shang and Western Zhou.'
11 Shaughnessy, *Sources*, p 223. In my opinion, Huang Yilong has effectively pricked the bubble of five-planet conjunctions as a sinological dating criterion, see his contribution to the Forum discussion in *Early China* 15 (1990), pp 97–112.
12 The brightness of stars is expressed in terms of *magnitude*. For example, a star of the first magnitude (+1, or mag.1) is bright, whereas a star of the sixth magnitude (+6, or mag.6) is faint. Stars over 2·5 times brighter than mag.1 are given negative (minus) magnitudes, such as Sirius, the brightest star in the sky, which has a magnitude of −1·46. Stars fainter than sixth magnitude are given progressively larger positive magnitudes; the faintest objects capable of being seen from Earth-bound telescopes have magnitudes of about 24.
13 Personal communication from Dr Krupp to Patrick Poitevin by e-mail, September 26, 1996, forwarded to the author October 27, 1996.
14 *Han Shu*, 30/62b–63a.
15 *Ibid.*, 99C/27a.
16 Stellar omens play a part in the Conquest in two texts of the Warring States period, the *Xunzi* (4/11A) and the *Shizi* (3/4B). Here the Conquest is said to have been completed against an astrologer's advice not to advance on the Shang because the baleful star 'Lord Great Year', *Taisui*, the planet Jupiter, was presiding over that direction, prohibiting military adventures to the east. Great Year was a powerful protector of the army of the state he resided above, but King Wu ignored the astrologer's counsel. See Hou, 'The Chinese Belief in Baleful Stars'. According to Chapter 15 of the *Huainanzi*, compiled 139BC, a comet appeared as King Wu was marching on Zhou Xin, with its tail pointing to the east, which was supposed to be favourable to Yin (Morgan, *Tao: The Great Luminant*, p 194). Some contemporary Chinese astronomers took this to be a reference to Halley's comet and attempted to date the Conquest by it, but the idea has attracted little support. The *Huainanzi* also puts forward the strange idea that a comet appears when a whale dies.
17 Wu Jing-Nuan, *Yi Jing*, p 194.
18 Thales of Miletus, oddly enough, is also credited with the first accurate prediction of a solar eclipse.
19 The later technical term, similarly pronounced *shi*, is also absent. This character emerged after the Han and is still used today to refer to an eclipse, combining 'to eat' with the insect radical in order to convey the slow steady consumption of the sun or moon, much as a silkworm devours a mulberry leaf.

20 Fotheringham, *Historical Eclipses*, pp 24–27.

21 The earliest known description of the corona that can be reliably dated is quite late, coming from an observation of the total solar eclipse of Dec 22, AD968, at Constantinople: 'Everyone could see the disc of the Sun without brightness, deprived of light, and a certain dull and feeble glow like a narrow headband, shining round the extreme parts of the edge of the disc. However, the Sun gradually going past the Moon (for this appeared covering it directly) sent out its original rays and light filled the Earth again.' (Stephenson, *Historical Eclipses and Earth's Rotation*, p 390.)

22 The drawback of dulling the sun's brilliance by reflection in water, a method used by medieval Arab astronomers to view partial eclipses, is that a slight breeze easily distorts the image. The Roman author Seneca said in the first century AD that viscous liquids such as oil or pitch were better for viewing solar eclipses, as they are less susceptible to being disturbed.

23 Schove, *Chronology of Eclipses and Comets AD1–1000*, x–xi. In medieval European records of total solar eclipses the common people, fearing the Apocalypse, often thought that the last day had come. There is a particularly good description showing the religious overtones of a solar eclipse in a chronicle of Novgorod, May 1, AD1185: 'On the first day of the month, on the day of the Saint Prophet Jeremiah, on Wednesday, during the evening service, there was a sign in the Sun. It became very dark, even the stars could be seen; it seemed to men as if everything were green, and the Sun became like the crescent of the Moon, from the horns of which a glow similar to that of red-hot charcoals was emanating. It was terrible to see this sign of the Lord.' The reference to 'red-hot charcoals' is thought to allude to the chromosphere, which only becomes visible when an eclipse is on the verge of totality. (Stephenson, *Historical Eclipses and Earth's Rotation*, p 395.)

24 In a Chinese report of the total solar eclipse of June 25, AD1275, which was regarded as the omen for the 'extinguishing' of the Song dynasty, it was said that 'the chickens and ducks returned to roost' (*ibid.*, pp 257–258).

25 *Encyclopaedia Britannica*, 15th edition, *Macropaedia*, pp 866–875.

26 See Stephenson, *Historical Eclipses and Earth's Rotation*, p 385, for a report from 1860 where shocked observers lost all sense of the passage of time and were convinced totality had lasted two hours.

27 Nienhauser, *The Grand Scribe's Records*, Vol. 1, p 67, n150. See map 1 on p 82.

28 Schafer, *Pacing the Void*, p 161.

29 GSR entry 501f. Wang Bi defines *pei* in hexagram 55 as 'a pennant or curtain, something used to fend off extremely bright light' (Richard

Lynn's translation). As I pointed out in n8 of the last chapter, Wang Bi makes no reference to an eclipse taking place whatsoever. Lynn glosses *pei* as 'shade'.

30 On incremental repetition in the *Shijing*, see C H Wang's study, *The Bell and the Drum*. See Kunst, *The Original Yijing*, pp 71–81, for a discussion of incremental repetition in the *Zhouyi*.

31 In 1973 at Mawangdui, near Changsha in Hunan, a silk manuscript of the *Zhouyi* was excavated from a tomb that had been sealed in 168BC. This is the earliest actual copy of the *Yi*, though it appears to originate from a later textual tradition than the received text, as is evident, for instance, by its rearrangement of the order of the hexagrams, which disrupts the pair relationships found in the received sequence or 'King Wen order' (*e.g.* 41/5 and 42/2; 43/4 and 44/3). If read aloud, the Mawangdui manuscript would sound very similar to the received text, though on the written page it employs many homophones. A translation by Edward Shaughnessy was published in 1997.

32 Entry 531p.

33 The *Yijing* tried Karlgren's patience. *BMFEA* 35 (1963), p 120, preserves his only comment on it: 'The rigmarole of the *Yi* often defies analysis.'

34 Shelfmark OR 8133.

35 He presumably means the minor stars of *Ursa Major*.

36 The Chinese report of the total solar eclipse of Aug 20, AD1514, said it became so dark 'objects could not be discerned at arm's length' (Stephenson, *Historical Eclipses and Earth's Rotation*, p 261).

37 Oddly enough, with respect to the candle interpretation, there is a striking parallel reference in *The Anglo-Saxon Chronicle* to the total solar eclipse of March 20, AD1140: 'In Lent the sun darkened about noon-tide of the day, when men were eating; and they lighted candles to eat by... Men were very much struck with wonder.' Garmonsway has translated this work.

38 The 'Descent of Hoarfrost', one of the 24 fortnightly periods, begins October 24.

39 The heliacal rising of a star is when it rises with the sun, *helios*, at dawn.

40 Chalmers, 'Astronomy of the Ancient Chinese', p 93.

41 Kunst translates the third line as seeing 'dark spots' inside the sun. This may be criticised on two grounds. First, 'inside the sun' is how he now chooses to render *rizhong*, scrapping it as 'equinox'. Second, this is presumably intended to be a reference to sun-spots, which comes approximately a thousand years before sun-spots were discovered in China, in 28BC. But, like the Curate's Egg, parts of Kunst are excellent. He appears to have been the first to have noticed the presence of two characters in hexagram 55 that later became technical calendrical terms. The character *bu*, in the second and

fourth lines, which I have translated as 'obscured', was later used to refer to the 76-year Callippic Cycle, which Sivin translated as the 'Obscuration Cycle' constant. The character *zhang* in the fifth line, which has a number of meanings such as 'chapter, stanza of an ode, an elegant literary composition, memorial to the throne, statutes, rules', later became the 19-year Metonic Cycle, translated by Sivin as the 'Rule Cycle' constant. If only one of these calendrical constants appeared in hexagram 55, it would mean nothing special, but the presence of two of them is a mysterious coincidence. It is extremely doubtful that these terms were in use in the eleventh century BC. The *locus classicus* for the technical definitions, so far as I know, is the final section of the *Zhou Bi Suan Jing*, a collection of ancient Chinese texts on astronomy and mathematics, which has been translated by Christopher Cullen. The *Zhou Bi*, in which King Wen's son the Duke of Zhou is found expounding the Chinese proof of the Pythagorean right-angle triangle theorem before Pythagoras, is traditionally reputed to date from the Western Zhou around the time of the Conquest, but unlike the tradition surrounding the origin of the *Yijing* this one has nothing to support it. The *Zhou Bi* was probably assembled under the Western Han dynasty during the first century BC, reaching its final form in the first century AD. The section defining the calendrical terms may date at the earliest from the beginning of the Western Han. It is therefore unlikely that these characters are used in their technical sense in the *Zhouyi*. While it is unknown precisely when these cycles were first discovered in China, it is well-known that the Metonic Cycle is associated with Meton of Athens, who flourished 430BC, and the Callippic Cycle is linked with Kallippos of Kyzikos, who flourished 330BC. Given the rate of unfoldment of knowledge in the ancient world it again seems unlikely that these cycles could be referred to in the *Zhouyi* some six centuries earlier. The Metonic Cycle of 19 years, after which the moon's phases recur on the same days of the year, and the four-fold 76-year Callippic Cycle that corrects it (four Metonic Cycles less one day), were counted to calculate lunar eclipse predictions, inadequately, in the Han (see Nathan Sivin's *Cosmos and Computation in Early Chinese Mathematical Astronomy*, pp 28–32, for examples of such calculations). Richard Rutt suggests these terms were probably used in hexagram 55 as puns, adding that though the history of the terms *bu* and *zhang* is unknown it is thought by some scholars that the cycles had been noticed as early as Shang times (*Zhouyi*, p 350). David S Nivison, stretching credulity somewhat, cites a passage in Chapter 3 of the *Zhuangzi*, about a cook whose knife has stayed sharp for 19 years, as evidence for knowledge of the 19-year cycle in the Warring States period (Nivison and Pang, 'Astronomical Evidence', p 93).

Chapter VI – The army carries the corpse

1 Serruys, 'The Language of the Shang Oracle Inscriptions', p 41. The translation is by Chang Tsung-tung.

2 Though this is certainly its meaning today, the actual character consists of three components, *dusk/night* between the *roof* and the *ground*. I mention this only because of its aptness to an eclipse.

3 Entry 21a.

4 Maspero, *China in Antiquity* (English translation), p 160.

5 *Ibid.*, pp 99–100.

6 Wilhelm-Baynes translates *jiu* generally as 'blame', though as 'mistake' in 55/1; Wilhelm masks the oracle-bone formula by running two phrases into one.

7 The term 'charge' (*mingci*) is used by modern scholars to refer to the topic of the divination inscription. See Keightley, *Sources of Shang History*, pp 33–36. A forum discussion on whether or not the charge constituted a question appeared in *Early China* 14 (1989). On the magical dimension of the Shang divination charge, see Keightley's paper 'Late Shang Divination: The Magico-Religious Legacy'.

8 According to Kunst's glossary, Appendix F of his PhD dissertation, *heng* occurs 47 times in the *Zhouyi*, thus substantially altering the meaning of many passages from that traditionally accepted for the past 2,000 years. See Kunst's thesis, pp 181–190, for a detailed discussion of the original etymology of this character. Kunst translates it as 'treat', in the sense of both a sacrificial offering and a ceremonial feast for an honoured guest. In the late Zhou it meant 'success', as it does today, but the evidence provided by the discovery of the Shang oracle-bone divination record in the early years of the twentieth century has made it clear that where it appears in the *Zhouyi* it must be read as referring to the practice of making sacrificial offerings in the context of the cult of ancestor worship.

9 Bodde, *Essays on Chinese Civilization*, p 97. Bodde points out, with a proviso, that the classical study of this cult still remains that of E Chavannes, 'Le Dieu du Sol dans la Chine antique', appendix to his *Le Tai Chan* (Paris, 1910).

10 *Mencius* 5A/4 reports Confucius as saying: 'There cannot be two kings for the people just as there cannot be two suns in the heavens.' D C Lau translation.

11 William Savage in 'The Confucian Gentleman', p 12, points out that the character *wen* appears in most early sources in reference to the dead.

12 In the *Wu Yi*, 'Against Luxurious Ease', a chapter of the *Documents*, the Duke of Zhou states that King Wen reigned for 50 years.

13 Ode 237 depicts King Tai's arrival at Mount Qi and his efforts to build up a capital from the bare earth. *Mencius* 1B/15 explains that

King Tai wished to avoid causing suffering to his people by engaging in a war with the Di tribe, who had invaded his territory at Bin. When attempts to buy off the invaders with precious gifts failed, King Tai realised that what the Di wanted was his land, so he voluntarily took himself off to Mount Qi, leaving his people to decide for themselves what they wished to do. The majority flocked after him as if to market. Bin was about 70 miles north of modern Xi'an on the Jing River in Shaanxi. See map 1 on p 82.

14 According to Wang Chong, King Wen was born with supernumerary nipples, which may have been the sign by which he was recognised as being special. The *Huainanzi*, Chapter 19, notes that King Wen had four nipples (Morgan, *Tao: The Great Luminant*, p 230.)

15 Creel, *The Origins of Statecraft in China*, p 122, n80. According to Sima Qian's 'Basic Annals of the Zhou', the two brothers tattooed their bodies, cut their hair short, and joined the Jing Man tribe.

16 Mentioned in odes 236 and 240, see Appendix II.

17 See Hsu and Linduff, *Western Chou Civilization*, p 64 and p 250; and Creel, *Origins*, p 63, n26.

18 Waley, *The Book of Songs*, p 258. Han Feizi records the curious detail that during the Siege of Chong King Wen's shoelaces came undone and he tied them up himself, rather than get an attendant to do it, because he regarded everyone as his equal. This is all Han Fei says about the Siege of Chong. (Liao, *The Complete Works of Han Fei Tzu*, Vol. II, p 72.)

19 In hexagram 42/2, the king makes a sacrificial offering to Di, the only reference to this deity in the *Zhouyi*. The character *tian* appears eight times in the *Zhouyi*, where it means either 'sky' or 'heaven', with the exception of hexagram 38/3, where it is taken to mean 'a brand on the forehead'. Creel suggests the character may have originated as a collective designation for the ancestors of the Zhou kings. See 'The Origin of the Deity T'ien', Appendix C of his book *The Origins of Statecraft in China*, pp 493–506.

20 Legge, *Chinese Classics*, Vol. V, p 177.

21 The exact location of Chong is not known. Some have speculated that Feng was built on top of it. See Hsu and Linduff, *Western Chou Civilization*, p 91.

22 *Mencius* 4B/1 and 2A/1, respectively.

23 Fung Yu-lan, *A History of Chinese Philosophy*, Vol. II, p 149.

24 Nienhauser, *The Grand Scribe's Records*, Vol. I, p 59, n53.

25 *Ibid.*, p 62, n73. This is a curious statement because the Hyades, a scattering of faint stars, does not lend itself well to graphical representation.

26 Creel, *The Birth of China*, pp 251–252.

27 Creel, 'On the Birth of *The Birth of China*', *Early China* 11–12, pp 1–5.

28 *Tian Wen, ll.*161–162. Translation by David Hawkes.
29 Hawkes, *The Songs of the South,* pp 148–149.
30 *Mencius* 4A/13 and 7A/22. D C Lau translation. The latter section explains that under King Wen there were no old folk who were cold or hungry.
31 *GSR* entry 89j.
32 Rutt, *Zhouyi: The Book of Changes,* p 300.
33 The character translated by David Keightley as 'perhaps' in the Shang oracle-bone inscriptions is *qi,* but nonetheless the principle is the same.
34 Birrell, *Chinese Mythology,* p 261. From *Lunheng* 24. The 'Great Lord' is Great Lord Jiang, also known as Taigong, King Wu's military adviser.
35 Wilhelm, *Heaven, Earth, and Man in the Book of Changes,* p 21, n28. Also in his *Change,* p 94. Hellmut Wilhelm doesn't cite his source in these two publications, but from his brief communication to *JAOS* 91 (1971), pp 504–505, it appears that this story originates from the fourth century BC *Shizi* (Sun's ed.), fragment 41.
36 The *Han Shi Wai Zhuan* also mentions the bad omens of King Wu's shield breaking in three places and it raining continuously for three days, which Taigong re-interpreted favourably to spur both the king and the troops on to victory (Birrell, *op. cit,* p 262). Taigong literally means 'Grand Duke'. There is only one authentic reference to him in Western Zhou sources, in ode 236, where he is called Shang Fu. He appears here as the general of King Wu's army at the Battle of Muye. The ode says 'he was an eagle, a hawk'. The next mention is by Mencius, who twice says that Taigong fled from the tyrant Zhou Xin to settle on the edge of the Eastern Sea, but, on hearing of the rise of King Wen, went to serve him (*Mencius* 4A/13 and 7A/22), paralleling the references to Bo Yi and his brother. In recognition of Taigong's role in the Conquest, he was enfeoffed in Qi (*Mencius* 6B/8). Later sources present him in a semi-legendary fashion. In the most popular version, King Wen comes across the elderly Taigong fishing on the riverbank. Believing he represents the fulfilment of a prophecy made by his grandfather—that a wise man will appear to help the Zhou defeat the Shang—King Wen elevates him from his lowly status and calls him Taigong Wang, 'Grand Duke Expected' (see *Shi Ji* 32; Sawyer, *The Seven Military Classics of Ancient China,* p 28; Birrell, *op. cit,* p 260). The story has variants. *Li Sao ll.*293–294, for instance, says Taigong was a butcher in the Shang town of Zhao Ge when King Wen met him, which is echoed in *Tian Wen ll.*159–160. In the former text he is called Lu Wang ('Lu the Expected'), and in the latter he is Shi Wang ('The Expected Commander'). He is also known as Lu Shang and Great Lord Jiang. Sarah Allan has written at length on

Taigong in 'The Identities of Taigong Wang in Zhou and Han Literature'.

37 Feng here means 'seal'; it is a different character to the name of King Wen's capital.

38 King Wen is said to have had ten sons. Kangshu was the ninth son and King Wu the second (*shu* simply means 'younger of brothers'). Some scholars believe that the king addressing Kangshu in the *Kang Gao* is King Wu's son, King Cheng, and that the Duke of Zhou, the alleged speaker, is simultaneously conveying King Cheng's words while referring to Kangshu as his own younger brother, rather than his uncle if he were faithfully reporting King Cheng's words. The first paragraph naming the Duke of Zhou as the speaker, however, is repeated verbatim at the beginning of the *Luo Gao*, 'The Announcement Concerning Luo', a chapter further on in the *Documents*, and appears entirely misplaced at the head of the *Kang Gao*, having no bearing on the text that follows. The paragraph makes perfect sense, however, at the head of the *Luo Gao*. If this repeated text is removed from the *Kang Gao*, the chapter attains a faultless integrity and presents the unnamed king as speaking directly to his younger brother, Feng, and thus the king can only be King Wu. If it is supposed that the king is King Cheng, it has to be asked why he repeatedly mentions King Wen by name but not King Wu. Legge discusses these difficulties in *Chinese Classics*, Vol. III, pp 382–383, explaining why he changed his former view that it was King Wu speaking to the notion that the Duke of Zhou was speaking on behalf of King Cheng. H G Creel, on the other hand, puts forward a far better argument for establishing the speaker as King Wu in *The Origins of Statecraft in China*, pp 450–451. For information about the other sons of King Wen, see Appendix II, 'Genealogical matters', and Chapter XI, 'King Wen is fed his own son'.

39 It is worth pointing out that the term *dajun*, 'great prince', bears a close written resemblance to *xianjun*, 'my deceased father' (Mathews' Dictionary, entry 1715–40).

40 The translation in Wilhelm-Baynes is generalised: 'The great prince issues commands, founds states, vests families with fiefs.' *Ming*, besides being *the* Mandate, can also mean the command or commands of a ruler; 'vests families with fiefs', *cheng jia*, is literally 'to inherit the house', if it is agreed that *ming* is *the* Mandate, then *jia* is *the* House.

41 Eberhard points out in *The Local Cultures of South and East China*, p 361, that the sedan-chair was allegedly invented by the last Xia Emperor, adding that the oldest form of the sedan-chair may have been a cloth sack on a carrying pole. In later literature the *yu* was the name given to the carriage used by Daoist transcendents to ride through the clouds.

42 Granet, *Danses et Légendes de la Chine Ancienne*, p 551.
43 I believe the hemiplegia of Yu the Great is alluded to in the *Zhouyi*. See Chapter XIV, 'No skin on his thighs'.
44 Josephus, Book 5, Chapter 11, translation by William Whiston. In the *Old Testament*, the 2nd Book of Samuel (sometimes called '2 Kings'), Chapter 6, mentions the awesome power unleashed by *shaking* the Ark of the Covenant.
45 See *The Bulletin of the Museum of Far Eastern Antiquities* 2 and 3.
46 In the factual Ming novel *Three Kingdoms*, set in the period AD187–280, the great general Zhuge Liang dies of an illness at an inopportune moment, his army pitched against an opponent, but on his deathbed he instructs his officers to silence all mourning cries among his troops. He tells them to dress in his clothes a wooden statue of himself he has had carved, set it in his wagon, and to push it out to the front ranks of the army. The enemy have intelligence Zhuge Liang has died and so advance to attack, but when they see the wooden statue they think he is still alive and that they have been lured into his trap. Thus they are panicked into flight by a dead Zhuge. See Luo Guanzhong, *Three Kingdoms*, pp 1254–1261.
47 The meaning of *bin* in the context of an ancestral rite is 'play host to', or 'receive as a guest'. Hexagram 20/4 may refer to this ritual: 'Beneficial for the king to perform the *bin* rite.' *Bin* also means a straightforward 'guest', as opposed to the guest being an ancestral spirit, and features again in hexagram 44/2, where it may also carry its sacrificial meaning (see Chapter X). Sarah Allan discusses the *bin* rite in *The Shape of the Turtle*, p 56 and p 60. Henri Maspero in *China in Antiquity*, pp 149–158, provides a marvellous reconstruction of a sacrifice involving impersonators of the dead, with the 'corpses', including Kings Wen and Wu, getting drunk at a ritual banquet. Maspero further refers to the rite on p 109 and pp 130–131. Impersonators of the dead appear to have been present, though it is not explicitly stated, at the funeral rites for King Cheng, described in a chapter of the *Documents* entitled *Gu Ming*, 'The Deathbed Commands', where the guests' staircase is featured.
48 *Analects* 7/15 and 18/8. *Mencius* 2A/2, 5B/1, and 7B/15. Not everyone thought Bo Yi a saint. The hedonistic fourth century AD 'Yang Zhu' chapter of the *Liezi*, ever delighting in contrariness and mocking of sacred cows, says Bo Yi was not acting as selflessly as everyone supposes: 'It is not that [Bo Yi] had no desires, his was the worst sort of pride in one's own purity, and because of it he starved to death.' (Graham, *The Book of Lieh-tzu*, p 141.) 'Yang Zhu' also says that the virtuous sage-rulers of antiquity, admired by all, are as dead now as the tyrannical kings Jie and Zhou, reviled by all, but at least these two villains led merry lives enjoying pleasures up to the end,

whereas the sages led miserable lives full of trial and tribulation, without a single day's joy. 'Yang Zhu' adds 'death was the last home of them all' (*ibid.*, pp 150–152).

49   *Shi Ji* 61. *Tian Wen*, *l.*175, contains a fragment Sima Qian does not mention. Birrell, *op. cit*, pp 220–221, translates a version of the story casting light on this fragment.

50   Watson, *Records of the Grand Historian of China*, Vol. 2, pp 468–475. 'The Biography of Bo Yi' has also been translated in Nienhauser's *The Grand Scribe's Records*, Vol. VII, pp 1–8. (Indiana University Press, 1994.)

51   *Tian Wen*, *l.*175.

52   *Analects* 16/12.

53   Morgan, *Tao: The Great Luminant*, p 158.

54   Gao Heng felt *xiong* meant nothing less than a 'major catastrophe' and Edward Schafer pointed out it was death-related. David Keightley noted in his 1978 *Sources of Shang History*, p 40, n64, that this particular prognostication word, the standard *Yijing* notation for 'inauspicious', does not appear in the Shang oracle-bone inscriptions. Wilhelm-Baynes translates it as 'misfortune'.

55   I no longer give credence to the traditional idea that the line texts were written after the judgment texts. In my view, both texts took shape simultaneously, hexagram 55 being a case in point.

56   A photograph of the He *zun* and its inscription appears in Hsu and Linduff's *Western Chou Civilization*, pp 96–98. In Wilhelm-Baynes, the 'jug' in hexagram 29/4 is specifically a *zun*.

57   Nienhauser, *The Grand Scribe's Records*, Vol. I, p 59.

58   I have translated *fu* as 'verification' following its usage in the *Book of Documents* (Karlgren's *GSR* entry 1233a); this is in preference to the blanket-reading of the character as 'captives' by the modernists. The last section of the line could alternatively be translated: 'Fa trusted in accordance with the auspicious omen.' Given the parallels between the fall of the Xia and Shang dynasties pointed out in the final note of Chapter III, it is worth recalling that the end of the Xia is presaged in solar myths. One myth is recorded in the *Bowu Zhi*, or *The Treatise on Research into Nature*, which originates from about the fourth century AD. A clansman of King Jie, the last Xia ruler, was travelling by the river one day when he observed two suns in the sky, one rising brilliantly in the east, the other sinking with fading light in the west, and he heard a sudden clap of thunder. He asked a soothsayer: 'Which sun is the Yin, which the Xia?' The soothsayer interpreted the observation as an omen of the ascendancy of the Yin and the decline of the Xia: 'The one in the west is the Xia, in the east the Yin.' On hearing this, the clansman changed loyalties and took his tribe over to the Yin. This story ironically echoes King Jie's blasphemous oath,

found in the *Tang Shi*, 'The Harangue of Tang', a chapter of the *Documents*. King Jie, displeased that his people did not approve of his indiscriminate massacres (in one source he lets loose tigers in the marketplace to amuse himself watching the people's terror), tempts fate by arrogantly swearing: 'When that sun dies, you and I, we'll all perish!' See Birrell, *op. cit*, pp 108–110; the *Bowu Zhi* has been translated by Roger Greatrex, see p 140 of that work. The sense of Birrell's translation of this section of the *Tang Shi*, which I have favoured above, differs from that of Legge and Karlgren. Legge has the people speaking, not Jie: 'When wilt thou, O sun, expire? We will all perish with thee.' Karlgren, strangely for him given his familiarity with Chinese legends, misses the point by translating *ri* not as 'sun' but as 'daily', and also appears to have the people speaking: 'That one (*i.e.* Jie) daily injures and destroys, you and I shall all together perish.' *Mencius* 1A/2 quotes this part of the *Tang Shi*, in D C Lau's translation: 'O Sun, when wilt thou perish? We care not if we have to die with thee.' Here again the people are speaking, not King Jie. Lau explains that the 'sun' is synonymous with Jie himself, whom the people did not dare name openly. He provides in a footnote a quotation from the *Han Shi Wai Zhuan* 2/22, in which Jie is said to have remarked: 'My possession of the Empire is like there being a sun in Heaven. Is there a time when the sun will perish? If the sun perishes, then I shall perish.'

Chapter VII – Battling in the Wilds

1 From Chapter 12 of the *Huainanzi*, compiled in 139BC. See Morgan, *Tao: The Great Luminant*, p 140.

2 The character translated in the *Zhouyi* as 'to cross', *she*, specifically means 'to ford a stream', *i.e.* to *wade* across rather than use boats. Chapter 6 of the *Huainanzi* preserves a folkloric fragment about King Wu crossing the great water at the Fords of Meng in which the river god tries to oppose his passage by whipping up strong waves and a fierce wind. The sky turns pitch black, horses and men cannot see each other. King Wu brandishes his yellow battle-axe in his left hand and the white ensign in his right, glaring ferociously as he demands: 'I have been entrusted with the protection of the world. Who dares oppose my will?' Whereupon the winds die down and the waves subside. See Birrell, *Chinese Mythology*, p 262, and Le Blanc, *Huai-nan Tzu: Philosophical Synthesis in Early Han Thought*, pp 104–105.

3 The basic threads of the story in this chapter have been picked up from the *Shi Ji* of Sima Qian. Details have been woven in from other sources as specified.

4   *Mencius* 7B/4 says King Wu marched on Yin with 300 war chariots
    and 3,000 braves, not mentioning the 45,000 troops. The *Mozi* just
    mentions 100 chariots and 400 braves (Watson, *Basic Writings of Mo
    Tzu*, p 106).
5   The personal name of Zhou Xin.
6   This sentence is Karlgren's translation. Legge has 'follows the words
    of his wife'. The character *fu* means 'a wife; a lady; a woman' and is
    generally supposed to allude to Da Ji. *Fu* is followed by *yan*, however,
    and *fuyan* is 'women's conversation'. The sentence may simply be
    intended as an insult, 'he only listens to women's conversation'.
7   The concept of measured constraint described here is said to be a
    strategy of King Wu's general, Taigong; it features in the fourth
    century BC military classic *Sima Fa*, which has been translated by
    Ralph D Sawyer in *The Seven Military Classics of Ancient China*.
    Legge feels that King Wu is admonishing his men, 'lest they should
    be hurried on in their rage by a desire for slaughter' (*Chinese Classics*,
    Vol. III, p 304). A late Tang work of military strategy, *Questions and
    Replies Between Tang Taizong and Li Weigong*, claims Taigong
    established a training ground before the Conquest to teach battle
    tactics to 300 'tiger braves', where they practised advancing 'six paces,
    seven paces' and making 'six attacks, seven attacks'. As a result, when
    Taigong deployed the army at Muye, he needed just 100 officers to
    control the field and defeat King Zhou's far larger army. See Sawyer,
    op. cit, p 328.
8   The 'leopard' here is *pi*, rather than the more usual *bao*. *Pi* is defined
    in Mathews' dictionary as either a white fox or a kind of leopard. It
    seems to have been the male of a fabulous fierce beast like a
    leopard—used to describe brave troops. Compare 'be like tigers, like
    leopards' to the fifth and sixth lines of hexagram 49, containing the
    expressions *hu bian* and *bao bian*, 'tiger change' and 'leopard change',
    respectively. The 3,000 'tiger braves' in King Wu's army are the
    huben, which has sometimes been translated as 'palace guards'.
    Possibly they wore tiger pelts. After the Conquest, according to the
    Li Ji, the *Record of Rites*, King Wu wrapped up the shields and spears
    of his army in tiger pelts and made it known he would no more have
    recourse to weapons of war (Legge, *The Sacred Books of China*, Part
    IV, p 124).
9   Creel, *The Origins of Statecraft in China*, pp 455–456.
10 In Wilhelm-Baynes, the 'two small bowls for the sacrifice' in the
    judgment of hexagram 41 are specifically *gui* vessels, as is the 'bowl'
    in hexagram 29/4.
11 A photograph of the Li *gui* and its inscription appears in Hsu and
    Linduff's *Western Chou Civilization*, pp 94–96. These authors
    believe that a problematic section of the inscription refers to a

divination that Li is thought to have made for King Wu. The auspiciousness of it encouraged Wu to launch his attack, hence the reward of bronze. Edward Shaughnessy discusses the seven vague characters of the inscription in *Sources of Western Zhou History*, pp 87–105.

12 Sawyer, *op. cit*, p 64.

13 Wilhelm-Baynes provides an interpretation rather than a translation, ignoring *jia* as a day-name in order to draw out of it a general understandable meaning for the non-sinologist. Hence *jia* becomes 'the starting point' because it is the first day of the *xun*, or ancient ten-day week. This of course has severely limited understanding of hexagram 18, about which I write more in Chapter XII.

14 The reader is referred to Appendix IV, 'The sexagenary cycle', to get a better idea of these 60 days. There are 60 days rather than 120 days because even stems can only be paired with even branches and odd stems with odd branches. Derek Walters provides an introduction to stems and branches in his *Chinese Astrology*.

15 This is also stated in the spurious *Wu Cheng* chapter of the *Documents*. This passage, unfortunately, was not quoted by Mencius (who quoted other sections of the original *Wu Cheng*), or, to my knowledge, any other early author before Sima Qian.

16 Wilhelm, 'I-Ching Oracles in the *Tso-Chuan* and the *Kuo-Yu*', p 276. It is impossible to know for sure whether *she he* was the original wording. The diviner in the *Zuo* could have read *da chuan* in the text before him and simply translated it to the situation he was divining about as 'the He'. For translations of the relevant section of the *Zuozhuan*, see Legge, *Chinese Classics*, Vol. V, p 167, and Rutt, *Zhouyi*, pp 179–180.

17 Wilhelm-Baynes again attempts to make what is essentially nomenclature generally appreciable by translating the *geng* stem-name: 'Before the change, three days. After the change, three days.' Richard Wilhelm's interpretation of *geng* and *jia* is anachronistic and misleading (p 684 and pp 477–479, respectively, in the 3rd edition of his *I Ching*). He explains them over-ingeniously in terms of trigrams and seasons, missing their original and simple meanings as day-names. For further details on the translation of *geng* as 'change', see Bodde, *Essays in Chinese Civilization*, p 378.

18 Richard M W Ho discusses these stem-name expressions in hexagrams 18 and 57 in his article 'Where Cross-Fertilization Fails: A Short Critique of the Wilhelm/Baynes Translation of the *Book of Changes*'. He not unreasonably supposed that the third day after *geng* was meant, *i.e. gui*, the last day of the ten-day week. Similarly, he takes *ding* as the third day after *jia*, rather than taking the next day, *wu*, the day after three whole days have passed. This is also how it was

interpreted in the Han dynasty. See the quotation of the judgment of hexagram 18 in the *Han Shu*, 6/21a, under the year 112BC (Dubs, *The History of the Former Han Dynasty*, Vol. II, p 78). In the Han, sacrifices were offered on *xin* and *ding* days, *i.e.* the third day before and after *jia*, respectively. Apparently, this was based on hexagram 18. But it begs the question: why name *jia*? In the final period of the Shang dynasty the ancestors received sacrifices on the day of the ten-day week corresponding to their stem-name; Father Jia would be sacrificed to on a *jia* day, for instance, Father Geng on a *geng* day. Naming a stem-day, therefore, suggests that it is the day of the sacrifice. By the Han this understanding of hexagram 18 appears to have been lost. For the three days before the named day, ritual preparation probably took place, such as the vegetarian regime suggested by the *Liu Tao*.

19   This is the most convincing example that moving-line relationships to the second hexagram were to some extent 'worked out', as opposed to simply being an accident of chance (bearing in mind what Heraclitus said: 'The fairest order in the world is a heap of random sweepings.').

20   Ode 180 describes a hunt in which three types of game are caught, deer, boar, and wild ox.

21   Wilhelm-Baynes translates *tongren* as 'fellowship with men', Richard Rutt has 'mustering men'; I favour 'fellow-countrymen' or 'compatriots', or even 'confederates'. In modern Chinese *tongren* means 'colleagues' and 'person of same belief/conviction'.

22   Legge translated the title of this chapter as 'The Successful Completion of the War', in accordance with traditional commentaries, which I have also followed above with the more literal 'Military Completion'. But it must be pointed out that the character *wu* of *Wu Cheng* is the same character as in King Wu, the 'Military King', whereas *cheng* is the same character as the name of the son who succeeded him, King Cheng, the 'Completing King'. Tang, who brought down the Xia dynasty to found the Shang, was called Cheng Tang, 'Tang the Completer'. The title of the *Wu Cheng* chapter, I suspect, should really be translated as 'Wu Completes' (*i.e.* the Conquest), or 'Wu's Completion'.

23   *Mencius* 3B/5. In the 'five elements' theory from the Warring States period yellow became the colour of earth and black that of heaven. On this basis, following traditional commentaries, Richard Wilhelm identified yellow with the false earthly dragon and black with the true heavenly dragon. When dragons did battle it was an omen portending disorder, war, and even the fall of the dynasty. There are a number of reports of dragons fighting in early Chinese annals that appear to be intended quite literally. See, for instance, de Visser, *The Dragon in China and Japan*, which collects together much of the folklore of

dragons. De Visser saw the top line of hexagram 2 as a meteorological omen. He claims that when black storm-clouds gathered against a yellow-tinged sky, with violent thunder and lightning, the ancient Chinese would say: 'The dragons are fighting; look at their blood spreading over the sky.' See also Chapter XIII, 'Clouds follow the dragon', where I interpret the dragon of hexagram 1 in terms of rain magic. Yellow and black, oddly enough, are the only colours mentioned in the Shang oracle-bone inscriptions.

24 Ode 118 mentions that soldiers lived in dread of the arrival of 'those bamboo slips', on which was written the king's command.

25 The character *zheng* used in this line specifically refers to soldiers going away on a military expedition, Wilhelm-Baynes masks this context by simply translating it as 'goes forth'.

26 Waley, 'The Book of Changes', pp 128–129. See also Shaughnessy, 'Marriage, Divorce, and Revolution: Reading Between the Lines of the *Book of Changes*'.

27 The character *zheng* is used here to describe troops on a military expedition, just as in hexagram 53/3.

28 See Situ Tan, *Popular Chinese Idioms*, Vol. 2, pp 82–83, for the love story of the broken mirror.

29 Ode 236 says that at Muye 'The cohorts of Shang were massed like a forest', Karlgren's translation. Waley's version says that the *catapults* of Yin-Shang 'were like the trees of a forest'.

30 Though the figure of 700,000 Shang troops is likely to be an exaggeration, it is nonetheless true that the Zhou would have been vastly outnumbered, as they did not control as large a population as the Shang. Archaeological excavations have determined, however, that the Zhou at the time of the Conquest were military innovators, having recently manufactured bronze swords, bronze helmets, and bronze armour, which, though heavy, allowed considerable freedom of movement. The Shang did not have the sword, only short bronze daggers; their armour was made of rawhide and greatly restricted movement. Given that the Shang had extensive bronze-casting capabilities, it is tempting to consider that the Zhou may have kept their new weaponry secret until the Conquest. Both sides possessed bows, shields, axes, chariots, and halberds, though the Zhou halberds were better designed for striking. Percussion instruments such as drums, gongs, and cymbals were also used for signalling, along with flags.

31 Ancient books were written on thin strips of bamboo tied together with string or leather, which were rolled up when not in use.

32 *Mencius* 7B/3. Translation based on Fung Yu-lan/Bodde, *A History of Chinese Philosophy*, Vol. I, p 109, and D C Lau.

33 *Dazhuan*, II, II, 9.

34 Small details such as this have a strangely poetic intensity. Compare
   the report in the *Zuozhuan*, when, in 597BC, the Jin soldiers were
   fleeing the army of Chu. They made for the boats to escape across the
   river, but there weren't enough. Those who got in first pushed off,
   hacking at the fingers of their compatriots attempting to board—
   'fingers could be scooped up by the double handful'.
35 *Lunheng* 7.14b–16a.
36 I find Legge's explanation, that the pestles were carried by the
   soldiers for preparing their rice rations, unconvincing (*Chinese
   Classics*, Vol. III, p 315). The actual phrase used in the *Wu Cheng*
   is *xue liu piao chu*, literally 'the bloodshed floated pestles', which one
   can today find in the dictionary as an idiom used for describing a
   dreadful carnage. The mortars, though not actually mentioned as
   such, are an assumption by Fung Yu-lan/Bodde, *op. cit*, p 109, which
   I have followed. It seems to make sense that the only way the pestles
   could have floated is if the blood collected in the mortars; I cannot
   imagine that the battlefield was ankle-deep in blood overall.
37 King Zhou's jade suit may have been like the one made for Prince Liu
   Sheng in the second century BC, exhibited at the British Museum in
   1996. A photograph appears in the exhibition catalogue, *Mysteries of
   Ancient China*, edited by Jessica Rawson, pp 170–171. This suit
   consists of 2,498 small rectangular plaques of jade pierced at each
   corner and sewn together with knots of gold wire. Jade is linked with
   immortality; it is generally thought that such suits were intended to
   preserve the bodies of their owners. Jade plugs were also made as
   stoppers for all the bodily orifices.
38 Watson, *Basic Writings of Hsun Tzu*, p 63. Xunzi says the expression
   'Zhou, the lone commoner' comes from the *Tai Shi* chapter of the
   Documents, the original now lost.
39 *Mencius* 7B/4. D C Lau's translation.
40 According to the *Shi Ji*, King Wu's sword was called *qinglu*, a name
   that is associated with sword worship in the steppes (Hsu and
   Linduff, *Western Chou Civilization*, p 81). This detail, however, is
   anachronistic to the time of the Conquest, it being unlikely this type
   of sword was introduced into China much before 300BC.
41 Watson, *op. cit*, p 123.
42 Watson, *Basic Writings of Mo Tzu*, p 107.
43 Nienhauser, *The Grand Scribe's Records*, Vol. I, p 52.
44 *Ibid.*, pp 61–62.
45 Legge, *Chinese Classics*, Vol. III, p 351.
46 See Appendix II.
47 Compare hexagram 16/5: 'Divining about illness: he will prevail, he
   won't die.'
48 Creel, *op. cit*, pp 457–458. See also *Mencius* 2B/9.

49 Jizi's response can be found in the *Hong Fan* or 'Great Plan' chapter of the *Book of Documents*. In the *Weizi* chapter of the *Documents* the Viscount of Ji had said that he would not serve the new dynasty when the House of Yin fell (see Chapter III). When King Wu released him from the tyrant's prison, Jizi refused to acknowledge his sovereignty and went into voluntary exile. King Wu respected his decision and did not treat him as a subject. Later King Wu sought to learn from Jizi the principles of government that had been passed down at the Shang court. The *Hong Fan*, containing this counsel, is an invention of the Warring States period. According to Sima Qian, when King Wu asked why Yin had been destroyed Jizi became so emotional he could not bear to speak of it. King Wu was embarrassed and instead asked about statecraft.

50 Sima Qian states Jizi paid homage to the Zhou, but this appears to have been a formality because he had accepted the fief in Korea, it should not be supposed he had gone back on his vow not to serve the new House.

51 Richard Rutt says that the story of the Viscount of Ji is no longer believed in Korea (personal communication, February 18, 1998).

52 In later literature the Shang capital after the Conquest became known as Yinxu, the 'Ruins of Yin'. This is the way Sima Qian refers to it. The character *xu*, however, is only ever translated as 'ruins' in this context. Primarily it means 'empty'. *Xu* appears once in the *Zhouyi*, in the third line of hexagram 46: 'Going up to the empty city.' I am inclined to think, therefore, that the 'empty city', one of the more haunting images in the *Book of Changes*, is almost certainly a reference to the abandoned ruins of Dayi Shang, 'Great City Shang'.

53 This episode is recorded in *Shi Ji* 38, the 'Hereditary House of Song'. See Chavannes, *Les mémoires historiques de Se-ma Ts'ien*, Vol. 4, pp 230–231. Chavannes translates the poem as follows:

> *Le blé en fleurs est tout humecté (de sève);*
> *Les céréales et le millet sont tout luisants (de prospérité);*
> *Ce garçon trompeur—n'a pas été bon pour moi.*

Chavannes pointed out that the expression '*ce garçon trompeur*/the deceitful boy' also occurs in ode 84 of the *Shijing*.

54 See 'The Parable of the Tares' in *Matthew* 13, v24–30.

55 *Grammata Serica Recensa*, entry 1181a.

56 Keightley, *Sources of Shang History*, p 38.

57 In 1983 the oracle-bone scholar Kenichi Takashima, who writes lengthy and extremely technical papers on single oracle-bone characters, said a startling thing in passing in a letter to *Early China* 9–10. He plainly admitted that he still failed to understand the judgment of hexagram 4. Takashima was responding to an article in

the same issue by the Western authority on the Shang oracle-bones, David N Keightley, who had translated the aforementioned passage as: 'It is not I who seeks the young fool, the young fool seeks me. When he first divines by stalks (the spirits) make report. But two or three times would be troublesome; and if he is troublesome, then they do not make report.' Takashima pointed out that 'much more precision is required in terms of grammar and semantics in the *Yijing* as a whole than is given by Keightley'. The character *gao*, 'report', highlighted by Keightley, is not straightforward. Keightley believed that the 'report' may have referred to the sounds produced by the cracking of an oracle-bone; that the word *gao*, common in the Shang inscriptions, may have been used for its onomatopoeic appropriateness. See Keightley's paper 'Reports from the Shang: A Corroboration and Some Speculation', and the 1955 paper by Wu Shi-ch'ang, 'On the Marginal Notes Found in Oracle Bone Inscriptions'. A further difficulty is that in modernist readings hexagram 4 is regarded as referring to the epiphytic dodder plant, a sacred plant like mistletoe in that it grows without the aid of roots (see entry 6116d–1 in Mathews' Dictionary, *tangmeng*, 'dodder'). Arthur Waley felt that the judgment was a magic spell for averting the dire consequences of tampering with the holy plant: 'It is not I who sought the stripling dodder; the stripling dodder sought me.' Certain plants reputed to have chthonic powers were tabooed in many early societies. See Waley's 1933 essay 'The Book of Changes', pp 130–131. Both Richard Rutt and Richard Kunst follow this reading in their translations of the *Zhouyi*. While this interpretation is certainly one of Waley's most fascinating ideas, it takes no account of the presence of the character *gao*, which appears to derive from the terminology of oracle-bone divination. (Though admittedly Waley's interpretation relies upon the idea that a peasant omen-text and a more sophisticated divination text, which were originally two separate works, have somehow become fused together.) Of further interest is the character *shi* used in the judgment, which specifically refers to divining by yarrow stalks rather than the tortoise. The implication from the use of *gao* appears to be that the words of the judgment were carried over from tortoise divination, but the presence of *shi* suggests it was slightly re-phrased for insertion in the *Zhouyi* at a later time. Hence the judgment of hexagram 4 probably represents an oral tradition of the story of King Zhou, 'the deceitful boy' with whom the oracle would no longer co-operate, being written down for the first time as a generalised idea, the original allusion being widely known at the time, but lost to history except for the reference in Jizi's poem, from which I have been able to reconstruct it. It does of course remain an interpretation, but not, I think, an unenlightening one; whereas the dodder interpretation leaves one wondering what relevance it has to the last part of the judgment about divining a second or third time, a question neither Waley nor his more recent followers have addressed. Note that Keightley does not adhere to modernist readings with his translation of 'the young fool'.

Chapter IX – The *mingyi* bird

1 Legge, *Chinese Classics*, Vol. V, p 604.
2 Waley, 'The Book of Changes', pp 127–128.
3 Liu Dajun and Lin Zhongjun, *The I Ching: Text and Annotated Translation*, pp 78–80.
4 Whincup, *Rediscovering the I Ching*, pp 125–127. There is a relationship between the Yin bone forms of the characters. See entry 560g in Karlgren's *Grammata Serica Recensa*.
5 Wilhelm-Baynes *I Ching*, p 566 in the 3rd edition. For various modernist interpretations of hexagram 36 see Shaughnessy's PhD dissertation, pp 221–227; Rutt, *Zhouyi*, pp 328–330; Sivin, *HJAS* 26 (1966), pp 290–298.
6 de Fancourt, *Warp and Weft*, p 29.
7 I happened to notice in the notes to Roger Greatrex's translation of *The Bowu Zhi*, p 226, n3, that the name Jizi has been mistakenly read as *qi zi*, 'his son'.
8 Presumably this association was made because of the reference to 'not eating' in the first line. Bo Yi and his brother Shu Qi starved themselves to death in protest against the Conquest, see Chapter VI.
9 See Chapter III. Bi Gan, who had his heart cut out by Zhou Xin, might be a more apt association than the Viscount of Wei, given the reference in this line to entering the left side of the belly and taking the heart.
10 The *Tang Shu* contains a number of examples, which are discussed briefly by Schafer in *Pacing the Void*.
11 An alternative translation may be made of hexagram 36/6 that is more suggestive of a solar eclipse: 'Not bright, dark. First ascending in the sky, later entering into the earth.'
12 This bird omen is reminiscent of the storks of Aquileia, which left their nests shortly before the city was taken and burned by the Huns.
13 Watson, *Basic Writings of Mo Tzu*, p 57.
14 Hellmut Wilhelm felt that three words had dropped out of the *Zuozhuan* text, and that the hexagram arrived at on this occasion was not an unchanging Fu but Mingyi changing into Fu, *i.e.* the third line of hexagram 36 changing to hexagram 24. In other words, that the quoted text was an alternative version of 36/3. See his essay 'I-Ching Oracles in the *Tso-Chuan* and the *Kuo-Yu*', p 276.

15 In simple terms, the radicals (usually 214 of them) are familiar
    elements that constantly recur throughout Chinese characters,
    forming pigeon-holes by means of which characters may be located
    in a dictionary if one does not know how the character is romanised in
    pinyin. ('Radical' is a misnomer, it wrongly conveys the impression it
    is an etymological root. Nonetheless, the word is still widely used and
    so I retain it here. The terms 'signific', 'classifier', 'determinative',
    and 'semantic element' are also used.) Broadly speaking, characters
    that take the 'water' radical, for instance, are often something to do
    with liquids, those that take the 'heart' radical tend to appear in words
    to do with the emotions, plant names usually carry the 'grass' radical,
    insects have the 'insect' radical. This is best thought of, however, as a
    rough guide to the scope of a large number of characters, rather than
    an infallible rule, as many characters dealing with more abstract
    matters cannot be so simply categorised. In addition, characters
    borrowed for their sound no longer conform to the rule. In other
    words: just because a character has the 'grass' radical doesn't mean it
    is definitely a plant, but plants often have the grass radical.
        The interpretation for sense of hexagram 33 as a 'sucking pig'
    instead of 'retreat' depends upon dropping an erroneously supplied
    radical. This manner of character 'substitution' is perfectly acceptable
    in that it is not strictly a 'replacement': it was the style of ancient
    Chinese writing to make little use of radicals and sometimes the
    wrong one was supplied when texts were later copied by scribes. This
    is a process that to some extent is still going on. In hexagram 31, for
    instance, Arthur Waley supplies the heart radical to the title, making
    it 'feelings', interpreting the hexagram to be about the category of
    omens derived from involuntary tingling sensations in the body that
    mean something, *e.g.* when your ears are burning it means someone is
    talking about you behind your back ('The Book of Changes', p 123).
    The test of restoring a potentially dropped radical, or supposing a
    radical has been incorrectly supplied and so dropping it again or
    changing it, ultimately depends on whether the resultant interpreta-
    tion can make sense of things previously senseless. In the top line of
    hexagram 33, for instance, *fei dun* is translated in Wilhelm-Baynes as
    'cheerful retreat'. But this is a forced translation because *fei* actually
    means 'fat, plump', and, as Waley points out, this really does clinch
    the matter because what is a 'fat retreat'? The simpler interpretation
    is that originally the hexagram was about a sucking pig being fattened
    up, the other lines also fitting this reading. It must not be forgotten, of
    course, that hexagram 33 has been read as 'retreat, withdrawal' for a
    very long time. Wang Bi (AD226–249) read it this way, as did Zhu Xi
    in the Song. Zhu Xi, who wrote extensively on the *Yijing*, appears to
    have rarely consulted it to resolve personal matters. There is only one

instance on record, where, after receiving hexagram 33, Zhu Xi decided not to submit a controversial memorial to the Emperor but instead chose to retire from public office, whereupon he became known as 'The Old Man Who Has Withdrawn' (Smith *et al.*, *Sung Dynasty Uses of the I Ching*, p 205).

16 See Chapter VI for the evidence that a tortoise shell was cracked in hexagram 55.

17 See, for instance, Hsu and Linduff, *Western Chou Civilization*, p 93. In the third century BC *Liu Tao, Six Scabbards*, the military strategist Taigong advises King Wu: 'If you wish to take the western flank, attack the eastern one.' See Sawyer, *The Seven Military Classics of Ancient China*, p 52.

18 Translation based on Legge, *Chinese Classics*, Vol. III, p 292. Legge missed the name of the Yi tribe in the *Tai Shi*, translating it as 'ordinary men' according to one of the meanings of *yi* mentioned earlier. No-one appears to have noticed before that there is a meeting with the Lord of the Yi tribe in hexagram 55/4. Wilhelm-Baynes translates the sentence as meeting a ruler 'of like kind'; Legge also has 'like himself'; Wu Jing-Nuan has a meeting with a 'pleased' lord; Kunst has a meeting with an 'ordinary' master; Rutt has meeting the master 'now'; Whincup has meeting a 'true' lord. None of these renderings of *yi* seem particularly meaningful.

19 See entry 760e in Karlgren's *Grammata Serica Recensa*.

20 *Mencius* 4B/1 says 'King Wen was a West Barbarian'.

21 The character for 'east', *dong*, where the sun rises, is a pictograph of the sun in a tree.

22 Anne Birrell has collected together the myths of Yi the Archer in Chapter 7 of her *Chinese Mythology*. Wolfram Eberhard discusses Yi the Archer in Chain 6 of his *Local Cultures of South and East China*, as does Derk Bodde in his essay 'Myths of Ancient China'.

23 Personal communication, April 10, 1996.

24 Field, *Tian Wen: A Chinese Book of Origins*.

25 Hawkes, *The Songs of the South*, p 129. Hawkes tries to guess a solution to the riddle: 'Perhaps their feathers were meteorites.'

26 Karlgren omitted the question mark. See 'Legends and Cults in Ancient China', pp 268–269. Notice that Karlgren has 'shoot at' not 'shoot down'.

27 Needham, *Science and Civilization in China*, Vol. III, p 411(a). *Tian Wen l.*56 is the *locus classicus* for the idea a crow lives in the sun, though it does not mention that it had three legs. In the Han the moon acquired a three-legged toad that was believed to be responsible for lunar eclipses (*Huainanzi*, Chapter 7).

28 Such beliefs still exist. As recently as 1974, during a lunar eclipse, 16 people were killed in the Cambodian capital, Phnom Penh, when

soldiers fired guns to scare off what they believed was a monkey eating the moon.

Chapter X – Melons, willows, hoarfrost, and creepers

1 'Bride abduction' has already been mentioned in Chapter III, n18.
2 Karlgren, *The Book of Odes*, p 67.
3 The translation of *bao* as 'tank' in lines 2 and 4 in Wilhelm-Baynes is incorrect. Wilhelm originally translated *bao* as *Behälter* in lines 2 and 4, meaning 'container', and Cary F Baynes presumably thought of a fish tank. Legge's translation of 44/4 conjures up a surreal image: 'The fourth line, undivided, shows its subject with his wallet, but no fish in it.' Wang Bi (AD226–249) glosses *bao* as *chu*, 'kitchen', in lines 2 and 4.
4 *Grammata Serica Recensa*, entry 1113a; Wieger, *Chinese Characters*, p 144.
5 Eberhard, *Local Cultures of South and East China*, p 281; Schafer, *Pacing the Void*, p 147.
6 There are a number of versions of the story. See, for instance, Wolfram Eberhard's telling of it in his *Chinese Festivals*.
7 River goddesses were drowned girls who subsequently attracted a cult and became deified. Slave-girls and concubines were sacrificed to the river, He, in Shang times. Later the river god, Hebo, the Earl or Elder of the Yellow River, each year demanded a 'bride', the last form of human sacrifice to be prohibited in China, as late as the third century BC. (See Waley, *The Nine Songs*, pp 47–52; also Whalen Lai's study of 'Mr Ho Po' in *History of Religions* 29/4, May 1990, pp 335–350.) A personal sacrifice was made to Hebo by nobles who wished to 'cross the great water'; a jade ring or an embroidered cap might be tossed into the water to ensure a safe crossing. Peasants, who could not afford such luxuries, hoped to placate Hebo with an annual bride, who was actually dressed up as if for her wedding and launched on the treacherous river on a raft decked out to resemble a bridal bed. She would float downriver ten miles or so before sinking, whereupon she was 'wedded' to Hebo. Even in the early years of the twentieth century anyone in danger of drowning in the Yangtze could not expect to be rescued by local sampan men, lest the river god, Lord Yang, take revenge for being cheated of his accidental sacrifice (personal observation of C P Fitzgerald, *China: A Short Cultural History*, p 52).
8 See Maspero, *China in Antiquity*, pp 76–77.
9 Different characters are used for 'willow'; hexagram 44 has *qi*, hexagram 28 *yang* (which Wilhelm-Baynes translates as 'poplar').
10 Waley, 'The Book of Changes', p 129.

11 A more sexually explicit interpretation of 'a melon wrapped with willow' might be advanced. In Chinese poetry 'in depths of willow shade' means a woman's pubic hair. 'Floating alone on the orchid boat', to give another example of this genre, is clitoral self-stimulation (see Rexroth, *Love and the Turning Year*, p 95). I mention these ideas not because I actually think 'a melon wrapped with willow' is intended in hexagram 44 to be a reference to the vulva, but rather to avoid the potential embarrassment of the classical scholar who wrote a learned and philosophical treatise on an obscure sentence in an ancient Chinese text without realising it was actually a sexual position. Even 'clouds and rain' and 'shooting pheasants' can have sexual connotations, the former referring to the sexual act itself and the latter being a quaint euphemism for visiting low-class brothels. 'Fish-trap' is also used as a metaphor and rebus for the vagina. The peach, pomegranate, peony, and lotus have all been used in Chinese literature to designate the vulva in addition to the melon. The expression *pogua*, 'the broken melon', means a girl who has reached womanhood. Chinese commentators explain this to mean 'the character *gua* broken in two'. *Gua*, 'melon', can be read as two *ba*, 'eight', placed side by side, and two eights are sixteen, the marriageable age for a girl. In van Gulik's opinion, however, this is a secondary explanation: he suggests *pogua* originally just meant 'broken red melon', an image of a girl's first menstruation, or a virgin's defloration (van Gulik, *Sexual Life in Ancient China*, p 275). While sexual interpretations can lead to reading all manner of things into a text, it is well to remember that in this case hexagram 44 is actually entitled 'Copulation'. (A somewhat unusual interpretation of 'a melon wrapped with willow' has been proposed by the modernist scholar Liu Dajun, who believes it is a UFO sighting. See *The I Ching: Text and Annotated Translation*, p 97.)

12 Marcel Granet has convincingly shown in *Festivals and Songs of Ancient China* (1919) that there existed a courtship festival held on the banks of rivers in the spring; young men and women from different villages lined up on opposite sides of the river singing songs to each other, the women tempting the men to make the crossing. Granet showed that this custom explained a number of odes that had previously been poorly understood and overlaid with all manner of absurd political allegories. Men would brave the rapids hopping from rock to rock to reach the girl of their choice, sometimes getting stranded because the river was in spate due to the spring thaw. Successful unions would result in betrothal, with marriage in the autumn. (Note that both hexagrams 28 and 44 have river settings, the top line of hexagram 28 mentioning a drowning.)

13 Eberhard, *Local Cultures*, p 119.

14   Chow Tse-tung discusses the context of the expression 'stepping on hoarfrost' in the *Shijing*, and its use in hexagram 2/1, in 'The Childbirth Myth and Ancient Chinese Medicine: A Study of Aspects of the *Wu* Tradition.'

15   King Wen went to meet his bride at the river. See Appendix II.

16   On the winter seclusion, see Maspero, *op. cit*, pp 70–72, and ode 154, where a cricket under the bed is a sign it is time to shut up the house for the winter.

17   Wilhelm-Baynes has 'leans on' thorns; literally it is 'to take into the hands'. *Xiong*, which I have usually translated as 'disastrous' when a line resembles an oracle-bone divination, I here translate as 'sorrow'. Wilhelm-Baynes has 'misfortune'.

18   Possibly he has spent three years in the 'dark valley' mentioned in hexagram 47/1, which might have been a prison.

Chapter XI – King Wen is fed his own son

1   These novels have been translated under the titles *The Water Margin* and *The Dream of the Red Chamber*, respectively.

2   I have already mentioned in the notes to Chapter III that *l*.157 of the fourth century BC *Tian Wen* may allude to King Wen being fed Yi Kao, rather than to King Zhou sending Chang the 'sliced and salted' flesh of Mei Bo, referred to in *l*.148. Stephen Field clearly thought so, he translated the line: 'Zhou served Chang a Thyestean stew, so the Western Duke appealed to Heaven.' (Field, *Tian Wen: A Chinese Book of Origins*.)

3   In this fictional account King Wen was imprisoned because he had dared to admonish the tyrant at the Shang court, having divined beforehand the consequences of doing what he regarded as his duty. The only reason he wasn't immediately executed, like others before him, was because all the palace officials pleaded with King Zhou to spare his life.

4   Though it is doubtful that a sexual connotation was intended, it might be noted that 'plucking the strings of the zither' has a rather colourful meaning in manuals on 'the art of the bedchamber'.

5   One gets the impression that Da Ji would have said this no matter what Yi Kao played, that this was the purpose of the exercise.

6   In the *Wu Wang Fa Zhou Binghua* it is autumn and some falling elm leaves float into King Wen's cell, which he uses instead of coins to perform the divination.

Chapter XII – The curse of the ancestors

1   One can today in China buy tee-shirts with the five poisonous animals embroidered on them.

2 Feng and Shryock, 'The Black Magic in China Known as *Ku*'. Particularly fascinating is the genre of 'golden caterpillar' tales. A man finds riches left in a basket in the street, which he naturally takes home, only to discover he has also 'willingly' taken the dreaded *jincan*, the golden caterpillar. The only way he can rid himself of this evil spirit is to leave out the basket in the street again, but with far more riches in it than he found. If he hasn't the means, he is fated to a life as a murderer to satisfy the spirit, which rewards him handsomely for these deeds. There are occasional examples of a poor virtuous man eating the golden caterpillar fully prepared to die rather than succumb to its noxious influence, but suffering no ill effects, providing the clear moral lesson that good triumphs over evil. Presumably the underlying message of these tales is to be happy with one's lot and not to wish for sudden wealth, for one never knows what it may entail. *Gu* stories are written as if they actually happened. Wolfram Eberhard has written about later *gu* practices in Chain 14 of his *Local Cultures of South and East China*. Also see de Groot, *The Religious System of China*, Vol. V, pp 826–861; Schafer, *The Vermilion Bird*, pp 102–103. The signs of *gu* poisoning are described in hideous detail in a thirteenth century manual of forensic medicine, see Sung Tz'u, *The Washing Away of Wrongs*, p 136. This shows *gu* was not merely the stuff of folklore. Nathan Sivin in *Chinese Alchemy*, p 302, speculates that *gu* poisoning could be schistosomiasis.

3 Waley, 'The Book of Changes', p 132. Waley derived his maggots in a carcass from the idea of worms in a vessel. Richard Rutt, thinking around the hexagram in a similar way, conceived the idea that *gu* may be mildew appearing on wooden ancestral tablets, as an ominous sign (*Zhouyi*, p 312). 'Mildew', however, is based on the later meaning of *gu* as 'decay' and has no relation to the original graph of worms or snakes in a vessel.

4 Entry 52b in Karlgren's *Grammata Serica Recensa*. Also see Allan, *The Shape of the Turtle*, p 163.

5 According to the *Record of Accounts of Marvels*, the *Shu Yi Ji* of Ren Fang (AD460–508), the dragon evolved from a water-viper (de Visser, *The Dragon in China and Japan*, p 72). In Shang bronze art the earliest representations of the dragon show a serpent with horns, an identification that is particularly apparent from round ritual washing basins (*pan*) where the horned dragon is coiled on the inside like a snake. See Chapter XIII, 'Clouds follow the dragon', for a discussion of the dragon of hexagram 1.

6 Allan, *op. cit*, p 163; Creel, *The Birth of China*, p 196.

7 *Yibian* 7797. Allan, *op. cit*, p 119.

8 Keightley, 'The Religious Commitment: Shang Theology and the Genesis of Chinese Political Culture', p 218.

9 See Hellmut Wilhelm, *Heaven, Earth, and Man in the Book of Changes*, pp 89–90; Nienhauser, *The Grand Scribe's Records*, Vol. I, p 63.

10 Keightley, *Sources of Shang History*, p 153, n81.

11 *Ibid.*, p 177, and Table 29 on p 222, showing frequency of divination topics over time. See also Allan, *op. cit*, p 119–120.

12 See Chapter VII.

13 Translation of Feng and Shryock, *op. cit*, p 2.

14 Translation by Kidder Smith, '*Zhouyi* Interpretation from Accounts in the *Zuozhuan*', pp 444–445. The 'wind blowing down a mountain' is based on the constituent trigrams of hexagram 18. Note that the reference to *gu* being a woman bewildering a man can no longer be found in the *Zhouyi*. Though Kidder Smith has suggested that this too is based on trigram correspondences, I think the doctor is referring to something like the bewitching effect the concubine Da Ji had on Zhou Xin. It can't be ruled out that hexagram 18 as known by the doctor may have contained an allusion of this kind that has been lost. There is another reference to hexagram 18 in the *Zuozhuan*, for the year 645BC. Here the quotation of the judgment is completely different to that found in the received text: 'A thousand chariots retreated thrice. As a result of the three retreats a male fox is captured.' See Rutt, *Zhouyi*, pp 179–180; Legge, *Chinese Classics*, Vol. V, p 167.

15 Allan, *op. cit*, p 163; Keightley, *Sources of Shang History*, p 86.

16 Five-pair divination sets might appear on a single bone or shell, or, as in the case of *Bingbian* 11–20, on five separate shells (Keightley, *Sources of Shang History*, p 39).

17 Keightley examines these inscriptions in great detail in Chapter 3 of *Sources of Shang History*, and in his preamble at the start of the book provides a marvellously imaginative reconstruction of the circumstances surrounding this incident of divination.

Chapter XIII – Clouds follow the dragon

1 The *Wenyan* is called the 'Commentary on the Words of the Text' in Wilhelm-Baynes. 'Clouds follow the dragon' is found in Book III under hexagram 1, p 382 in the 3rd edition. In Book I, p 9, the expression is wrongly attributed to Confucius. See Appendix I, 'The sinological maze of Wilhelm-Baynes'.

2 In Wilhelm-Baynes this is found in the 'Commentary on the Decision' of hexagram 1 in Book III, p 370.

3 Another translation of this expression can be found on p 379 of Wilhelm-Baynes.

4 See Lynn's translation of Wang Bi's commentary, *The Classic of Changes*, p 139, for another rendering of this statement.

5 See Hellmut Wilhelm's *Change*, pp 87–88, for a translation of Section 4 of the *Zhouyi lueli*, from which this quotation comes. Lynn, *op. cit*, pp 25–46, translates the *Zhouyi lueli* in its entirety as 'General Remarks on the *Changes of the Zhou*'.

6 In this regard, Wang Bi's Neo-Daoist philosophy is not without appeal. A line of the *Great Treatise* reads: 'Did not the makers of the *Changes* become concerned about calamities?' (Part II, Chapter VII). Wang Bi simply comments: 'If they had not become concerned about calamities then it would have been sufficient for them to deal with things through nonpurposeful action (*wuwei*).' Lynn, *op. cit*, p 87.

7 The winged dragon is known as the *ying long*, about which there is a separate tradition. Clay effigies of the *ying long* were still being whipped in town squares in China in the early years of the twentieth century to shame the dragon into bringing rain during times of drought. The pearl symbolism associated with the unwinged flying dragon is preserved in the 'Lantern Festival', the closing ceremony of the long drawn-out Chinese New Year celebrations. Here the pearl is represented by a separate ball lantern carried ahead of the grotesque carnival *long*, with its gold and blue eyes, silver horns decorated with red tassels, long green beard, and gaping mouth with a red tongue, chasing the pearl lantern in rhythmic writhings through the crowded fire-crackered streets. Eberhard argues that the Lantern Festival is a survival of the original Spring rain rite put back in the calendar to address the need for a closing ceremony. Eberhard in *The Local Cultures of South and East China*, and de Visser in *The Dragon in China and Japan*, have collected much of the folklore of the *long* dragon, so it need not be repeated here. See also the separate papers by Cohen, Davidson, Dragan, Glum, and Loewe, listed in the bibliography.

8 An alternative method of arousing the dragon, considered more efficacious, was to throw powdered tiger bones into the dragon pool, the tiger being the deadly enemy of the dragon, *yin* to the dragon's *yang*. In one Song dynasty report collected by de Visser, *op. cit*, p 120, a tiger's bone was lowered into the water tied to a rope as a precaution, but still it could not be hauled out fast enough. The storm was so quick in coming it threatened to destroy the government buildings before the bone broke the surface and was pulled out, quelling the typhoon (a word partly derived from the Chinese for 'great wind', *taifeng*). Just as clouds follow the dragon, 'winds follow the tiger'. This was explained in a lost work by Dong Zhongshu from the second century BC, preserved by the Han dynasty cynical rationalist Wang Chong, who had a 'hatred of fictions and falsehoods': 'The *Yijing* says: "Clouds follow the dragon, winds follow the tiger". They are invited to come by means of their likenesses and clouds and rain arrive of their own accord.'

9 'The Dragon of the Black Pool' has been translated by Arthur Waley in *170 Chinese Poems*, pp 121–122.

10 Glum, 'Rain Magic at Anyang?', p 246.

11 Wilson, *A Naturalist in Western China*.

12 When one realises it is raining in hexagram 5—Wilhelm-Baynes makes it sound as if one were waiting for rain, rather than waiting *because* it is raining—it becomes obvious why sand on the bank of a river, mud, and a primitive pit-dwelling are foolhardy places to wait. A pit-dwelling, *xue*, a common form of habitation in early Zhou China, had to be vacated every time it rained heavily. The fourth line, 'waiting in blood', appears to depict someone who is wounded and shedding blood into rainwater puddles forming in the pit. How the occupant came to be injured may be answered by hexagram 62/5. In Wilhelm-Baynes this is translated: 'The prince shoots and hits him who is in the cave.' The 'cave' here, however, is a further meaning of *xue*. I would translate the line: 'The duke's sharpened stake takes another in a pit-dwelling.' *Yi* means both a corded arrow and a sharpened stake. The interpretation of this line as shooting a bird in a cave is unconvincing.

13 Wilhelm-Baynes translates the line as: 'Hidden dragon. Do not act.' Though the interpretation that it is not yet the time for action is derived from the *Wenyan* commentary, de Visser and de Groot suggested the line would be more accurately translated as: 'A hidden dragon is of no use.' While the dragon is still submerged it is of no use for bringing rain, it has to be awakened to fulfil its potential. If this translation is followed, then in a consultation of the *Changes* the line can be interpreted to mean that hidden talent must be brought out, not sat on.

14 *Jiao* is the first mansion of the Chinese Azure Dragon constellation that stretches across seven lunar mansions through the zodiacal constellations of Virgo, Libra, Scorpio, and Sagittarius. The Azure Dragon includes the appropriately named asterisms *Kang*, 'Gullet', *Xin*, 'Heart', and *Wei*, 'Tail'.

15 De Saussure noticed that the full moon in Spring sits in the mouth of the Azure Dragon constellation and suggested that this may be the origin of the pearl symbolism connected with the dragon, the moon being commonly referred to as a pearl in Chinese poetry. The pearl is a fairly late motif in connection with the dragon; it doesn't appear, for instance, in Shang dragon designs.

16 This translation is Wilhelm-Baynes. The same expression is used in hexagram 62/5. The character *wo*, meaning 'my' or 'our' in this phrase, appears in the Shang oracle-bone inscriptions as a term of self-address on the part of the king or the state. The reference to the 'western region', the homeland of the Zhou, has led to this sentence

being seen as an allusion to the time King Wen was imprisoned at Youli by the Shang tyrant Zhou Xin. Richard Wilhelm mentions this in his translation, but also see p 106 of his *Lectures on the I Ching*.

17 Hellmut Wilhelm thought the dragon was already out of the water by the second line, he visualised it plodding about in a wet field (*Heaven, Earth, and Man in the Book of Changes*, p 203).

18 Creel, *Studies in Early Chinese Culture (First Series)*, pp 237–239.

19 Waterbury, *Early Chinese Symbols and Literature: Vestiges and Speculations*.

20 The 13th day of the sixth moon was in later times regarded as the birthday of the Dragon King, *Long Wang*. Then he prepares to distribute water to the sun-baked earth during the period of greatest heat, corresponding to the 'dog-days', when Sirius, the Dog Star, rises and sets with the sun.

21 See, for instance, Shaughnessy, 'Composition of the *Zhouyi*', pp 266–287; Kunst, 'The Original *Yijing*', pp 369–420. Both these commentators provide more developed astronomical interpretations of hexagram 1 than myself.

Chapter XIV – No skin on his thighs

1 Other potential allusions to myths in the *Changes* are not as compelling as the one I have devoted this chapter to, but they deserve mention. The most well-known mythological interpretation concerns Wang Hai, a Shang ancestor. Wang Hai was a nomadic king who lost his sheep and cattle in a place called Yi. This mythological fragment has been widely accepted as the explanation of hexagrams 34/5 and 56/6. The story of Wang Hai appears in *Tian Wen ll*.109–120. Another possible allusion to a myth is the 'dark man', *you ren*, of hexagrams 10/2 and 54/2. Hellmut Wilhelm in *Heaven, Earth, and Man in the Book of Changes*, p 74, was the first to draw attention to this expression: 'The "dark man" might well be an historical allusion that can no longer be explained.' Hellmut Wilhelm may not have been able to explain it, but on p 144 of *The Songs of the South* David Hawkes mentions the 'Dark Man' (though not the *Yijing*) and identifies him as Tai Jia Wei, whose name Wei means 'dark' or 'faint'. Wei was one of the pre-dynastic ancestors worshipped by the Shang kings, he features in *l*.119 of the *Tian Wen*. Hawkes translated this line as: 'The Dark Man lay with her adulterously and destroyed his elder brother.' Stephen Field provides a quite different translation: 'Corrupted too was the addled youth who imperilled the elder brother.' The elder brother of Tai Jia Wei was Wang Hai. The 'dark man' of hexagrams 10 and 54 seems to be connected with the 'one-eyed man' and the 'lame man', who also appear in the same

two hexagrams. My guess is that there is a fragmented story here that it may be possible to reconstruct with further research. The only other myth that I am aware has been linked with the *Changes* is that of *hundun*, which Hellmut Wilhelm felt was alluded to in the 'tied-up sack' of hexagram 2/4. Girardot has written at length on *hundun* in *Myth and Meaning in Early Taoism*. The 'tied-up sack' could equally well allude to the story of the Shang king Wu Yi, who filled a leather sack with blood, tied it to the branch of a tree, and shot arrows at it.

2 Lynn, *Classic of Changes*, p 408.

3 *Ibid.*, p 413.

4 Eberhard, *Local Cultures*, p 350.

5 Bodde deals with the Yu flood myth in 'Myths of Ancient China'; Birrell collects various strands of the Yu myth in Chapter 8 of *Chinese Mythology*, as does Eberhard in Chains 5 and 33 of *Local Cultures*.

6 Granet, *Danses*, p 467, n2; Schafer, *Pacing the Void*, p 239.

7 *Mencius* 3A/4. Translation by D C Lau.

8 Translation by Anne Birrell, *op. cit*, p 83. Note the similarity to Richard Lynn's translation of hexagrams 43/4 and 44/3: 'This one's thighs are without skin, and his walking falters.' *Op. cit*, p 408 and p 413.

9 Watson, *Basic Writings of Han Fei Tzu*, p 98 and p 129.

10 *Mencius* 7A/26. Translation by Bodde in Fung Yu-lan, Vol. II, p 203.

11 Graham, *The Book of Lieh-tzu*, pp 148–149.

12 Translation by Bernhard Karlgren, *Legends and Cults in Ancient China*, p 303. Karlgren notes that it was also said of the legendary sage-emperors Yao and Shun that 'their thighs had no white flesh, their shanks had no hair'. There is a discrepancy in the length of time Yu was away from home. The *Shizi* says it was ten years, whereas Mencius has eight years. Sima Qian says it was 13 years (Nienhauser, *The Grand Scribe's Records*, Vol. I, p 22).

13 Personal communication, April 10, 1996.

14 Eberhard, *Local Cultures*, pp 72–80. The shamanic Dance of Yu was later taken over by Daoists who superimposed a shambling set of steps upon the Big Dipper, attempting to pace like Yu between its stars. Laszlo Legeza in *Tao Magic*, plate 48, reproduces a map of these steps from the *Daozang*, the *Daoist Canon*; as does Schafer in *Pacing the Void: T'ang Approaches to the Stars*, p 240, the title of his book being derived from these practices.

15 Karlgren, *Book of Documents*, p 68; Waltham/Legge, *Shu Ching*, p 199.

16 Fung Yu-lan, *A History of Chinese Philosophy*, Vol. II, p 440.

17 See Berglund, *The Secret of the Luo Shu*, for a monographic treatment of this subject.

18 In the 3rd edition of the Wilhelm-Baynes *I Ching* the *Luoshu* is reproduced on p 310 and the *Hetu* on p 309.

19 The connection of Yu the Great with both a dragon and a tortoise also occurs in the *Shi Yi Ji*, where a yellow dragon and a dark tortoise help Yu clear the flood. The dragon cuts channels by dragging its tail through the green mud in front of Yu, who piles the mud onto the back of the tortoise following behind (Birrell, *op. cit*, p 148).

20 Karlgren, *Legends and Cults in Ancient China*, p 273.

21 Birrell, *op. cit*, p 158.

22 *Great Treatise*, Part I, Chapter XI, Verse 8. The esoteric Daoist walk known as the 'Steps of Yu' also has versions based on the *Luoshu* and the *Hetu*. See Saso, 'What is the *Ho-T'u?*'.

23 *Analects* 9/9.

24 Rutt, *Zhouyi: The Book of Changes*, p 301.

25 The *Tuanzhuan* is the 'Commentary on the Decision' in Wilhelm-Baynes, the section commenting on hexagram 43 comes from Part 2, otherwise known as the Second Wing (see Appendix I, 'The sinological maze of Wilhelm-Baynes'). For a convenient Chinese source, see Sung, *The Text of Yi King*, p 183. Karlgren points out in his *Grammata Serica Recensa* that *jue* (entry 312b) is used as a loan for *guai* (312a). Hexagram 44 also refers to rivers (see Chapter X).

Appendix I – The sinological maze of Wilhelm-Baynes

1 Needham, *Science and Civilisation in China*, Vol. II, p 308 (a).

2 Swanson, 'The Great Treatise' (PhD dissertation), pp 5–6. He repeated the error a decade later in his article 'The Concept of Change in the *Great Treatise*', pp 84–85, n2.

3 Though 6 × 64 = 384, hexagrams 1 and 2 each have an extra line, hence the poem has 386 lines.

4 Ritsema and Karcher, *I Ching: The Classic Chinese Oracle of Change*, p 92.

5 Willard Peterson in his paper on this section translated the *Xicizhuan* as *Commentary on the Attached Verbalizations*.

6 The extract attached to hexagram 14/6 comes from the beginning of Part I, Chapter XII.

7 The comments on 21/1 and 21/6 are found in a footnote to this hexagram, not in the main text.

8 There are three further 'Confucius says' quotations in Book I that do not come from the *Dazhuan*. 1/5 is from the *Wenyan*, the Seventh Wing; 3/6 reformulates line text (b) from Book III, *i.e.* it is from the Third Wing; and the Confucius quote found under THE IMAGE of hexagram 16, a reference to the Di sacrifice, comes from *Analects* 3/11. Note that Confucius actually said that he didn't understand this sacrifice, which is presumably why he never ruled the world as if it was spinning on his hand. *Mencius* 2A/1 says King Wu Ding ruled the Empire as easily as rolling it on his palm.

9   In this extract Wilhelm rather tellingly forgot to change the formula found in the *Dazhuan*, *i.e.* it has 'The Master said' instead of 'Confucius says'.

10   Here the *Dazhuan* quotes *Analects* 6/3.

11   'The Master said' is a common formula seen in the *Analects*; a device used by the disciples of Confucius after his death to convey things they had heard the great sage say. There is only one example in the *Analects* where Confucius appears to be quoting the *Zhouyi*. In 13/22 he quotes the third line of hexagram 32, though the source is not named. He could simply be quoting a common saying that happened to derive from the *Yi*, it does not prove that he was familiar with the text. The solitary reference to the *Yi* in 7/7 appears to be an interpolation. If Confucius rated the *Zhouyi* as highly as some believe it is surprising that he didn't appear to talk about it with his students. His enthusiasm for the *Odes*, by contrast, is indisputable. Richard Rutt provides a succinct summary of the evidence against the claim that Confucius knew and admired the *Yi*. See his *Zhouyi: The Book of Changes*, pp 33–34. See also Shchutskii, *Researches on the I Ching*, pp 212–214. Dubs, 'Did Confucius Study the "Book of Changes"?' (1927), was an influential paper.

12   Rutt, *op. cit*, pp 433–439.

13   Loewe, ed., *Early Chinese Texts*, p 221.

14   Rutt, *op. cit*, Appendix.

Appendix II – Genealogical matters

1   Legge, *Li Ki*, p 120.

2   Morgan, *Tao: The Great Luminant*, p 145.

3   Chavannes, *Les mémoires historiques de Se-ma Ts'ien*, Vol. 4, p 153.

4   Waltham/Legge, *Shu Ching*, pp 188–189.

5   Nienhauser, *The Grand Scribe's Records*, Vol. 1, p 64.

6   Chavannes, *op. cit*, Vol. 4, p 153.

7   Legge, *Chinese Classics*, Vol. III, p 420.

8   *Zuozhuan*, Chao 28, translation by Savage, 'The Confucian Gentleman', p 20. In Legge's translation, *Chinese Classics*, Vol. V, pp 725–727.

9   Wilhelm-Baynes oddly misidentified Di Yi as the first Shang king Cheng Tang and for some equally strange reason mistranslated *mei* as 'daughter' instead of 'younger sister'. Richard Rutt says the character can also mean 'cousin', a translation he favours in his *Zhouyi: The Book of Changes*: 'Diyi gives his cousin in marriage.' Referring to hexagram 54/5 on p 137, however, he writes of 'the wedding of Diyi's daughter'.

10   Gu Jiegang, 'Historical events in the judgment and line texts of the *Book of Changes*' (Chinese). See Shaughnessy, 'Marriage, Divorce, and

Revolution: Reading Between the Lines of the *Book of Changes'*. Gu Jiegang was not the first to suggest hexagrams 11/5 and 54/5 refer to King Wen's wife, simply the most influential. James Legge rejected the notion on the grounds of lack of evidence, attributing it to the Latin translation of Regis (Legge, *I Ching*, 2nd edition, pp 83–84).

11 Cyrille J-D Javary is said to be a 'leading authority' on the *Yijing*, yet his account of the Zhou Conquest is littered with clumsy errors and inventions. He stresses that a crucial element of the story is that King Wen was the brother-in-law of the tyrant Zhou Xin and that therefore King Wu established the Zhou dynasty on the foundation of murdering his own uncle, the elder brother of his mother (he takes *mei* as the 'younger daughter' of Di Yi). He states all these relationships as if they were facts. See Javary, 'Un meurtre familial fondateur' ('The foundation laid by a familial murder'). Javary cannot even get well-attested facts correct; given his emphasis on familial relationships it is astonishing how many he has got wrong. He says that King Wen's father was King Tai, who was actually his grandfather; King Ji is not mentioned. He compounds the error by a family tree. He says Jizi and Bi Gan were younger brothers of Zhou Xin, which is not so. *Mencius* 6A/6 says King Zhou was Bi Gan's nephew. Jizi was probably also Zhou's uncle, he certainly wasn't his younger brother. Javary doesn't mention Zhou Xin's elder brother Weizi. And, presumably because he has only heard of King Wu, the Duke of Zhou, and the Marquis of Kang, King Wen is presented as having just three sons.

12 Wilhelm, *Heaven, Earth, and Man in the Book of Changes*, pp 61–62.

13 Recent adherents to this theory are: Edward Shaughnessy, 'Marriage, Divorce, and Revolution: Reading between the lines of the *Book of Changes'*, also his PhD dissertation, pp 239–244; Cyrille Javary, *op. cit*, repeats the basic idea; Richard Rutt appears to find value in it, *op. cit*, pp 347–349.

Bibliography

Abbreviations:

BMFEA: Bulletin of the Museum of Far Eastern Antiquities.
BSOAS: Bulletin of the School of Oriental and African Studies.
HJAS: Harvard Journal of Asiatic Studies.
JAOS: Journal of the American Oriental Society.
JRAS: Journal of the Royal Asiatic Society.
UMI: University Microfilms International.

Allan, Sarah. 'Drought, Human Sacrifice, and the Mandate of Heaven in a Lost Text from the *Shang Shu.*' *BSOAS* 47 (1984), pp 523–539.
——. 'Review: Edward L Shaughnessy: *Sources of Western Zhou History: Inscribed Bronze Vessels.*' *BSOAS* 55 (1992), pp 585–587.
——. 'The Heir and the Sage: A Structural Analysis of Ancient Chinese Dynastic Legends.' PhD dissertation, University of California, 1974. (Microfilm, British Library Document Supply Centre, Boston Spa.)
——. 'The Identities of Taigong Wang in Zhou and Han Literature.' *Monumenta Serica* 30 (1972–1973), pp 57–99.
——. *The Shape of the Turtle: Myth, Art, and Cosmos in Early China.* Albany: State University of New York Press, 1991.
——. *The Way of Water and Sprouts of Virtue.* Albany: State University of New York Press, 1997.
Allen, Richard Hinckley. *Star-Names and their Meanings.* New York: G E Stechert, 1899.
Anthony, Carol K. *A Guide to the I Ching.* Massachusetts: Anthony Publishing Company, 1988. (3rd edition.)
Bakich, Michael E. *The Cambridge Guide to the Constellations.* Cambridge: Cambridge University Press, 1995.

Berglund, Lars. *The Secret of the Luo Shu: Numerology in Chinese Art and Architecture.* Lund, Sweden: Lund University, 1990.

Birch, Cyril, ed. *Anthology of Chinese Literature.* Harmondsworth: Penguin Books, 1967.

Birrell, Anne. *Chinese Mythology: An Introduction.* Baltimore: The John Hopkins University Press, 1993.

Blofeld, John, trans. *I Ching: The Book of Change.* London: George Allen & Unwin, 1965.

——. *Taoism: The Quest for Immortality.* London: Mandala, 1986.

Bodde, Derk. *Essays on Chinese Civilization.* New Jersey: Princeton University Press, 1981.

——. *Festivals in Classical China: New Year and Other Annual Observances During the Han Dynasty 206BC–AD220.* New Jersey: Princeton University Press, 1975.

——. 'Myths of Ancient China.' In his *Essays on Chinese Civilization,* pp 45–84. New Jersey: Princeton University Press, 1981.

Boltz, William G. 'Perspectives on Literacy in Ancient China.' Paper from the conference at the British Museum, 'Mysteries of Ancient China', December 6–8, 1996, 5pp.

Bredon, Juliet, and Igor Mitrophanow. *The Moon Year.* Oxford: Oxford University Press, 1982. (First published 1927.)

Carus, Paul. *Chinese Thought.* Chicago: Open Court, 1907.

Chalmers, John. 'Astronomy of the Ancient Chinese.' In James Legge, *The Chinese Classics,* Vol. III, pp 90–102. London: Trübner & Co, 1895.

Chang Cheng-lang. 'An Interpretation of the Divinatory Inscriptions on Early Chou Bronzes.' *Early China* 6 (1980–81), pp 80–96.

Chang, Kwang-chih. *Art, Myth, and Ritual: The Path to Political Authority in Ancient China.* Cambridge, Massachusetts: Harvard University Press, 1983.

——. *Shang Civilization.* New Haven: Yale University Press, 1980.

——, ed. *Studies of Shang Archaeology: Selected Papers from the International Conference on Shang Civilization.* New Haven: Yale University Press, 1986.

——. *The Archaeology of Ancient China.* New Haven: Yale University Press, 1986. (4th edition: revised and enlarged.)

——. 'T'ien Kan: A Key to the History of the Shang.' In David T Roy and Tsuen-hsuin Tsien, eds, *Ancient China: Studies in Early Civilization,* pp 13–42. Hong Kong: The Chinese University Press, 1978.

Chatley, Herbert. 'Ancient Chinese Astronomy.' Offprint from *The Asiatic Review* (January 1938), pp 1–8.

——. 'The Date of the Hsia Calendar *Hsia Hsiao Cheng.*' *JRAS* (1938), pp 523–533.

Chavannes, Édouard, trans. *Les mémoires historiques de Se-ma Ts'ien.* Paris: Ernest Leroux, 1895–1905. (5 vols.)

Chen, Shih-chuan. 'How to Form a Hexagram and Consult the I-Ching.' *JAOS* 92 (1972), pp 237–249.

Ch'en, Ch'i-yun. 'A Confucian Magnate's Idea of Political Violence: Hsun Shuang's (128–190AD) Interpretation of the Book of Changes.' *T'oung Pao* 54 (1968), pp 73–115.

Ching, Julia. *Mysticism and Kingship in China: The Heart of Chinese Wisdom.* Cambridge: Cambridge University Press, 1997.

Chow Tse-tsung. 'The Childbirth Myth and Ancient Chinese Medicine: A Study of Aspects of the *Wu* Tradition.' In David T Roy and Tsuen-hsuin Tsien, eds, *Ancient China: Studies in Early Civilization*, pp 43–89. Hong Kong: The Chinese University Press, 1978.

Cohen, Alvin P. 'Coercing the Rain Deities in Ancient China.' *History of Religions* 17, Nos. 3 and 4 (February–May 1978), pp 244–265. Chicago: The University of Chicago Press.

Creel, Herrlee Glessner. 'Bronze Inscriptions of the Western Chou as Historical Documents.' *JAOS* 56 (1936), pp 335–349.

———. 'On the Birth of *The Birth of China.*' *Early China* 11–12 (1985–1987), pp 1–5.

———. *Studies in Early Chinese Culture (First Series).* Baltimore: Waverly Press, 1937.

———. *The Birth of China: A Study of the Formative Period of Chinese Civilization.* London: Peter Owen, 1958. (First published 1936.)

———. *The Origins of Statecraft in China.* Vol. I: *The Western Chou Empire.* Chicago: The University of Chicago Press, 1970.

Cullen, Christopher, trans. *Astronomy and Mathematics in Ancient China: The Zhou Bi Suan Jing.* Cambridge: Cambridge University Press, 1996.

Davidson, J LeRoy. 'The Riddle of the Bottlehorn.' *Artibus Asiae* 22 (1959), pp 15–22.

de Fancourt, William. *Warp and Weft: In Search of the I-Ching.* Chieveley, Berkshire: Capall Bann, 1997.

de Harlez, Charles Joseph, trans. *The Yih-king: A New Translation from the Original Chinese.* Woking: Publications of the Oriental University Institute, 1897. (A translation by J P Val d'Eremao of *Le Yih king: Texte primitif rétabli, traduit et commenté.* Brussels: F Hayez, 1889.)

de Groot, J J M. *The Religious System of China.* Leiden: E J Brill, 1892–1910. (6 vols.)

de Saussure, Léopold. *Les origines de l'astronomie chinoise.* Paris: Maisonneuve, 1930.

de Visser, M W. *The Dragon in China and Japan.* Amsterdam: Johannes Müller, 1913.

DeFrancis, John. *The Chinese Language: Fact and Fantasy.* Honolulu: University of Hawaii Press, 1984.

Doré, Henri. *Researches into Chinese Superstitions.* Shanghai: T'usewei Printing Press, 1914–1929. (A translation by M Kennelly of *Recherches sur les Superstitions en Chine,* 14 vols.)

Dragan, Raymond. 'The Dragon in Chinese Myth and Ritual: Rites of Passage and Sympathetic Magic.' In Julia Ching and R W L Guisso, eds, *Sages and Filial Sons,* pp 135–162. Hong Kong: The Chinese University Press, 1991.

Dubs, Homer H. 'Canon of Lunar Eclipses for Anyang and China, −1400 to −1000.' *HJAS* 10 (1947), pp 162–178.

——. 'Did Confucius Study the "Book of Changes"?' *T'oung Pao* 24 (1927), pp 82–90.

——. 'The Beginnings of Chinese Astronomy.' *JAOS* 78 (1958), pp 295–300.

——. 'The Date of the Shang Period.' *T'oung Pao* 40 (1951), pp 322–335.

——. 'The Date of the Shang Period—A Postscript.' *T'oung Pao* 42 (1954), pp 101–105.

——, trans. *The History of the Former Han Dynasty, by Pan Ku.* Baltimore: Waverly Press, 1938, 1944, 1955. (3 vols.)

——, trans. *The Works of Hsuntze.* London: Arthur Probsthain, 1928. (Reprinted by AMS Press, New York, 1977.)

Eberhard, Wolfram. *A Dictionary of Chinese Symbols.* London: Routledge, 1988. (Translated from the German by G L Campbell.)

——. *Chinese Festivals.* New York: Abelard-Schuman, 1958.

——. 'Contributions to the Astronomy of the Han Period III: Astronomy of the Later Han.' *HJAS* 1 (1936), pp 194–241. (With the astronomical collaboration of Rolf Mueller.)

——. *The Local Cultures of South and East China.* Leiden: E J Brill, 1968. (A translation by Alide Eberhard of a greatly revised version of the second volume of *Lokalkulturen im Alten China.*)

Eno, Robert. 'Was There a High God Ti in Shang Religion?' *Early China* 15 (1990), pp 1–26.

Erkes, Eduard. 'Some Remarks on Karlgren's "Fecundity Symbols in Ancient China".' *BMFEA* 3 (1931), pp 63–68.

Feng, Gia-fu, and Jane English, trans. *Chuang Tsu: Inner Chapters.* London: Wildwood House, 1974.

——, trans. *Lao Tsu: Tao Te Ching.* London: Wildwood House, 1972.

Feng, H Y. 'The Chinese Kinship System.' *HJAS* 2 (1937), pp 141–275.

Feng, H Y, and J K Shryock. 'The Black Magic in China Known as *Ku.*' *JAOS* 55 (1935), pp 1–30.

Field, Stephen. 'Cosmos, Cosmograph, and the Inquiring Poet: New Answers to the "Heaven Questions".' *Early China* 17 (1992), pp 83–110.

——, trans. *Tian Wen: A Chinese Book of Origins.* New York: New Directions, 1986.

Fitzgerald, C P. *China: A Short Cultural History.* London: The Cresset Press, 1961.

Fotheringham, John Knight. *Historical Eclipses, Being the Halley Lecture Delivered 17 May 1921.* Oxford: Clarendon Press, 1921.

Fung Yu-lan. *A History of Chinese Philosophy.* Vol. I: *The Period of the Philosophers (from the Beginnings to circa 100BC).* Peiping: Henri Vetch. London: George Allen & Unwin, 1937. Vol. II: *The Period of Classical Learning (from the Second Century BC to the Twentieth Century AD).* Princeton: Princeton University Press, 1983. (Both volumes translated by Derk Bodde, Vol. II first published 1953.)

Garmonsway, J N, trans. *The Anglo-Saxon Chronicle.* London: Dent (Everyman Library), 1953.

Girardot, N J. *Myth and Meaning in Early Taoism: The Theme of Chaos (hun-tun).* Berkeley: University of California Press, 1988.

Glum, Peter. 'Rain Magic at Anyang?' *BMFEA* 54 (1982), pp 241–265.

Gould, Charles. *Mythical Monsters.* London: W H Allen, 1886.

Graham, A C. *Disputers of the Tao: Philosophical Argument in Ancient China.* Illinois: Open Court, 1989.

——, trans. *The Book of Lieh-tzu: A Classic of Tao.* London: Mandala, 1991.

Granet, Marcel. *Danses et Légendes de la Chine Ancienne.* Paris: Librairie Félix Alcan, 1926. (2 vols.)

——. *Festivals and Songs of Ancient China.* London: George Routledge & Sons, 1932. (Translated by E D Edwards, first published 1919 in French as *Fêtes et chansons anciennes de la Chine.*)

——. *La Pensée Chinoise.* Paris: La Renaissance du Livre, 1934.

Greatrex, Roger, trans. *The Bowu Zhi: An Annotated Translation.* Skrifter utgivna av Föreningen för Orientaliska Studier 20, Stockholm, 1987.

Gu Zhizhong, trans. *Creation of the Gods.* Beijing: New World Press, 1992. (A translation of the *Feng Shen Yan Yi.* 2 vols.)

Hacker, Edward A. *The I Ching Handbook: A Practical Guide to Logical and Personal Perspectives from the Ancient Chinese Book of Changes.* Brookline, Massachusetts: Paradigm, 1993.

Harper, Donald J. 'The Han Cosmic Board (*shih*).' *Early China* 4 (1978–79), pp 1–10. (Also follow-up discussion in *Early China* 6 and 7.)

Hartner, Willy. 'Das Datum der Shih-ching-Finsternis.' *T'oung Pao* 31 (1935), pp 188–236.

Hawkes, David, trans. *The Songs of the South: An Ancient Chinese Anthology of Poems by Qu Yuan and Other Poets.* London: Penguin Books, 1985.

Henricks, Robert G, trans. *Lao-Tzu: Te-Tao Ching. A New Translation Based on the Recently Discovered Ma-wang-tui Texts.* London: Rider, 1991.

Herrmann, Albert. *An Historical Atlas of China.* Edinburgh: Edinburgh University Press, 1966.

Ho Peng Yoke, trans. *The Astronomical Chapters of the Chin Shu.* Paris and The Hague: Mouton, 1966.

Ho, Richard M W. 'Where Cross-Fertilization Fails: A Short Critique of the Wilhelm/Baynes Translation of the *Book of Changes.*' In Roger T Ames, Chan Sin-wai, and Mau-sang Ng, eds, *Interpreting Culture Through Translation: A Festschrift for D C Lau,* pp 145–153. Hong Kong: The Chinese University Press, 1991.

Hopkins, L C. 'The Dragon Terrestrial and the Dragon Celestial— A Study of the *Lung* and the *Ch'en.*' Part I: *JRAS* (October 1931), pp 791–806. Part II: *JRAS* (January 1932), pp 91–97.

Hou, Ching-lang. 'The Chinese Belief in Baleful Stars.' In Holmes Welch and Anna Seidel, eds, *Facets of Taoism: Essays in Chinese Religion,* pp 193–228. New Haven: Yale University Press, 1979.

Houtgast, Jakob. 'Eclipse, Occultation, and Transit.' In *Encyclopaedia Britannica,* 15th edition, *Macropaedia,* Vol. 17, pp 866–875.

Hsu, Cho-yun, and Katheryn M Linduff. *Western Chou Civilization.* New Haven: Yale University Press, 1988.

Huang, Kerson, trans. *I Ching: The Oracle.* Singapore: World Scientific, 1984.

Hughes, E R. *Chinese Philosophy in Classical Times.* London: J M Dent, 1942.

Inwards, Richard. *Weather Lore.* London: Rider, 1950.

Javary, Cyrille J-D. 'Un meurtre familial fondateur: La germe historique du Yi Jing.' *Question de* 98 (1994), pp 78–91. (A special edition entitled *Les mutations du Yi King.*)

Joseph, George Gheverghese. *The Crest of the Peacock—Non-European Roots of Mathematics.* London: Penguin Books, 1992.

Jou, Tsung Hwa. *The Tao of I Ching: Way to Divination.* Piscataway, NJ: Tai Chi Foundation, 1984.

Kahn, Charles H, trans. *The Art and Thought of Heraclitus: An Edition of the Fragments with Translation and Commentary.* Cambridge: Cambridge University Press, 1979.

Karlgren, Bernhard. 'Glosses on the Book of Documents.' Part 1: *BMFEA* 20 (1948), pp 39–315. Part 2: *BMFEA* 21 (1949), pp 63–206.

——. 'Glosses on the Kuo Feng Odes.' *BMFEA* 14 (1942), pp 71–247.

——. 'Glosses on the Siao Ya Odes.' *BMFEA* 16 (1944), pp 25–169.

——. 'Glosses on the Ta Ya and Sung Odes.' *BMFEA* 18 (1946), pp 1–198.

——. 'Grammata Serica Recensa.' *BMFEA* 29 (1957), pp 1–332.

——. 'Legends and Cults in Ancient China.' *BMFEA* 18 (1946), pp 199–365.

——. 'Some Fecundity Symbols in Ancient China.' *BMFEA* 2 (1930), pp 1–54.

——. 'Some Sacrifices in Chou China.' *BMFEA* 40 (1968), pp 1–31.

——. 'The Authenticity of Ancient Chinese Texts.' *BMFEA* 1 (1929), pp 165–183.

——, trans. 'The Book of Documents.' *BMFEA* 22 (1950), pp 1–81.

——, trans. *The Book of Odes: Chinese Text, Transcription, and Translation*. Stockholm: The Museum of Far Eastern Antiquities, 1950.

Keightley, David N. 'Late Shang Divination: The Magico-Religious Legacy.' In Henry Rosemont Jr, ed, *Explorations in Chinese Cosmology*, pp 11–34, JAAR Thematic Studies 50/2. Chico, California: Scholars Press, 1984.

——. 'Reports from the Shang: A Corroboration and Some Speculation.' *Early China* 9–10 (1983–85), pp 20–54. (Includes comments by Sarah Allan, David S Nivison, Edward Shaughnessy, Kenichi Takashima, and L Vandermeersch, with a reply by David Keightley.)

——. *Sources of Shang History: The Oracle-Bone Inscriptions of Bronze Age China*. Berkeley: University of California Press, 1978.

——. 'The Late Shang State: When, Where, and What?' In David N Keightley, ed, *The Origins of Chinese Civilization*, pp 523–564. Berkeley: University of California Press, 1983.

——. 'The Religious Commitment: Shang Theology and the Genesis of Chinese Political Culture.' *History of Religions* 17, Nos. 3 and 4 (February–May 1978), pp 211–225. Chicago: The University of Chicago Press.

——. 'The Shang State as seen in Oracle-Bone Inscriptions.' *Early China* 5 (1979–80), pp 25–34.

Krappe, Alexander H. *The Science of Folk-Lore*. London: Methuen, 1930.

Kunst, Richard Alan. 'The Original *Yijing*: A Text, Phonetic Transcription, Translation, and Indexes, with Sample Glosses.' PhD dissertation, University of California, 1985. (UMI facsimile.)

Lai Ming. *A History of Chinese Literature*. London: Cassell, 1964.

Lau, D C, trans. *Confucius: The Analects*. Harmondsworth: Penguin Books, 1979.

——, trans. *Lao Tzu: Tao Te Ching*. Harmondsworth: Penguin Books, 1963.

——, trans. *Mencius*. Harmondsworth: Penguin Books, 1970.

Laurin, Colin Mac. 'An Observation of the Eclipse of the Sun, on Feb 18, 1737, made at Edinburgh.' *Philosophical Transactions*, Vol. XL (1737–38), pp 177–195. London: The Royal Society.

Le Blanc, Charles, trans. *Huai-nan Tzu: Philosophical Synthesis in Early Han Thought*. Hong Kong: Hong Kong University Press, 1985.

Legeza, Laszlo. *Tao Magic: The Secret Language of Diagrams and Calligraphy*. London: Thames and Hudson, 1975.

Legge, James, trans. *The Chinese Classics*, Vol. III. London: Trübner & Co, 1865. (Translation of the *Bamboo Annals*, 'Current Text', and the *Shujing*, 2 parts.)

——, trans. *The Chinese Classics*, Vol. V. London: Trübner & Co, 1872. (Translation of the *Chunqiu* with the *Zuozhuan*, 2 parts.)

——, trans. *The I Ching: The Book of Changes*. New York: Dover, 1963. (Facsimile of the 1899 second edition.)

——, trans. *The Li Ki, or Collection of Treatises on the Rites of Propriety or Ceremonial Usages*. In Max Müller, ed, *The Sacred Books of the East*, Vols. XXVII–XXVIII. Oxford: Clarendon Press, 1885.

Li Xueqin. 'Basic Considerations on the *Commentaries* of the Silk Manuscript *Book of Changes*.' *Early China* 20 (1995), pp 367–380.

——. *Eastern Zhou and Qin Civilizations*. New Haven: Yale University Press, 1985. (Translated by K C Chang.)

Liao, W K, trans. *The Complete Works of Han Fei Tzu*. London: Arthur Probsthain. Vol. I, 1939 (reprinted 1959); Vol. II, 1959.

Liu Dajun. 'A Preliminary Investigation of the Silk Manuscript *Yijing*.' *Zhouyi Network* 1 (January 1986), pp 13–26. (Translated from *Wenshizhe* 1985, issue 4, pp 53–60, by Edward L Shaughnessy.)

Liu Dajun, and Lin Zhongjun, trans. *The I Ching: Text and Annotated Translation*. Jinan, China: Shandong Friendship Publishing House, 1995. (A translation from classical Chinese to modern Chinese, translated into English by Fu Youde.)

Liu Ts'un-yan. *Buddhist and Taoist Influences on Chinese Novels*. Vol. I: *The Authorship of the Feng Shen Yen Yi*. Wiesbaden: Otto Harrassowitz, 1962.

Loewe, Michael, ed. *Early Chinese Texts: A Bibliographic Guide*. Berkeley: The Society for the Study of Early China and The Institute of East Asian Studies, University of California, 1993.

——. 'Manuscripts Found Recently in China: A Preliminary Survey.' *T'oung Pao* 63 (1977), pp 99–136.

——. 'The Cult of the Dragon and the Invocation for Rain.' In Charles Le Blanc and Susan Blader, eds, *Chinese Ideas about Nature and Society*, pp 195–213. Hong Kong: Hong Kong University Press, 1987.

Loewe, Michael, and Carmen Blacker, eds. *Oracles and Divination*. Boulder: Shambhala, 1981.

Luo Guanzhong. *Three Kingdoms*. Beijing/Berkeley: Foreign Languages Press/University of California Press, 1994. (A translation of the *Sanguo* by Moss Roberts, 3 vols.)

Lynn, Richard John, trans. *The Classic of Changes: A New Translation of the I Ching as Interpreted by Wang Bi*. New York: Columbia University Press, 1994.

Lynn, William Thynne. *Remarkable Eclipses and Comets*. London: Samuel Bagster & Sons, 1911.

McClatchie, Rev. Canon, trans. *A Translation of the Confucian Yih King or Classic of Change.* Shanghai: American Presbyterian Mission Press, 1876.

Maspero, Henri. *China in Antiquity.* Massachusetts: The University of Massachusetts Press, 1978. (Translated from the 1927 French first edition *La Chine Antique* by Frank A Kierman Jr.)

———. 'L'astronomie chinoise avant les Han.' *T'oung Pao* 26 (1929), pp 267–356.

Mathews, R H. *Chinese–English Dictionary.* Cambridge, Massachusetts: Harvard University Press, 1943. (English Index, 1944.)

Mei, Yi-pao, trans. *The Ethical and Political Works of Motse.* London: Arthur Probsthain, 1929. (Reprinted by Hyperion, Connecticut, 1973.)

Meeus, Jean. *Astronomical Algorithms.* Richmond, Virginia: Willmann-Bell, 1991.

Meeus, Jean, and Hermann Mucke. *Canon of Solar Eclipses,* −2003 to +2526. Vienna: Astronomisches Büro, 1983.

Moore, Patrick. *Exploring the Night Sky with Binoculars.* Cambridge: Cambridge University Press, 1996. (3rd edition.)

Moore, Steve. *The Trigrams of Han: Inner Structures of the I Ching.* Wellingborough: The Aquarian Press, 1989.

Morgan, Evan, trans. *Tao: The Great Luminant—Essays from Huai Nan Tzu.* New York: Paragon Book Reprint Corp., 1969.

Moule, A C, and W Percival Yetts. *The Rulers of China 221BC–AD1949.* London: Routledge & Kegan Paul, 1957.

Murdin, Paul, and David Allen. *Catalogue of the Universe.* Cambridge: Cambridge University Press, 1979. (Photographs: David Malin.)

Needham, Joseph, and Wang Ling. *Science and Civilisation in China.* Cambridge: Cambridge University Press. Vol. II: *History of Scientific Thought,* 1956. Vol. III: *Mathematics and the Sciences of the Heavens and the Earth,* 1959.

Nienhauser, William H, Jr, ed, trans. *The Grand Scribe's Records.* Vol. I: *The Basic Annals of Pre-Han China,* by Ssu-ma Ch'ien. Bloomington and Indianapolis: Indiana University Press, 1994.

Nivison, David S. 'An Interpretation of the "Shao Gao".' *Early China* 20 (1995), pp 177–193.

———. '1040 as the Date of the Chou Conquest.' *Early China* 8 (1982–83), pp 76–78.

———. 'The Dates of Western Chou.' *HJAS* 43 (1983), pp 481–580.

Nivison, David S, and Kevin Pang. 'Astronomical Evidence for the *Bamboo Annals*' Chronicle of Early Xia.' *Early China* 15 (1990), pp 87–95. (Comments by Forum correspondents Huang Yilong, John S Major, David W Pankenier, and Zhang Peiyu, with responses from Nivison and Pang, pp 97–196.)

Obenchain, Diane B. 'Ministers of the Moral Order: Innovations of the Early Chou Kings, the Duke of Chou, Chung-ni and "Ju".' PhD dissertation, Harvard University, 1984. (UMI facsimile.)

Pang, Kevin, Kevin Yau, Hung-hsiang Chou, and Robert Wolf. 'Computer Analysis of Some Ancient Chinese Sunrise Eclipse Records to Determine the Earth's Past Rotation Rate.' *Vistas in Astronomy* 31 (1988), pp 833–847.

Pang, Sunjoo. 'The Consorts of King Wu and King Wen in the Bronze Inscriptions of Early Chou.' *Monumenta Serica* 33 (1977–78), pp 124–135.

Pankenier, David W. 'Astronomical Dates in Shang and Western Zhou.' *Early China* 7 (1981–82), pp 2–37.

——. '*Mozi* and the Dates of Xia, Shang, and Zhou: A Research Note.' *Early China* 9–10 (1983–85), pp 175–183.

——. 'Reflections of the Lunar Aspect on Western Chou Chronology,' *T'oung Pao* 78 (1992), pp 33–76.

——. 'The *Bamboo Annals* Revisited: Problems of Method in using the Chronicle as a Source for the Early Zhou.' *BSOAS* 55 (1992), Part 1 pp 272–297, Part 2 pp 498–510.

——. 'The Cosmo-Political Background of Heaven's Mandate.' *Early China* 20 (1995), pp 121–176.

Peterson, Willard J. 'Making Connections: "Commentary on the Attached Verbalizations" of the *Book of Change*.' *HJAS* 42 (1982), pp 67–116.

Porter, Deborah. 'The Literary Function of K'un-lun Mountain in the *Mu T'ien-tzu Chuan*.' *Early China* 18 (1993), pp 73–106.

Pound, Ezra, trans. *Confucian Analects*. London: Peter Owen, 1951.

Rawson, Jessica, ed. *Mysteries of Ancient China: New Discoveries from the Early Dynasties*. London: British Museum Press, 1996.

Reeves, John. *List of Chinese Stars*. In Part II, Vol. I, Morrison's *Dictionary of the Chinese Language*, 1819. (Original manuscript notebook kept at the British Library, shelfmark OR 8133.)

Rexroth, Kenneth, trans. *One Hundred More Poems from the Chinese: Love and the Turning Year*. New York: New Directions, 1970.

Ridpath, Ian, and Wil Tirion. *The Night Sky (Collins Gem Guide)*. Glasgow: HarperCollins, 1985.

Riegel, Jeffrey K. 'A Textual Note on the *I Ching*.' *JAOS* 103 (1983), pp 601–605.

Ritsema, Rudolf, and Stephen Karcher, trans. *I Ching: The Classic Chinese Oracle of Change*. Shaftesbury: Element, 1994.

Rutt, Richard, trans. *Zhouyi: The Book of Changes*. London: Curzon Press, 1996.

Saso, Michael. 'What is the *Ho-t'u*?' *History of Religions* 17, Nos. 3 and 4 (February–May 1978), pp 399–416. Chicago: The University of Chicago Press.

Savage, William E. 'Archetypes, Model Emulation, and the Confucian Gentleman.' *Early China* 17 (1992), pp 1–25.

Sawyer, Ralph D, trans. *The Seven Military Classics of Ancient China.* Boulder: Westview Press, 1993.

Schafer, Edward H. *Pacing the Void: T'ang Approaches to the Stars.* Berkeley: University of California Press, 1977.

———. *The Divine Woman: Dragon Ladies and Rain Maidens in T'ang Literature.* Berkeley: University of California Press, 1973.

———. *The Vermilion Bird: T'ang Images of the South.* Berkeley: University of California Press, 1967.

Schlegel, Gustave. *Uranographie Chinoise.* La Haye, Leyde, 1875. (2 vols.)

Schove, D Justin. *Chronology of Eclipses and Comets* AD1–1000. Bury St Edmunds, Suffolk: The Boydell Press, 1984.

Schuessler, Axel. *A Dictionary of Early Zhou Chinese.* Honolulu: University of Hawaii Press, 1987.

Serruys, Paul L-M. 'Studies in the Language of the Shang Oracle Inscriptions.' *T'oung Pao* 60 (1974), pp 12–120.

Shaughnessy, Edward L, trans. *I Ching: The Classic of Changes—The First English Translation of the Newly Discovered Second-Century* BC *Mawangdui Texts.* New York: Ballantine Books, 1997.

———. 'Marriage, Divorce, and Revolution: Reading Between the Lines of the *Book of Changes.'* *The Journal of Asian Studies* 51, No. 3 (August 1992), pp 587–599.

———. '"New" Evidence on the Zhou Conquest.' *Early China* 6 (1980–81), pp 57–79.

———. *Sources of Western Zhou History: Inscribed Bronze Vessels.* Berkeley: University of California Press, 1991.

———. 'The Composition of the *Zhouyi.'* PhD dissertation, Stanford University, 1983. (UMI facsimile.)

———. 'The "Current" *Bamboo Annals* and the Date of the Zhou Conquest of Shang.' *Early China* 11–12 (1985–87), pp 33–60.

———. 'The Duke of Zhou's Retirement in the East and the Beginnings of the Ministerial–Monarch Debate in Chinese Political Philosophy.' *Early China* 18 (1993), pp 41–72.

———. 'The Origin of an *Yijing* Line Statement.' *Early China* 20 (1995), pp 223–240.

———. 'Western Zhou Civilization: A Review Article.' *Early China* 15 (1990), pp 197–205. (A review of Hsu and Linduff.)

———. 'Zhouyuan Oracle-Bone Inscriptions: Entering the Research Stage?' (A review of *Xizhou jiagu tanlun* with comments by Wang Yuxin, Li Xueqin, and Fan Yuzhou, and 'Extra-Lineage Cult in the Shang Dynasty: A Surrejoinder'.) *Early China* 11–12 (1985–87), pp 146–194.

Shchutskii, Iulian K. *Researches on the I Ching.* London: Routledge & Kegan Paul, 1980. (Translated from the Russian by William L

MacDonald and Tsuyoshi Hasegawa with Hellmut Wilhelm, introduction by Gerald Swanson.)

Situ Tan. *Popular Chinese Idioms: Meaning and Origin.* Singapore: Asiapac Books, 1988. (Translated from the Chinese by Zhao Shuhan and Tang Bowen, 2 vols.)

Sivin, Nathan. *Chinese Alchemy: Preliminary Studies.* Harvard Monographs on the History of Science. Cambridge: Harvard University Press, 1968.

———. *Cosmos and Computation in Early Chinese Mathematical Astronomy.* Leiden: E J Brill, 1969. (Reprinted from *T'oung Pao* 55.)

———. 'Review of *The Book of Change* translated by John Blofeld.' *HJAS* 26 (1966), pp 290–298.

Smith, Kidder. 'The Difficulty of the *Yijing.*' *Chinese Literature* 15 (1993), pp 1–15.

———. '*Zhouyi* Interpretation from Accounts in the *Zuozhuan.*' *HJAS* 49 (1989), pp 421–463.

Smith, Kidder, Peter K Bol, Joseph A Adler, and Don J Wyatt. *Sung Dynasty Uses of the I Ching.* Princeton: Princeton University Press, 1990.

Smith, Richard J. *Fortune-Tellers & Philosophers: Divination in Traditional Chinese Society.* Boulder: Westview Press, 1991.

Soothill, William Edward. *The Hall of Light: A Study of Early Chinese Kingship.* London: Lutterworth Press, 1951.

Soper, Alexander C. 'King Wu Ting's Victory over the "Realm of Demons".' *Artibus Asiae* 17 (1954), pp 55–60.

Stephenson, F R. *Historical Eclipses and Earth's Rotation.* Cambridge: Cambridge University Press, 1997.

Stephenson, F R, and M A Houlden. *Atlas of Historical Eclipse Maps: East Asia 1500BC–AD1900.* Cambridge: Cambridge University Press, 1986.

Sung Tz'u. *The Washing Away of Wrongs: Forensic Medicine in 13th Century China.* Ann Arbor: Center for Chinese Studies, University of Michigan, 1981. (Translation by Brian E McKnight of the *Xi Yuan Ji Lu.*)

Sung, Z D. *The Text of Yi King.* New York: Paragon Book Reprint Corp., 1969. (First published: Shanghai, 1935.)

Swanson, Gerald. 'The Concept of Change in the *Great Treatise.*' In Henry Rosemont Jr, ed, *Explorations in Chinese Cosmology*, pp 67–93, JAAR Thematic Studies 50/2. Chico, California: Scholars Press, 1984.

———. 'The Great Treatise: Commentary Tradition to the *Book of Changes.*' PhD dissertation, University of Washington, 1974. (UMI facsimile.)

Terrien de Lacouperie, Albert Etienne Jean Baptiste. *The Oldest Book of the Chinese: The YH-King and its Authors.* Vol. I: *History and Method.* London: D Nutt, 1892.

The Times Atlas of the World. London: Times Books/HarperCollins, 1994. (9th comprehensive edition.)

Tjan Tjoe Som, trans. *Po Hu T'ung* (Comprehensive Discussions in the White Tiger Hall). Leiden: E J Brill, 1949, 1952. (2 vols.)

Tsien, Tsuen-hsuin. *Written on Bamboo and Silk: The Beginnings of Chinese Books and Inscriptions.* Chicago: The University of Chicago Press, 1962.

Tung Tso-pin. *Fifty Years of Studies in Oracle Inscriptions.* Centre for East Asian Studies, 1964.

———. 'Ten Examples of Early Tortoise-Shell Inscriptions.' *HJAS* 11 (1948), pp 119–129.

van Esbroeck, Guy. 'The So-Called Eclipse in the Shu-king.' Offprint from *Le Muséon: Revue d'études orientales,* LXXXIX, 1–2, pp 225–273. Louvain, 1971.

van Gulik, R H. *Sexual Life in Ancient China: A Preliminary Survey of Chinese Sex and Society from ca. 1500BC till 1644AD.* Leiden: E J Brill, 1961.

von Falkenhausen, Lothar. 'Ancilla to Hsu and Linduff, *Western Chou Civilization.*' *Early China* 15 (1990), pp 206–222.

Waley, Arthur, trans. *More Translations from the Chinese.* London: George Allen & Unwin, 1919.

———. 'Notes on Chinese Alchemy.' Offprint from *Bulletin of the School of Oriental Studies London Institution,* Vol. VI, Part I (1930), pp 1–24.

———, trans. *170 Chinese Poems.* London: Constable & Co., 1918.

———, trans. *The Analects of Confucius.* London: George Allen & Unwin, 1938.

———. 'The Book of Changes.' *BMFEA* 5 (1933), pp 121–142.

———, trans. *The Book of Songs: The Ancient Chinese Classic of Poetry.* New York: Grove Weidenfeld, 1987.

———, trans. *The Nine Songs: A Study of Shamanism in Ancient China.* London: George Allen & Unwin, 1955.

———, trans. *The Way and its Power: A Study of the Tao Te Ching and its Place in Chinese Thought.* London: George Allen & Unwin, 1934.

Walters, Derek. *Chinese Astrology.* London: The Aquarian Press, 1992.

Waltham, Clae. *Shu Ching: Book of History—A Modernized Edition of the Translations of James Legge.* London: George Allen & Unwin, 1972.

Wang, C H. *The Bell and the Drum: Shih Ching as Formulaic Poetry in an Oral Tradition.* Berkeley: University of California Press, 1974.

Wang Dongliang. 'Un chariot chargé de demons: Aperçu d'un tirage de Wang Fu-zhi (1619–1692).' *Question de* 98 (1994), pp 170–173. (A special edition entitled *Les mutations du Yi King.*)

Waterbury, Florence. *Early Chinese Symbols and Literature: Vestiges and Speculations.* New York: E Weyhe, 1942.

Waters, Geoffrey R. *Three Elegies of Ch'u: An Introduction to the Traditional Interpretation of the Ch'u Tz'u.* Madison: The University of Wisconsin Press, 1985.

Watson, Burton, trans. *Basic Writings of Mo Tzu, Hsun Tzu, and Han Fei Tzu.* New York: Columbia University Press, 1963, 1964. (Originally published as three separate books.)

——. *Early Chinese Literature.* New York: Columbia University Press, 1962.

——, trans. *Records of the Grand Historian of China,* Vol. 2. New York: Columbia University Press, 1961.

——, trans. 'The Biography of Po Yi and Shu Ch'i.' In Cyril Birch, ed, *Anthology of Chinese Literature,* pp 127–130. Harmondsworth: Penguin Books, 1967.

——, trans. *The Columbia Book of Chinese Poetry: From Early Times to the Thirteenth Century.* New York: Columbia University Press, 1984.

Watts, Alan. *Tao: The Watercourse Way.* Harmondsworth: Penguin Books, 1979.

Wei, Henry, trans. *The Authentic I-Ching.* California: Newcastle Publishing, 1987.

Wei Tat. *An Exposition of the I-Ching or Book of Changes.* Taiwan: Institute of Cultural Studies, 1970.

Welch, Holmes. *Taoism: The Parting of the Way.* Boston: Beacon Press, 1965.

Wheatley, Paul. *The Pivot of Four Quarters: A Preliminary Enquiry into the Origins and Character of the Ancient Chinese City.* Edinburgh: Edinburgh University Press, 1971.

Whincup, Greg, trans. *Rediscovering the I Ching.* Wellingborough: The Aquarian Press, 1987.

Whiston, William, trans. *The Works of Flavius Josephus.* Halifax: Milner and Sowerby, 1864.

Wieger, L. *Chinese Characters: Their Origin, Etymology, History, Classification and Signification.* New York: Dover, 1965. (Unabridged reprint of 2nd edition, 1927. Translated by L Davrout.)

Wilhelm, Hellmut. *Change: Eight Lectures on the I Ching.* London: Routledge & Kegan Paul, 1961. (Translated from the German by Cary F Baynes.)

——. *Heaven, Earth, and Man in the Book of Changes.* Seattle: University of Washington Press, 1977. (Seven Eranos Lectures.)

——. 'I-Ching Oracles in the *Tso-Chuan* and the *Kuo-Yu.*' *JAOS* 79 (1959), pp 275–280.

——. 'On Sacrifice in the *I Ching.*' *Spring,* 1972, pp 74–89.

——. 'On the Oracle Recorded in the Tso-chuan, Hsi 4 (656BC).' *JAOS* 91 (1971), pp 504–505.

Wilhelm, Richard. *A Short History of Chinese Civilization.* London: George G Harrap & Co., 1929. (Translated from the German by Joan Joshua.)

——, trans. *I Ging: Das Buch der Wandlungen*. Jena, 1924.

——. *Lectures on the I Ching: Constancy and Change*. London: Routledge & Kegan Paul, 1980. (Translated from the German by Irene Eber.)

——, trans. *Tao Te Ching: The Book of Meaning and Life*. London: Arkana, 1985. (Translated from the German by H G Ostwald.)

——, trans. *The I Ching or Book of Changes*. London: Routledge & Kegan Paul, 1968. (Translated from the German by Cary F Baynes, 3rd edition.)

——, trans, and C G Jung. *The Secret of the Golden Flower: A Chinese Book of Life*. London: Routledge & Kegan Paul, 1965. (Translated from the German by Cary F Baynes.)

Wilson, E H. *A Naturalist in Western China*. London: Methuen, 1913.

Wu Jing-Nuan, trans. *Yi Jing*. Washington, DC: The Taoist Center, 1991.

Wu Shih-ch'ang. 'On the Marginal Notes Found in Oracle Bone Inscriptions.' *T'oung Pao* 43 (1955), pp 34–74.

Wylie, Alexander. 'Eclipses Recorded in Chinese Works.' In his *Chinese Researches*. Shanghai, 1897.

——. 'List of Fixed Stars.' In his *Chinese Researches*. Shanghai, 1897.

Yang Wan-li. *Heaven My Blanket, Earth My Pillow: Poems from Sung Dynasty China*. New York: Weatherhill, 1975. (The poetry of Yang Wanli translated and introduced by Jonathan Chaves.)

Zhang Yachu, and Liu Yu. 'Some Observations about Milfoil Divination Based on Shang and Zhou *Bagua* Numerical Symbols.' *Early China* 7 (1981–82), pp 46–59. (Translated by Edward L Shaughnessy.)

Zirker, J B. *Total Eclipses of the Sun*. New Jersey: Princeton University Press, 1995.

Select glossary of Chinese characters

ba (eight) 八
bao (leopard) 豹
bao (wrapping) 包
bei (north) 北
bi (title hexagram 8; assembly) 比
bi (title hexagram 22; ornaments; brave) 賁
Bi (King Wen's burial place; Duke of Bi; Hyades) 畢
bian (to change) 變
Bi Gan (uncle of Zhou Xin) 比干
bin (guest; name of rite) 賓
Bo Yi (protester against Zhou Conquest) 伯夷
bu (obscuration; calendrical term) 蔀
Chang (name of King Wen) 昌
che (cart) 車
chen (character mistaken for eclipse in *Shujing*) 辰
cheng (inherit) 承
Cheng Tang (Tang the Completer, founder of Shang) 成湯
Cheng Wang (King Cheng, King Wu's son) 成王
chong (insect) 蟲
Chong (Siege of Chong; Marquis of Chong) 崇
chu (kitchen) 廚
chu (pestle) 杵
chuan (stream) 川
da (great) 大
Da Ji (concubine of Zhou Xin) 妲己

dajun (great prince) 大君
Dan (dawn; name of Duke of Zhou) 旦
dao (way; path) 道
Dayi Shang (Great City Shang) 大邑商
di (to be admitted to audience) 覿
Di (supreme deity; Shangdi) 帝
Di Yi (penultimate Shang King, father of Zhou Xin) 帝乙
dong (east) 東
dou (Big Dipper) 斗
dun (title hexagram 33; retreat) 遯
E (Marquis of E) 鄂
Fa (name of King Wu) 發
fan (turn back) 反
fei (flying) 飛
fei (fat) 肥
Fei Zhong (minister of Zhou Xin) 費中
Feng (seal; name of Marquis of Kang) 封
Feng (title hexagram 55; abundant; King Wen's capital) 豐
fengshui (wind and water) 風水
fu (trust; verify) 孚
fu (title hexagram 24; return) 復
fu (not) 弗
Fu Sang (mythical Leaning Mulberry tree) 扶桑
Fuxi (legendary originator of trigrams) 伏羲
fuyan (women's conversation) 婦言
gai (to change) 改
gan (stem of 'Ten Heavenly Stems') 干
gan (perform, carry out) 幹
gao (report) 告
Gaozong (Illustrious Ancestor) 高宗
ge (ge-creeper) 葛
ge (revolution; leather) 革
gou (title hexagram 44; copulation) 姤
gu (title hexagram 18; curse) 蠱
gua (melon) 瓜
gua (to divine; a trigram or hexagram) 卦
guai (title hexagram 43; to fork) 夬
gui (tortoise) 龜

gui (ghost) 鬼
Guifang (Demon's Territory) 鬼方
han (red pheasant feathers) 翰
Hao (King Wu's capital) 鎬
he (river; Yellow River) 河
Hebo (Earl of Yellow River) 河伯
heng (sacrifice; success) 亨
Hetu (Yellow River Map) 河圖
Hou Tu (deity of the soil) 后土
hu (tiger; name of Marquis of Chong) 虎
huang (yellow) 黃
huben (tiger braves) 虎賁
huo (fire) 火
huo (perhaps) 或
huo (calamity) 禍
ji (auspicious) 吉
jia (approaches) 假
jia (house) 家
jian (see; appear) 見
jiao (horn; constellation name) 角
Jie (King Jie, last Xia king) 桀
jing (warp of fabric; classic text) 經
jiu (calamity) 咎
Jiu (Marquis of Jiu) 九
Jizi (Viscount of Ji) 箕子
jue (bursting dykes; clearing water-ways) 決
kang (gullet; neck; constellation name) 亢
Kanghou (Marquis of Kang) 康侯
ke (able to) 克
li (third of a mile; village) 里
li (advantageous) 利
liang (millet) 梁
ling (magic; divine) 靈
ling (burial mound) 陵
linggui (magic tortoise) 靈龜
lingtai (Divine Tower; astronomical observatory) 靈臺
liu (to flow) 流
long (dragon) 龍

Luoshu (Luo Writing) 洛書
lutai (Deer Pavilion) 鹿臺
mei (faint light; so-called star-name) 沬
mei (dark; dim) 昧
mei (younger sister) 妹
meng (title hexagram 4; deceive; to cover) 蒙
meng (alliance) 盟
Mengjin (Fords of Meng, written two ways) 盟津 and 孟津
miao (ancestral temple) 廟
min (vessel; bowl) 皿
ming (mandate; command; fate) 命
ming (cry of bird) 鳴
mingyi (title hexagram 36; bird name?) 明夷
mo (saliva; froth; so-called star-name; Shang city) 沬
mo (white jasmine) 茉
Muye (Wilds of Mu) 牧野
nan (south) 南
pan (a rock) 磐
pei (darkened) 沛
pei (a pennon) 旆
peng (pair; set of cowries; friend) 朋
pi (white fox; kind of leopard) 貔
piao (to float) 漂
qi (that; his; Keightley's 'perhaps' in oracle-bone inscriptions) 其
qi (willow) 杞
qian (title hexagram 1; dry) 乾
qinglu (King Wu's sword) 輕呂
Qi Shan (Mount Qi) 岐山
ren (man) 人
ren (perfect virtue) 仁
ri (sun; day; daily) 日
rong (weapons; Rong tribe) 戎
san (three) 三
Shang (Shang dynasty) 商
Shangdi (deity of the Shang) 上帝
Shang Fu (Taigong's name in ode 236) 尚父
shangji (highly auspicious) 上吉
she (to ford a steam) 涉

shi (corpse) 尸
shi (to divine by stalks) 筮
shi (to eat) 食
shi (eclipse) 蝕
Shou (name of Zhou Xin) 受
shu (younger of brothers) 叔
Shu Qi (protester against Zhou Conquest) 叔齊
Taigong (Grand Duke, King Wu's counsellor) 太公
Tairen (King Wen's mother) 太任
Taisi (King Wen's wife) 太姒
Tai Wang (King Tai, King Wen's grandfather) 太王
Tang (Tang the Completer, founder of Shang) 湯
tangmeng (dodder) 唐蒙
tian (field; sow grain) 田
tian (Heaven; sky; deity of the Zhou) 天
tianming (Mandate of Heaven) 天命
tong (boy) 童
tongmeng (deceitful boy; young fool) 童蒙
tongren (title hexagram 13; fellow-countrymen) 同人
wang (king) 王
Wang Hai (Shang ancestor, early nomadic king) 王亥
Wang Ji (King Ji, King Wen's father) 王季
wei (oppose) 違
wei (weft of fabric; apocryphal text) 緯
Weizi (Viscount of Wei, elder half-brother of Zhou Xin) 微子
Wen Wang (King Wen) 文王
wo (my; our) 我
wu (crow; black) 烏
Wu Ding (early Shang king) 武丁
Wu Geng (Zhou Xin's son) 武庚
Wu Wang (King Wu) 武王
wuwei (Daoist concept of 'doing nothing') 無爲
Xia (Xia dynasty) 夏
xianjun (my deceased father) 先君
Xibo (Earl of the West, King Wen's Shang title) 西伯
xing (moving) 行
xing (star) 星
xiong (disastrous) 凶

xu (empty; ruins) 虛
xu (title hexagram 5; waiting; stopped by rain) 需
xuan (dark; black) 玄
xue (pit-dwelling; cave) 穴
xue (blood) 血
xun (ten-day 'week') 旬
yang (yang of 'yin and yang') 陽
yang (willow) 楊
Yao (mythical emperor) 堯
yi (change; easy; Yijing) 易
yi (appropriate; sacrifice to soil deity) 宜
yi (corded arrow; sharpened stake) 弋
yi (yi of 'mingyi'; barbarian; Yi tribe) 夷
Yi (Yi the Archer) 羿
Yi Kao (first son of King Wen) 邑考
yin (shady; yin of 'yin and yang') 陰
Yin (alternative name for the Shang) 殷
Yi-Yi (East Barbarian Yi) 夷羿
you (dark) 幽
you (grief; sad; mourning for a parent) 憂
Youli (place King Wen imprisoned) 羑里
yu (cart; sedan-chair; carry on shoulders) 輿
Yu (Yu the Great, mythical flood hero) 禹
yuan (depths; gorge) 淵
yuanji (most auspicious) 元吉
yue (moon; month) 月
zhang (rule; chapter; calendrical term) 章
Zhao Ge (Shang city) 朝歌
zheng (go on military expedition) 征
zhi (pheasant) 雉
zhi (it) 之
zhong (middle) 中
Zhou (Zhou dynasty) 周
Zhou Xin (last Shang king) 紂辛
zhu (lord) 主
zi (son; child; master; viscount) 子

Index

Jiu, Marquis of, 20–21, 176 n54
Jiu Gao, see Documents, Book of
Jizi, *see* Ji, Viscount of
Joel, Book of, 173 n39
Josephus, 77
Junior Master, 30–31, *see also* Bi Gan
Jupiter, 56, 183 n16

Kallippos of Kyzikos, 186 n41
Kang, Marquis of, 7–8, 45, 76, 164
    n13, 215 n11, *see also* Kangshu
Kang asterism, 143, 210 n14
Kang Gao, see Documents, Book of
Kanghou, *see* Kang, Marquis of
Kanghou *gui,* 7, 164 n11
Kangshu, 7–8, 76, 155, 156, 190 n38,
    see also Kang, Marquis of
Karlgren, Bernhard, *xiii,* 26, 42, 50,
    62, 63, 64, 68, 75, 77, 86, 96,
    111, 113, 175 n47, 177 n64, 185
    n33, 193 n58, 197 n29, 212 n12
Keightley, David N, 129, 174 n41,
    192 n54, 199–200 n57
knowing the seeds, 20, 169–170 n9
Korea, 95–96, 199 n50/n51
Krupp, E C, 54–55
Kunst, Richard A, *xi,* 9, 46, 47, 64,
    65–66, 106, 140, 185–186 n41,
    187 n8

lame man, 211 n1
Lantern Festival, 209 n7
Lao Can's Travels, 15
Lao Naixuan, 4
Laurin, Colin Mac, 57
Leaning Mulberry (Fu Sang tree),
    109
Legalism, *xiii*
Legge, James, *xiii,* 10, 14, 36, 38, 42,
    44, 61, 63, 94, 166 n23, 190
    n38, 193 n58, 194 n6/n7, 198
    n36, 203 n18, 204 n3, 215 n10
leopard, 20, 86, 194 n8
li (measure of distance), 25, 84, 92,
    172 n30
Li (bronze caster), 86, 194–195 n11
Li, Shang garrison city of, 27, 72, 82
    (*map 1*), 173 n40, 174 n41
Li gui, 86, 194–195 n11

Li Ji, 155, 157, 194 n8
Li Jingchi, 105, 106
Li Sao, 21, 189 n36
Li Si, *xiii*
Li Zheng, see Documents, Book of
Libra, 178 n6, 210 n14
Liezi, xiv, 19, 146, 191 n48
Lin Zhongjun, 105
ling (burial mounds), 91
linggui (magic tortoise), 174 n41
lingtai (astronomical observatory),
    26–27
Lintong, 86
litter, 76
Liu Dajun, 105
Liu E, 15
Liu Tao, 86–87, 196 n18, 203 n17
Liu Ts'un-yan, 126
Liu Xiang, 43
Liu Xin, 53
lizard, 13, 14
loa (voudoun), 77
lone commoner, motif of, 93, 198
    n38
long, see dragon
Lu Fu, 155, *see also* Wu Geng
Lu Shang, 118, 189 n36, *see also*
    Taigong
Lu the Expected, 189 n36, *see also*
    Taigong
Lu Wang, 189 n36, *see also* Taigong
Lucretius, 43
lunar mansions, 178 n6
lunar phase notations, 53
Lunheng, 19, 75, *see also* Wang
    Chong
Lunyu, see Confucius
Luo Gao, see Documents, Book of
Luo River, 23, 82 (*map 1*), 147, 172
    n23
Luo Writing, *see Luoshu*
Luoshu, 147, 212 n18, 213 n22
Luoyang, 37, 83 (*map 2*)
lutai, 26, 167 n2, *see also* Deer
    Pavilion
Lynn, Richard, 64, 140, 163 n4

Ma Rong, 9
maggots, 128